Tolerance and Risk

Muslim International

Sohail Daulatzai and Junaid Rana, Series Editors

With Stones in Our Hands: Writings on Muslims, Racism, and Empire
Sohail Daulatzai and Junaid Rana, Editors

Foucault in Iran: Islamic Revolution after the Enlightenment
Behrooz Ghamari-Tabrizi

Arc of the Journeyman: Afghan Migrants in England
Nichola Khan

Tolerance and Risk: How U.S. Liberalism Racializes Muslims
Mitra Rastegar

TOLERANCE AND RISK

HOW U.S. LIBERALISM RACIALIZES MUSLIMS

MITRA RASTEGAR

Muslim International

University of Minnesota Press

Minneapolis

London

Portions of chapter 2 are adapted from "Reading Nafisi in the West: Authenticity, Orientalism, and 'Liberating' Iranian Women," *WSQ: Women's Studies Quarterly* 34, no. 1–2 (2006): 108–28; copyright 2006 by the Feminist Press at the City University of New York; reprinted by permission of The Permissions Company, LLC on behalf of the publishers, www.feministpress.org; all rights reserved. Chapter 3 was originally published as "Emotional Attachments and Secular Imaginings: Western LGBTQ Activism on Iran," *GLQ* 19, no. 1 (2013): 1–29; copyright 2013 Duke University Press; reprinted by permission, www.dukeupress.edu.

Published by the University of Minnesota Press
111 Third Avenue South, Suite 290
Minneapolis, MN 55401-2520
http://www.upress.umn.edu

ISBN 978-1-5179-0484-5 (hc)
ISBN 978-1-5179-0485-2 (pb)

A Cataloging-in-Publication record for this book is available from the Library of Congress.

Printed in the United States of America on acid-free paper

The University of Minnesota is an equal-opportunity educator and employer.

To S and O

Contents

Introduction

Tolerance and Anti-Muslim Racism

The image by Shepard Fairey that I saw everywhere in the days, weeks, and months following the inauguration of President Donald Trump—in a full-page *New York Times* ad, attached to innumerable online articles, in storefronts, as Facebook profile pictures, and especially at protests—is a portrait of a striking woman gazing directly at the viewer. Her head is covered by a form-fitting head scarf, half in blue with white stars, the other half in red and white stripes. The red is repeated only in her lips, and the lipstick seems to extend slightly beyond the perimeter of her mouth. Thick eyelashes, arched eyebrows, and distinct cheekbones convey the beauty of the framed face. The U.S. flag hijab fully covers her shoulders and fills the bottom of the poster. Below reads "We the people / are greater than fear." The poster was first publicized as one of three images of women that circulated in relation to the Women's March on Washington the day after President Trump's inauguration. The other images are of a Black woman with a solemn, slightly downcast expression that reads "We the people / protect each other" and of a Latina woman smiling slightly and wearing a red rose in her hair that reads "We the people / defend dignity." The three images connect a feminine, presumably feminist, and multicultural image of the United States with an articulation of reenvisioned founding values and implicitly critique anti-Black violence, anti-immigrant policy, and Islamophobia. In the context of Trump's executive order banning the entry of visa holders (and initially green card holders) from several Muslim-majority countries, his adoption of explicit anti-Muslim rhetoric, and an increase in hate crimes in the United States against Islamic institutions and individuals perceived as Muslim, the image of the Muslim woman seems to articulate a perfect countermessage: Muslims are patriotic Americans, and hence Muslims do belong here. This message of inclusion resonated strongly among critics of the Trump regime.

This Shepard Fairey image also beautifully epitomizes the tensions implicit in predominant U.S. discourses of tolerance in relation to Muslims in the years since the September 11 attacks. These discourses are the object of analysis of this book. Among the three images, the Muslim woman is the only one that includes the colors and patterns of the American flag. All three images include the first three words of the U.S. Constitution: "We the people." Given that the American flag is often associated with a conservative perspective on U.S. cultural identity and global geopolitical role (compare the prevalence of U.S. flags at progressive versus conservative rallies), what does it mean to attach it to the Muslim woman only? If the goal is to reclaim the flag, and hence U.S. identity, as a liberal and inclusive symbol, why not repeat the flag in all three images? However, the flag

FIGURE 1. Women's March on Washington, January 21, 2017. Photograph by JohnJackPhotography.

seems to serve another purpose, which is to mark the figure as the one who most needs to be explicitly brought into the nation, to be seen as patriotic, to be seen as unthreatening. The Muslim woman *needs* the flag to become American—she needs not simply an association with the flag but to wear the flag as hijab, her body and religion literally transformed through the symbol of American patriotism. Given that Black and Latina women are also violently excluded from the privileges of the nation, why is it that the flag in particular is what needs to be attached to the Muslim woman? What does this tell us about the terms of inclusion and exclusion of Muslims as a relatively newly configured internal racial Other?

Before 2001, images of Muslims, who were commonly associated with the Middle East, served to exotify, mystify, and evoke a distant threat: flying carpets, belly dancers, harem women, wish-granting genies, camel-riding Arabs, oil-rich sheikhs, gun-toting hijackers, black-veiled women, and turbaned mullahs.[1] Whether magical, dangerous, or backward, what was clear was that, in the minds of many, Muslims were *foreign* and *distant*.[2] With the September 11, 2001, attacks, that wall of separation between Muslims and the United States was punctured. Suddenly people who had been living in the United States for years, decades, or generations began to be seen in a new light. Identified with the moniker "Muslim or Arab," people were called on to fill these categories. I remember my own wonder at suddenly seeing television programs filled with talking heads discussing "my" part of the world or speaking *as* Muslims themselves. I also remember being asked for the first time, from curious and supportive acquaintances, if I was Muslim. As an Iranian American with Muslim family members, even as someone who is not religious and has never self-identified (or dis-identified) as Muslim, it seemed like the world where I was from was coming into recognition in a new way. It was oddly affirming.

These memories seem naive looking back, as I am, from the era of Trump. Nevertheless, a mode of relating to Muslims took shape in the post-9/11 period that has left its indelible mark, especially on those who espouse inclusion and multiculturalism. In analyzing discourses of tolerance, one can see how the articulation of liberal values in the public sphere functions today. Do representations of Muslims as tolerable and sympathetic actually promote tolerance? Do they create space for Muslims to hold differing religious, cultural, and political perspectives and still be deemed acceptable? As should already be clear, this book is not about Muslims themselves. It is not about the more than one billion people globally who claim Islam as their faith, the millions of Americans who do, or the millions of Americans who come from countries where Islam is the predominant religion. It is also not about Islam as a faith with multiple denominations, sects, and schools of thought or Islam as comprising highly variable cultural norms associated with people who practice the religion. Rather, this book is about how Muslims are represented and perceived, and particularly how articulations of sympathy and tolerance for Muslims shape those perceptions.

In the post-9/11 moment, Muslims in the United States became more starkly an internal minority with an ambiguous status in the U.S. cultural and racial landscape. Notably, this representation tended to exclude Muslims who had previously been, in Su'ad Abdul Khabeer's words, "the prototypical Muslims on the domestic front." U.S. Black Muslims had previously filled this role due to their prominent role in antiracist movements and the fact that paths to integration into Whiteness were denied them, in contrast to some other smaller Muslim communities in the United States.[3] However, White Americans have often viewed Black Muslims less as representative of Islam globally and more as a product of the particularities of U.S. history. The 1959 documentary *The Hate That Hate Produced* typifies this thinking, portraying the Nation of Islam as a national menace that emerged with Black Nationalism in response to racism. Sohail Daulatzai describes how the global and internationalist politics of many U.S. Black Muslims was domesticated in the 1990s in part through the example of Muhammed Ali. The highly polarizing boxer was broadly criticized in the 1960s and 1970s for his refusal to fight in the Vietnam War, his support of Black Power as part of a Third World internationalist framework, and his conversion to Islam. However, in the 1990s, Ali was recuperated as an American hero, as his anti-imperialist vision of Black Freedom was reframed in terms of multiculturalism and benevolent imperialism.[4] Despite these attempts to separate U.S. Black Muslims from a global conception of Islam, Black Muslims have nevertheless been targeted in the War on Terror, particularly though the production of fears about "Homegrown Terrorism."[5] Perhaps because of these crosscutting perceptions of Black Muslims in the United States, and undoubtedly due to anti-Blackness, discourse of tolerance and sympathy for Muslims in the post-9/11 era did not generally focus on Black Muslims, whether in the United States or abroad. As Khabeer has noted, this predominant post-9/11 discourse, whether referencing "bad Muslims" or "good Muslims," largely ignored Black Muslims.[6]

In the post-9/11 period, it was Muslims of Middle Eastern and South Asian descent (as "the Middle East" seemed to grow) who were brought into focus. While "Muslim" suddenly in this moment emerged into public discourse as a particularly relevant category, the precise content of the category, or what it means to be Muslim, would be debated for years to come. However, the dominant meanings associated with Muslims were not new but built on histories and stereotypes that extended back decades and centuries, reflecting the uneven power relations between Europe, the United States, and Muslim-majority countries. Nevertheless, the shock of 9/11 disrupted existing sedimented frameworks and offered an opportunity to reconfigure ideas about what it means to be Muslim and to relate differently to the actual immense diversity contained within this category.

Perceptions of Muslims have been deeply shaped by the War on Terror, a war that has been so normalized that it continues to be waged globally with notably little concern from U.S. publics. The enemy in this war has been produced through both the ideological framings of the war and the diverse "counterterrorism" activities that constitute the war. The enemy has been intentionally ill defined and malleable: a murky terrorist network, Islamic militants on battlefields, rogue states, and/or independent "self-radicalized" individuals who could strike almost anywhere. This enemy construction has been used to justify many warfronts, most prominently in Afghanistan and Iraq, and also in Pakistan and Yemen, in the form of military interventions and drone strikes that have produced innumerable displacements, injuries, and deaths.[7] The geographic extent of this U.S.-led War on Terror was documented by the Brown University Watson Center, which estimated that between 2015 and October 2017, U.S. counterterror activities occurred in 39 percent of the world's countries, including through air and drone strikes in seven countries, combat troops in fifteen, U.S. military bases in forty-four countries, and U.S.-led counterterrorism training in fifty-eight countries.[8] Beginning under the Bush and Obama administrations, the United States incorporated a range of tactics, including extended imprisonments, torture, extraordinary renditions, and targeted killings, including of U.S. citizens. Domestically, the government has targeted Muslims, and many non-Muslim Arabs, with the threat and reality of extensive surveillance, raids into homes and businesses, entrapment, indefinite detentions, and mass deportations. Citizens from Muslim-majority countries seeking to visit the United States have been banned outright or subject to stringent visa processing requirements.

Therefore, on one hand, the production of the category of Muslim has been interdependent with the production of an enemy in the global War on Terror. On the other hand, a more marginal discourse about "good" Muslims has also been integral to War on Terror discourses and a construction of what it means to be Muslim. President G. W. Bush framed the war as a war for "our freedoms," including among them the freedom to practice one's religion, and American Muslims were put forth as evidence that the United States was fighting a war for civilization and not against Islam. President Obama revived and expanded this tradition as evident in his Cairo address, dubbed "The Muslim World Address." As Zareena Grewal has analyzed, Obama presented Muslim Americans as "moral examples of modern, democratic, and productive citizens for Muslims in the Muslim World to emulate but also as proof to the Muslim World of the American government's exceptional benevolence and tolerance of minorities."⁹ Even as Bush and Obama discourses acknowledged and valued Muslims, in stark contrast to Trump's exclusionary and dehumanizing rhetoric and policies, the War on Terror's construction of a murky, fluid, and flexible enemy long provided cover for U.S.-led policing and violence against Muslim populations in the United States and abroad. Furthermore, rather than separating "good" Muslims from "bad" Muslims, the fluid construction of enemy Muslims has subjected all Muslims to assessment practices that operate as forms of policing. As I will argue further, the enemy construction intimately shaped the terms of inclusion of Muslims.

This book is an analysis of broadly circulating media discourses about tolerating and sympathizing with Muslims. Moving between media representations of Muslims in the United States and abroad, my analysis considers how tolerance for Muslim Americans interacts with sympathy for the suffering of Muslims in, or displaced from, Muslim-majority societies. My cases are eclectic, traversing a period of fifteen years (2001–16) and moving between media genres and issue areas. Nevertheless, they cohere around a question of how Muslims are represented as tolerable or sympathetic. I find that these articulations of liberal values create lines of distinction, between Muslims and non-Muslims and among Muslims themselves, as they put forth only some Muslims as worthy of tolerance or sympathy. These discourses articulate a set of standards by which Muslim trustworthiness, or alternately riskiness, must be assessed, and they circulate a notion of the *distinct problems* of Muslims as a population. They also construct a "we" of liberal multiculturalists who become those who can and should know and assess the tolerability of Muslims. In certain forms, these discourses function as alibis for U.S. war and violence, particularly by articulating a civilizing mission, where U.S. cultural or military involvement creates the possibility of the production of more "good" Muslims. They more broadly function as a policing and disciplining discourse that casts Muslims as tolerable only if they exhibit particular characteristics. In these broadly circulating media discourses, tolerance is transformed from a political ethos that should protect a space for those whose beliefs or cultures are different, even objectionable, into an assessment tool that facilitates the intimate surveillance of Muslims who are constructed as a population of risk.

In this chapter, I situate my analysis theoretically in relation to the concepts of tolerance and sympathy, on one hand, and racism, on the other. Whereas tolerance and sympathy suggest cohabitation and inclusion and racism suggests discrimination and exclusion, I outline my theoretical framework for arguing that discourses that seem to espouse liberal values function through charged media representations to produce Muslims as a racialized population. I also examine scholarship on the racialization of Muslims and propose the concept of population racism to explain the circulation of anti-Muslim racism that aligns with what Jodi Melamed has termed "neoliberal multiculturalism."[10] I then discuss how liberal values circulate in the media and how emotional representations of Muslims contribute to their racialization, concluding with a brief overview of the specific cases that make up the book.

TOLERANCE AND SYMPATHY IN LIBERAL SUBJECTIVITY

Following the successes of the civil rights movement in the 1960s, official anti-racism was unevenly integrated into U.S. governance.[11] By the 1980s, a clear pushback was evident, as laws and policies with racist effects were promoted through discourses that were facially race neutral by evoking racist stereotypes, for example, through the figures of the "gang member," the "welfare queen," and the "illegal alien." Multiculturalism was disseminated through superficial recognition and token inclusivity and through emotional articulations of the liberal subjectivity, as one who cares and feels for the other. Bill Clinton expertly presented himself as a *feeling* president who viscerally connected to the American people. G. W. Bush garnered more moderate and Latino voters—crossing the political aisle—by presenting himself as a compassionate conservative and rebranding the Republican Party as concerned with issues of poverty and racial equality. An ostensible commitment to multiculturalism took the form of the inclusion of at least some token women and people of color within positions of power, even as people like Madeleine Albright, Condoleezza Rice, Colin Powell, and Clarence Thomas served to maintain the system's misogyny, White supremacy, and imperialism. These shifts laid the groundwork for the election of the first African American president, Barak Hussein Obama, who would continue the American tradition of imperial warfare while extending its multicultural rhetoric to Muslims in the United States and abroad. These state discourses of tolerance, sympathy, compassion, and respect for those who are different speak to the broad legitimacy and acceptance of liberal multiculturalism. One of Trump's distinguishing characteristics was his rejection of the official rhetorical anti-racism and multiculturalism of his Democratic and Republican predecessors. The fact that Trump was able to quickly achieve such a dramatic shift away from this official discourse speaks to the relative superficiality of this discourse, which never challenged the racial and neoliberal logics of U.S. domestic and foreign policies.

Nevertheless, these earlier discourses of state power shaped expectations for citizenship and neoliberal subjectivity, aligning with a liberal tradition that attaches significance to tolerance and sympathy even as it expresses ambivalences about culture and religion as repositories of anti-liberal values. By way of example, philosopher Richard Rorty points to the centrality of sympathy and tolerance for liberal self-conceptions:

> Our bourgeois liberal culture . . . is a culture which prides itself on constantly adding more windows, constantly enlarging its sympathies. It is

a form of life which is constantly extending pseudopods and adapting itself to what it encounters. Its sense of its own moral worth is founded on its tolerance of diversity. The heroes it apotheosizes includes those who have enlarged its capacity for sympathy and tolerance. Among the enemies it diabolizes are the people who attempt to diminish this capacity, the vicious ethnocentrists.[12]

It is the liberal's flexibility and malleability, not to mention mobility, that constitutes her own sense of morality and identity. Even as this expansionist liberalism goes beyond seeing and knowing others, to organically assimilate into others, one's liberalism becomes a way to distinguish oneself from the Other. Writing in the 1990s, Rorty accepts that liberals must, in a postmodern age, give up the presumption of the universality of their values yet feels they can recognize the superiority of their framework for allowing for civil cultural and economic exchange among people with incompatible values. Notably, the Muslim is presented as the most problematic case for liberal tolerance. Rorty describes a Kuwaiti in a bazaar, whom he imagines as preferring to die than to share the beliefs of others at the bazaar. However, liberal market relations redeem the Kuwaiti by allowing him to profit from economic intercourse with others, transforming a "vicious ethnocentric" into someone who at least temporarily is tolerant and tolerable. Tolerance and sympathy presented as core values of liberalism thereby reinforce a notion of the division and incompatibility between Islamic and liberal cultures. Effacing the violence of neoliberal economic expansionism and imperialism—while projecting violence onto the Kuwaiti—Rorty positions tolerance as a litmus test for civilization, one that the Kuwaiti can only pass when brought into those global market relations.

The slippage between tolerance and sympathy in Rorty's writing also obscures important distinctions between these concepts that should make them inapplicable to the same context. Tolerance in political philosophy is the withholding of one's disagreement, disapproval, or dislike of particular practices, beliefs, or categories of persons.[13] As such, tolerance should be reserved for that which offends and must be tolerated for the sake of civility, inapplicable to those we find sympathetic, especially when sympathy means feeling *with* another. However, as Marjorie Garber has argued, though sympathy initially implied "a condition of equality or affinity," it has shifted to suggesting "inequality, charity, or patronage," or feeling *for* another.[14] Amit Rai notes that sympathy often implies a distinction: "there must be at least two, non-identical subjects of sympathy: the active, often empowered and privileged sympathizer, and the seemingly passive, disempowered and often suffering object of sympathy."[15] "Empathy" emerged in the twentieth century to address this apparent flaw, emphasizing a self-conscious act of "projecting one's personality into the object of contemplation."[16] In my research, however, tolerance, sympathy, and empathy often blend into each other, as similarity between the (liberal) subject and (Muslim) object often serves as the basis of making a Muslim worthy of these dispositions. As a result, the dividing line is less explicitly between "us" and "them"; rather, it is *between* Muslims who are deemed worthy or unworthy of tolerance, sympathy, or empathy. In essence, true tolerance disappears, as likeness with oneself becoming the requisite of acceptability.

At the same time, discourses of tolerance and sympathy establish a hierarchy between the liberal subjects and the Muslim objects in part through the claim of being distinctly liberal dispositions. Wendy Brown describes how a notion of the tolerant West, as opposed to an intolerant Islamic East based on an essentialized concept of cultural differences, has reinforced a notion of a civilizational divide.[17] This self/Other conceptualization erases or justifies the violence conducted in the name of liberalism and neoliberalism, while casting Muslim-majority societies as irrational and barbaric. Joseph Massad goes further to show how liberalism historically constituted itself by projecting its anxieties about its own contradictions— including persistent despotism, misogyny, and intolerance in Europe and the colonies—onto Islam. He argues that liberalism and secularism did not simply grow out of internal dynamics of European modernity but rather were formed in opposition to European constructions of "Islam," providing justification for the colonial domination and coercive assimilation of Muslims.[18]

I analyze discourses of tolerance and sympathy as discourses of power that reinforce the legitimacy of liberal and neoliberal projects. Talal Asad has argued that the heart of liberalism is a violence that eliminates particular practices, meanings, and forms of life, which is justified in the service of protecting liberal values.[19] This universalizing agenda is intimately connected to the rise of capitalism, expressing market-based conceptions of choice and freedom and seeking to eliminate traditions perceived as oppressive to create liberals in its stead. Consistent with this perspective, Hester Eisenstein has argued that liberal feminism has acted as a "solvent" dissolving social and economic relations seen as traditional and sexist, resulting in women's mass entry into low-wage work, which has been highly compatible with the forces of neoliberal globalization.[20] As such, liberalism cannot be seen as a neutral framework that, through tolerance and sympathy, allows for a multiplicity of paths, perspectives, and cultures. Rather, it has been articulated with neoliberalism and imperialism in ways that lead to the destruction of many existing ways of life.

Nevertheless, Rorty's notion of tolerance and sympathy as key to liberal self-conceptions is useful to understanding the centrality of discourses of tolerance and sympathy to produce a liberal positionality in relation to the War on Terror, and also in opposition to Trump's anti-Muslim rhetoric and policies. While discourses of tolerance and sympathy have at times served as alibis for the self-interested actions of neoconservative advocates of war, they have also been integral to the predominant critiques of the War on Terror. Indeed, tolerance and sympathy have been the most common positive modes of relating to Muslims in public discourse in the United States. Although leftist activists tend to prefer to articulate their relationships to allies in terms of solidarity, such discourses rarely enter more mainstream arenas, and as Rai points out, even calls for solidarity often depend on evocations of sympathy.[21] Furthermore, these liberal discourses of tolerance and sympathy play an important role in relation to the broader discursive context: by identifying the terms in which Muslims are deemed worthy of tolerance and sympathy, they delineate and reinforce particular measures of acceptability that I argue are intrinsic to the racialization of Muslims.

RACIALIZING RELIGION

What does it mean to say that Muslims have been racialized in the United Sates, particularly in the period since September 11, 2001? Anti-Muslim racism is not just fear of Islam as a religion, as the term *Islamophobia* implies, and cannot be reduced to rationally grounded animosity caused by political conflicts and differences of interest. Race and racism have been traditionally understood as constructs based on a perception of innate biological difference, where specific physical traits are viewed as indicators of different bodily, mental, and moral capacities. Noting the challenges in applying a biological concept of race to Muslims, a number of scholars have developed a concept of cultural racism to explain the racialization of Muslims as based on a perception of unbridgeable *cultural* divides. My research builds on both these frameworks, while overlaying a concept of population racism to explain the dynamics by which notions of biological and cultural difference are mobilized to produce a construct of Muslims as a distinct and coherent—yet diverse—racial population. Population racism operates in and through biological and cultural racism; however, the concept of population racism draws emphasis to the flexibility of racism, accounting for mechanisms by which notions of essential difference persist in discourses that might otherwise seem antiracist, or at least nonracist. The figure of the tolerable or sympathetic Muslim—the patriot, the liberal, the feminist—can appear to be an antiracist rejoinder to stereotypes of Muslims. However, representations of tolerable Muslims contribute to the racialization of all Muslims by reinforcing stereotypes as risk factors of a population. Rather than understanding race primarily as an attribute attached to an individual or a type of person, I see it as attached to populations, serving as a sifting mechanism by which people are placed on a spectrum of value.

From one perspective, the notion that anti-Muslim sentiment should be conceptualized as a form of racism may seem strange. Most obviously, there has been little attempt among anti-Muslim activists to designate Muslims as a biologically or genetically distinct "race." After all, Muslims are identified in terms of the religion of Islam, and religion in today's secularized context is often understood as a chosen identity, whereas race is seen as an unchangeable attribute of birth. Furthermore, Islam is a highly diverse religion that encompasses various traditions of belief and practice followed by people of innumerable ethnicities, nationalities, and phenotypical appearances. In the U.S. context, Muslims are people who can be identified by any of a range of official race categories, most predominantly White, Asian, and African American/Black. While South Asian and Black Americans are racialized as non-White regardless of their religious identities, people from West Asia (the "Middle East") and North Africa[22] are categorized as White by the U.S. Census, notwithstanding efforts to add a

Middle Eastern/North African category. The official designation as White was first established through early twentieth-century court decisions that, while variable, ultimately determined Arabs as White and hence eligible for U.S. citizenship.[23] In 1978, this designation was codified in the federal classification of White as indicating people of European, Middle Eastern, and North African descent. However, such official designations have frequently conflicted with lived realities that demonstrate much more complex relationships to Whiteness, as Arabs, Iranians, and others from the Middle East and North Africa have at times assimilated into Whiteness as an "invisible minority" and at other times being subject to discrimination, racial profiling, and vigilante violence on the basis of their identities.[24]

Neda Maghbouleh has described Iranian Americans as a test case demonstrating "the limits of whiteness," where even as Iranians have been one of the most well integrated immigrant communities, based on such socioeconomic indicators as educational attainment, economic success, intermarriage, and spatial integration, they have also been the objects of suspicion and intense overt hostility, especially since the 1979 Islamic Revolution and the ensuing hostage crisis. Maghbouleh uses the concept of "racial loopholes" to describe the paradoxical status of Iranians and other Middle Easterners who experience discrimination, harassment, and violence and yet are seen as too White to warrant legal protections against such acts. Parallel dynamics are evident in relation to other communities, as economic integration of Arab Americans, and South Asians, has historically led to a model minority narrative of successful assimilation.[25] Nevertheless, there is increasing evidence that today, regardless of class or official racial designation, Iranian and Arab "bodies are rejected from whiteness,"[26] including through the violation of civil and human rights by the U.S. government.

Although in the immediate post-9/11 era, "Muslims and Arabs and those perceived as such" was one inelegant way to reference a still shifting set of associations, "Muslim" would emerge as the predominant, although not sole, racial formation aligning with the War on Terror. Though this racialization, or the production of "Muslim" as a racial category, certainly interacted with and influenced how specific communities came to identify themselves as communities, my analysis focuses exclusively on the external production of the category of "Muslim." I do not consider how the communities being referenced have responded to this racialization or how they constituted themselves as communities, "Muslim" or otherwise; hence my language, such as my use of *Muslim* and *Muslim American,* should be seen as referring to the construction of racial categories, rather than the production of religious or ethnic identities.[27]

Although I focus on the production of "Muslim" as a racial category, I see race, religion, ethnicity, gender, and sexuality as interacting, crosscutting conceptualizations, and organizations of life, that should be analyzed through their, at times paradoxical, coarticulations and enactments. As Nikhil Singh writes,

> race is a fungible assemblage rather than a coherent, preconstituted entity . . . race is heterogeneous, and it also works through heterogeneity. Gender, religion, economic conditions, sexuality, dis/ability and other key markers of social and embodied difference are the modalities in which race is lived; they are also selectively accented in processes of ascribing racial characteristics to groups.[28]

Race dynamically configures and reconfigures markers of difference to incorporate, exclude, and manage, while also producing and justifying the differential valuing of lives. I offer population racism as a conceptual framework that can capture dynamics of racialization that are consistent with post-racial ideologies. However, population racism does not supersede but rather builds on and bridges biological and cultural conceptualizations of Muslim racial differences, to which I turn first.

BIOLOGICAL AND CULTURAL RACISM

It is a sociological truism that race is a social construct, meaning that there is no objective scientific basis to racial categories. Race as a concept and material reality is produced through social relations, rather than as an outgrowth of genetic or biological differences. Therefore, racialization, or what the sociologists Michael Omi and Howard Winant describe as "the extension of racial meaning to a previously racially unclassified relationship, social practice, or group,"[29] is always a possibility. The term *racialization* highlights not only the social construction of race but the fact that these constructions are ever-unfolding processes rather than static, historically produced frameworks and relations. This is especially true in relation to the othering of Muslims, which has morphed in concordance with developing U.S. geopolitical interests, taking a harsher tone in the period since the 1967 Israeli–Arab War, developing an ideological apparatus since the end of the Cold War, and intensifying domestically in the period since 2001. As Omi and Winant note, race is "an unstable and 'decentered' complex of social meanings constantly being transformed by political struggle."[30] Racism as a structure of power has always been inherently tied to and shaped by the political. Nevertheless, racism cannot be reduced to rationally grounded political conflicts over territory, economic power, or status; rather, it has a distinct logic of its own.

One of the key logics of race in the United States has been a conception of biologically grounded difference, evident through physical markers like phenotype. Indeed, Omi and Winant define race as "a concept that signifies and symbolizes social conflicts and interests by referring to different types of human bodies."[31] However, as notions of biological racial differences have been deemed scientifically invalid, socially unacceptable, and racist following the successes of the civil rights movement, cultural ideas have emerged to reestablish notions of racial inferiority and superiority on more acceptable grounds. Eduardo Bonilla-Silva notes that culture increasingly serves as explanation for structural inequality.[32] For example, Daniel Patrick Moynihan in 1965 argued that African American socioeconomic inequality was a result of a "culture of poverty" manifest in cultural traits, such as matriarchal family structures, that originated under conditions of slavery. Despite significant work that has demonstrated that systemic racism, such as housing and employment discrimination, segregation, and lack of access to equal education, produces these inequalities, the periodically revived "culture of poverty" thesis offers one way to place blame on African Americans, while avoiding an argument of genetic inferiority. Such cultural arguments appear nonracist, if racism is understood as rooted in perceptions of biological difference.

Scholars of the racialization of Muslims have drawn on both biological and cultural notions of race to explain the process by which Muslims have been constituted as a racial group. Erik Love, in *Islamophobia and Racism in America*, emphasizes race as an ascription that is based on a notion of biological difference, arguing, "Race is a social process that makes reference to biology. It is a socially derived classification for human bodies."[33] Hence anti-Muslim racism is primarily directed against those who "look Muslim" based on their physical appearance, an argument supported by research on daily experiences of anti-Muslim bias.[34] While Love notes that cultural items, such as "prayer beads or a *taqiyah* cap," can mark someone as Muslim, he emphasizes what he terms "racial cues," such as skin color, facial features, and hair texture, as primary in the racialization process.

Other scholars have given greater emphasis to what has been termed *cultural racism*, whereby real or imagined cultural differences are treated as inherent and immutable traits of a collective—a form of cultural, rather than biological, determinism.[35] This scholarship builds on the work of Etienne Balibar, who wrote in the early 1990s about the French relationship to Arab immigrants, arguing that culture can "function as a way of locking individuals and groups a priori into a genealogy, into a determination that is immutable and intangible in origin."[36] Anti-Muslim cultural racism builds on Orientalist notions of civilizational difference that became predominant in nineteenth-century European scholarly and artistic work, what Edward Said described in *Orientalism* as a style of thought that produces a binary opposition between Islamic or Arab civilization and European civilization. Orientalism constructs "the Orient" as static, backward, irrational, depraved, and incapable of self-governance and, in opposition, "the West" as dynamic, modern, liberal, rational, civilized, and self-disciplined.

Such notions of cultural difference, when essentialized, form the basis of cultural racism whereby, as Amaney Jamal says, "the racialization of Arabs and Muslims is not simply contingent on phenotypical differences . . . [but] is driven by a perceived clash of values and exacerbated by cultural ethnocentrism."[37] Nadine Naber similarly argues that those "perceived as 'Arab/Middle Eastern/Muslim' were rendered as inherently connected to a backward, inferior, and potentially threatening Arab culture, Muslim religion, or Arab Muslim civilization."[38] Cultural racism explains why a mutable trait—like a headscarf, beard, or name—can be read as signifying an essential difference. This analysis suggests that bodily traits compose one of multiple axes through which racialization of individuals occurs. However, even as this body of work emphasizes notions of cultural difference as central to casting Muslims as inherently different, as Naber's work demonstrates, "culture" may not sufficiently capture the operating framework of racialization.[39] Naber describes a second logic in the racialization of Muslims, what she terms "nation-based racism," that emphasizes a perception of difference and threat rooted in a permanent foreign status. This latter racial logic connects with the work of other scholars who place more emphasis on the political dimensions of the racialization of Muslims, where a threat deemed unique to Muslims marks their racial difference.

Sherene Razack describes a process whereby Muslims are cast as culturally and religiously threatening to "modern enlightened, secular people," becoming "communities without the right to have rights."[40] This construction casts Muslims out of humanity and the protections of law, producing them as rightless people who may be subject to surveillance, internment, torture, and war. Junaid Rana describes the racialization of Muslims today operating primarily through the production of "the terrorist militant" and "the labor migrant," who are "woven together in the figure of 'the Muslim' as a racial type" and become a means to manage and contain Muslim populations.[41] While notions of cultural difference may be evoked in these figures, Razack's and Rana's analyses suggest that it is primarily through the construction of an enemy threat that Muslim racialization occurs. Falguni Sheth similarly argues that racialization of Muslims occurs through defining Muslims as an "unruly," and therefore threatening, population that must be cast out of the political community.[42]

Because scholars have understandably focused on the significant dynamics by which Muslims have been excluded, or in Razack's words, "cast out," racialization of Muslims is often represented as a process of homogenization, where all Muslims are made to fit a distinct stereotype or profile. Such an analysis also fits longer-standing and still-operant typological understandings of race where all members of a racial group are seen as sharing certain essential characteristics. Indeed, it is often true, as Love notes, that the "vibrant diversity [of Muslim Americans] is simply ignored by the racialization process." However, I find that racialization of Muslims also occurs in discourses of tolerance and sympathy that highlight the diversity of Muslims while nevertheless reinforcing the association of Muslims as a population with a pattern of problematic characteristics. The concept of *population racism,* which rests on a shift from a typological to a population-based understanding of race, analytically captures the dynamics through which this process occurs.

POPULATION RACISM

Population racism is a framework that situates racism in relation to the rise of demography, statistics, and risk management in governance and the economy. I borrow the term from Patricia Clough[43] to explain how cultural, biological, or political determinism functions not at the level of the individual but rather at the level of the population. Population racism manifests through the uncritical delineation of one population from another (e.g., Muslims vs. Judeo-Christian Whites) and the ascription of specific problematic characteristics to a population, even while allowing for diversity within that population. While the construction of a population can follow a binary us–them logic, population racism allows for diversity and multiplicity within each side of the binary. Populations are assumed to vary internally, yet a population's internal diversity never undermines the coherence of the population category. Rather, statistical analysis of a population reveals distinct patterns of characteristics and probabilities of outcomes that reinforce the notion that the population category is meaningful. The oft-repeated claim that "not all Muslims are terrorists, but most terrorists are Muslim" encapsulates the logic of population racism, where terrorism is a risk ascribed to Muslims as a population, even as most Muslims may be deemed law abiding, moderate, and patriotic. Whether the statement is true or false is less relevant than the belief that it is meaningful. Such a belief rests on problematic assumptions, including that of the coherence of the category of Muslim vis-à-vis terrorism.

While my focus on media representations emphasizes the ideological manifestations of population racism, it is important to note that racism is in the first instance a system of domination, exclusion, and negligence that, as Ruth Wilson Gilmore says, produces and exploits "group-differentiated vulnerability to premature death."[44] Racism is not only articulated through concepts of population but also enacted through and on populations. As Jodi Melamed describes, racialization is the "process that constitutes differential relations of human value and valuelessness according to specific material circumstances and geopolitical conditions while appearing to be (and being) a rationally inevitable normative system that merely sorts human beings into categories of difference."[45] In other words racial distinction-making creates hierarchies of value that justify distributions of power, resources, and life chances within and between populations. Such hierarchies and differentiations can take absolutist form, where racialization necessarily produces direct consequence, for example, the exclusion of immigrants from Muslim-majority countries; however, they more frequently operate through gradations of distinction, where inclusion of some racialized people can justify or produce exclusions of others, for example, the incorporation of communities into policing efforts that result in self-surveillance and targeting of members within the community. The concept of population racism emphasizes that inclusion and exclusion are not opposing dynamics but rather contained within a single logic.

From the perspective of the social sciences, a population is potentially any collection of humans, or nonhumans, who have been identified as sharing some kind of social or natural designation. A population can be defined or produced along the lines of any characteristic deemed significant, such as ethnicity, gender, or employment status. In the nineteenth century, as Michel Foucault has described, the science of demography and statistics created the population as a new object of biopolitical governance, which it revealed to "possess[] its own regularities."[46] No longer simply that which "populates" a territory, the population became, as Tiziana Terranova describes, "a dynamic quasi-subject constituted by a great number of variables" akin to a natural phenomenon that must be allowed to follow its own laws but can be manipulated or indirectly intervened upon.[47] Within the biopolitical mandate to maximize life, Foucault argues that racism is that which distinguishes one population from another and legitimates the exposure of a population to death in the name of the life of the population as a whole. Sheth, building on Foucault, describes a more subtle dynamic whereby race has become an "instrument by which to channel an element that is perceived as threatening to the political order into a set of classifications";[48] because of the apparently objective nature of classifications used to divide populations, these technologies operate "in less conspicuous and more insidious ways than through identity or social stigma."[49] Such techniques are consistent with neoliberal governmentality in which calculation of individual and population-level capacities produces a flexible racialization that does not always align with a color line, even as it justifies existing inequalities.[50] They also legitimate systems of policing and war-making in the name of apparently race-neutral goals of risk management and global security.

Population racism marks a shift away from typological thinking as foundational to the construction of race. As philosopher of science Lisa Gannett, writing on race and genetics, explains,

> "typologists" assume that racial and ethnic groups are genetically homogeneous, at least for certain "essential" characteristics, and that the differences among them are absolute. This leads to stereotyping—assigning properties to individuals on the basis of their group membership. It also encourages the hierarchical rankings of groups. "Population thinkers," in contrast, recognize that populations are genetically heterogeneous, that differences among populations are overwhelmingly statistical, and that within-group variation far exceeds between-group variation. This means that individuals from different populations will often be more alike in certain characteristics than individuals from the same population.[51]

Nevertheless, population thinking is susceptible to *statistical racism,* or stereotyping that is articulated in terms of a greater probability that someone of a particular group will manifest certain characteristics. Gannett describes this dynamic in relation to genetic sciences, where race has been dismissed as a scientific concept since the 1950s. However, even while scientists have found that humans are 99.9 percent genetically identical, "the remaining 0.1 percent is distributed across populations in an overwhelming statistical pattern—this statistical distribution represents the empirical foundations of 'population thinking.'"[52] That said, the majority of genetic differences occur within a single geographical population, rather than between populations, and such differences are not absolute but rather differences of degree. Nevertheless, Gannett notes that those interested in locating a biological basis for racial difference focus on the relatively small percentage of gradient genetic differences found *between* populations. Therefore preexisting beliefs shape the lines of division drawn between populations, and the kinds of analysis populations are subject to, leaving room for the continuing reassertion of notions of inherent difference through preexisting racial categories.

While population racism exhibits a distinct logic, it builds on preexisting frameworks of biological and cultural racism in justifying what constitutes a discrete population and in producing the variables of assessment deemed relevant to a population. Muslims are racialized first by being separated from other populations. However, as a population, Muslims are also recognized to be internally differentiated and therefore in need of being analyzed in terms of the population's characteristics, capacities, and threats. A racialized population can be recognized as highly diverse, yet analysis of its distribution of characteristics and capacities will show patterns that can distinguish it from other populations. What defines the population, then, is not its homogeneity but this presumed *distribution* of characteristics. Population-based thinking is disseminated to neoliberal citizen-subjects through an invitation to monitor and assess individuals in relation to the characteristics and capacities deemed problematic for that population, often manifest through distinct figures or profiles.[53] These profiles are multiple and ever shifting, constructed through the assemblage of distinct *variables of assessment.*

Variables of assessment are relatively consistent repeated measures that are deemed relevant to a population and become the basis by which the worthiness or threat of any particular individual can be measured. While these variables often coalesce into a profile, such as the "Muslim terrorist" or the "Muslim American patriot," the multiplicity of profiles and different ways in which variables can be assembled lead me to emphasize the variables themselves. Variables of assessment emerge from constructed oppositions with roots in Orientalist binaries: religiosity–secularism, gender equality–gender oppression, sexual liberation–sexual oppression, tolerance–intolerance, and politically aligned with the West–politically aligned with the Muslim or Arab East. Each opposition points to an arena of presumed problematic characteristics associated with Muslims as a population that requires monitoring. As variables of assessment, not only do they emerge in coherent narratives about Muslims but they can also be separated, measured, evoked, and/or circulated in fragmented and disjointed ways. Variables of assessment emerge in human interest stories, opinion polls, news programs, advertisements, Facebook posts, and many other places to temporarily evoke the tolerability or threat of a specific Muslim. Discourses of tolerance regularly traffic in these variables of assessment to demonstrate the tolerability of their subjects; they thereby attune audiences to the measures by which the potential threat of all Muslims must be assessed. By identifying and circulating these distinct variables of assessment, these discourses produce Muslims as a population of risk. Population racism, therefore, points to a logic whereby a discourse that holds up the diversity of Muslims can simultaneously reproduce a conception of Muslims as risky due to its distribution of characteristics and capacities.

Returning for a moment to the question of whether what is popularly termed *Islamophobia* is racism, it may be useful to consider that George Fredrickson, a historical sociologist of race, argues for a distinction between religious intolerance and racism. Fredrickson offers that wherever an "escape hatch" exists that allows for entry into the mainstream, for example, through religious conversion or cultural assimilation, the marginalization in question should be thought of as a form of intolerance rather than as racism.[54] This formulation leads me to ask whether an "escape hatch" of religious, political, or cultural conversion exists for Muslims. Discourses of tolerance seem to imply that some Muslims have passed a litmus test— that some individuals are patriotic, abide by Western values, or have in fact crossed a "civilizational" divide. As such, these discourses might imply an opening through which Muslim Americans who assimilate properly can lay claim to equal citizenship. My analysis in the following chapters suggests otherwise: that even when Muslims are deemed acceptable, tolerable, and sympathetic, they never lose their association with Muslims as a population and hence continue to retain the potentiality of threat associated with that population. As a result, they may at any point be judged differently, transformed from friend into foe. This is not primarily a product of the "success" of intolerant Islamophobia but rather evinces a racialization internal to discourses of tolerance and sympathy, which circulate variables of assessment in a highly affective media environment.

MEDIA CIRCULATIONS OF TOLERABLE MUSLIMS

In November 2013, reports of an attention-grabbing billboard on Sunset Boulevard in Los Angeles featured an image of a White male soldier embracing a Muslim woman wearing a black head scarf and facial veil (*niqab*), along with a wedding band and black polish on her long fingernails. Advertising a nasal spray called SnoreStop, the caption read "keeping you together." Responses ranged from whole-hearted support to incredulous outrage, some defending the advertisement as a statement of tolerance and multiculturalism, others deeming it offensive to military service members and arriving "too soon" after the September 11, 2001, attacks.

FIGURE 2. SnoreStop advertisement, displayed as a billboard on Sunset Boulevard in Los Angeles in October 2013.

The company explained the campaign, which included video commercials featuring interracial and same-sex couples, as a celebration of diversity and equality. My examination of the circulation of discourses of tolerance toward Muslims demonstrates how such discourses contribute to the racialization of Muslims. In a context where most other Americans have little to no direct contact with Muslims, the media is an important realm in which perceptions of Muslims are produced. In this case, a conservatively dressed yet tantalizingly made up Muslim woman's embrace of U.S. militarism became the terms of her ostensible inclusion. However, attention, rather than tolerance, was the real object of the advertisement, which elicited it by emphasizing characteristics—patriotism, religiosity, gender rights, sexual norms—deemed to be uniquely "of concern" in relation to Muslims, thereby contributing to the production of Muslims as a racial population. The debate that ensued joined images, captions, and reactions that circulated swiftly through news reports, op-eds, and reader comments, each seeking to capture the attention of distracted audiences, while also reinforcing preexisting associations with Muslims.

Discourses and representations are important realms in the construction of racial categories and the justification of racial policies.[55] While racism is a system of institutional and structural power, this power is both expressed in and justified by discursive and ideological constructions.[56] These discourses and representations also have material effects, producing the self-disciplining, policing, and exclusion of populations. Discourses of tolerance and sympathy focus on individuals, even as I argue that they reference populations. As Clough notes, "population racism often needs to appear behind a human figure."[57] As such, the figure or the profile, whether the Muslim terrorist, the Muslim American patriot, the *niqab*-wearing woman, or the agentive Muslim feminist, comes to stand for or in relation to the population, referencing it and helping to constitute it. Some questions I consider are, Why and how do Muslim figures come to circulate and resonate? Are these figures presented as representative of or exceptional to the Muslim population as a whole? What associations do these representations reference and reinforce for Muslims as a population? What variables of assessment do they circulate and reinforce?

Sympathetic media representations of Arabs and Muslims in the post-2001 United States, as Evelyn Alsultany has demonstrated, "appear to challenge or complicate former stereotypes and contribute to a multicultural or post-race illusion" but nevertheless "promote logics that legitimize racist policies and practices."[58] More specifically, Alsultany describes "simplified complex representations" as a strategy used by television dramas to create a sense of balanced representation, without undermining the major assumptions of the War on Terror. Her analysis of reality television shows finds that shows seeking to create sympathy for Muslim subjects subtly reference the "problem" of Muslims as threatening by emphasizing the patriotism or secularism of their subjects.[59] Arguing that sympathy is an important public emotion in the Obama-era "post-race" United States, Alsultany demonstrates how representations that garner sympathy, for example, for Muslim women, often maintain an association between Muslims and violence.

Hence discourses of tolerance, as Wendy Brown has argued, are an element of governmentality, which articulates lines of inclusion and exclusion, along with forms of disciplining and managing those deemed to compose risky populations.[60] I engage liberalism not as an abstract political philosophy but rather as a popular discursive repertoire that makes claims to values and dispositions perceived as particular to liberalism. I focus on mediated articulations of tolerance and diversity, sympathy and empathy, autonomy and freedom, and civility and rationality. While at times these ideas are articulated to justify policies that in fact promote the opposite, I am not primarily interested in articulations of tolerance as indicative of hypocrisy. Rather, I see discourses of tolerance as a technology of governance that disseminates standards of assessment to publics, producing them as responsible citizens and empowered experts.

I find that despite liberalism's attachment to reason and rationality, the circulation of liberal discourses of tolerance and sympathy is determined in large part by the emotional and affective resonances of these discourses. In an increasingly fragmented, competitive media environment, a multiplicity of narrative and nonnarrative representations seek to capture attention.[61] For liberals, the media is ideally an arena of rational discourse and debate that facilitates the free circulation of information, contributing to a vibrant civil society and acting as a watchdog of state power. This idea is contradicted by the innumerable ways that economic and political interests shape the media and media discourses. It also ignores that media is a technology that connects to audiences through tapping into emotions and affects. I understand emotions and affects as distinct but interconnected bodily responses that can function at the conscious and preconscious levels. Where emotions tend to be narratively structured responses to an interpretation of a situation, affects are unstructured "proto-thoughts"[62] that are felt as intensities of the body, moving people before or without conscious thought.[63] Mark Poster argues that "wherever individuals deploy media, they are in the midst of a system of power relations that remains out of phase with their conscious mind."[64] As such the public sphere is not a space of dispassionate debate but rather an arena in which thought and action are constituted and activated by emotions and affects via the circulation of images, stories, sound bites, and statistics.[65]

Indeed, the idealized notion of the media and media consumer has been increasingly upended by the recognition of immense political polarization, the segmentation of media markets, and increased propagandization, including the wide circulation of fake news. In a time when we are aware that "click-baiting" headlines grab our attention through the use of superlatives and Facebook encourages us to react to our friends' posts through emotion emojis, it is easy to see how central the activation of emotions is to the circulation of the media. However, even in my cases that precede this social media–dominated era, we see how the media harnesses emotions and affects to gain attention and, in the process, produce unstable and shifting parameters of us–them—the tolerable and intolerable, the sympathetic and unsympathetic. Ultimately, my analysis demonstrates a disjuncture between liberal values and how such values have been articulated and circulated in media discourses. I argue that articulations of tolerance and sympathy for Muslims function not as value-claims that create space for a diverse range of Muslims to participate in public life but rather as speech acts that incite and move audiences, in large part by circulating racializing variables of assessment by which individual Muslims may be deemed tolerable or not.

In the following chapters, I present particular moments when the figure of the tolerable or sympathetic Muslim becomes the focus of attention, especially in broadly accessible and more mainstream media sources that circulate widely. In each case, I account for the dynamics manifest in that particular construction of the tolerable or sympathetic Muslim; moving between the cases, I also track similarities, differences, and the interplay between these different constructions. By consistently focusing on the construction of Muslims as objects of tolerance or sympathy, I come to analyze a more or less coherent phenomenon from a variety of angles. My selection of cases is neither systematic nor exhaustive, yet the cases represent a diversity and range that speak to the pervasiveness of the dynamics that I describe. While I could have logically chosen other cases, a few considerations framed my selection, including an interest in examining (1) the early formative periods in the construction of the tolerable and sympathetic Muslim, namely, the six months following the September 11 attacks and the start of the 2003 Iraq War; (2) the relationship between representations of Muslim Americans and of Muslims in Muslim-majority societies in the construction of variables of assessment, given that conceptions of Muslims in the United States build on and reference perceptions of a global Muslim population; and (3) the relationship between narrative, truncated narrative, and nonnarrative representations, such as human interest stories, statistics, memoirs, images, news articles, and Facebook posts, which allows me to consider the different ways in which emotions and affects facilitate the circulation of variables of assessment and create a feeling of affiliation or disaffiliation.

My chapters are organized loosely chronologically, although some chapters traverse different time periods. Beginning with the post-9/11 moment, in chapter 1, "News Stories, Police Profiles, and Opinion Polls: Muslims as a Population of Risk," I examine *New York Times* human interest stories published in the six months following the attacks that seem to document the diversity of Muslims and Arabs in the United States. Putting these stories in relation to debates about racial profiling, policing efforts to construct a terrorist profile, and later Pew Research Center opinion polls of Muslim Americans, I argue that these stories, profiles, and polling data all shared in the logic of population racism, disseminating variables of assessment by which the threat of Muslims can and must be measured.

The next two chapters consider representations of sympathetic Muslims in Muslim-majority societies, with a repeated, but not exclusive, focus on representations of Iran in the period 2003–6. In this period, Iran was dubbed a major adversary in the War on Terror, as an "axis of evil" nation with threatening nuclear ambitions, building on fears of Iran that were rooted in its image as the progenitor of the first manifestations of "Islamic terrorism" that threatened the United States. The Iran hostage crisis, which began in 1979 with the seizure of the U.S. embassy and its employees, was a highly televised event lasting 444 days, embroiling U.S. audiences in an emotional drama that positioned Islam as against the West.[66] The two chapters consider a shift in U.S. discourses about Iran, with a focus on sympathetic Muslims, specifically women and gay Iranians, who were deemed victims of a repressive theocratic state.

Chapter 2, "From Reading Lolita to Reading Malala: Sympathy and Empowering Muslim Women," is an analysis of the production of the agentive Muslim woman who resists sexism and seeks to create liberation for other Muslim women and girls through literature and education. Focusing on the reception of Azar Nafisi's *Reading Lolita in Tehran,* published in 2003, and representations of Malala Yousafzai, including through her memoir, *I Am Malala,* published in 2013, I analyze how the stories told in these memoirs are distilled and circulated. Even as these two women's stories and positions are quite different, my analysis highlights a tendency toward reading Muslim societies through a binary framework of good Muslims and bad Muslims, a framework that does not so much challenge a culturally racist notion of civilizational divides as it brings some Muslims over that divide. The chapter also demonstrates the gendered aspect of anti-Muslim racism, where a specific acceptable role for Muslim women is produced, while conservative views on gender become circulating markers of both backwardness and threat deemed particular to Muslims.

Chapter 3, "'Iran, Stop Killing Gays': Queer Identifications and Secular Distinctions," offers a close reading of Western lesbian, gay, bisexual, transgender, and queer (LGBTQ) activist responses to the execution of two teenage boys in Iran, interrogating why activists insisted on, amplified, and elaborated on a narrative that the boys were executed for being gay, despite reason for doubt. I find that the strong emotional identification with the boys through the projection of a universal gay identity, along with the story's resonance with the activists' secularist assumptions, produced a narrative that was exceedingly difficult to challenge. Furthermore, even as these boys were brought over a civilizational divide, as being "just like us," their story served to reinforce that divide, one that undergirds cultural racism. At the same time, the reinforcement of an association of Islam with barbaric and violent homophobia supports population racism by producing views on homosexuality as a variable of assessment used to measure the acceptability or threat of Muslims in a wide range of other contexts.

Chapter 4, "Defamed and Defended: The Precarity of the 'Moderate' Muslim American," returns to the U.S. context to consider public controversies in New York City in which widely respected Muslims were quickly, if temporarily, transformed into potential threats. Addressing the Park51, aka Ground Zero Mosque, controversy, and more substantively a preceding controversy surrounding plans to create a dual-language Arabic–English public school in Brooklyn, I demonstrate how the media used the figure of the moderate Muslim to garner attention through highly affective right-wing attacks and dispassionate liberal defenses. Even as media outlets seemed to represent divergent positions on the controversies, they circulated the same variables of assessment by which the moderate status of a Muslim was to be measured, leaving public figures open to attacks that drew power from their association with Muslim populations.

Chapter 5, "Making Muslims Worth Saving: Humanitarianism and the Syrian Refugee Crisis," asks when and how refugees are made worthy of attention and care. It focuses on the production of sympathy for the Muslim refugee in the period of the 2015–16 U.S. presidential campaign, during which Syrian refugees were cast as terrorist threats by Donald Trump and other Republican candidates. Through a close reading of the very popular Humans of New York, which produced three series profiling Syrian and Iraqi refugees, I find that although the project humanized refugees through ascription of voice and agency, it also circulated variables of assessment by holding up a few exceptional individuals who aligned with an image of the good immigrant and patriotic Muslim American, even without having set foot in the United States. I end with a reading of Ai Weiwei's film *Human Flow* to suggest other modes of representing refugees that elicit an ethical obligation without reinforcing a conception of Muslims as a population of risk.

In the Conclusion, I bring together my analyses to demonstrate the flexibility and durability of the variables of assessment that racialize Muslims, while establishing the interconnections between different forms of representation, including of Muslims "here" in the United States and Muslims "there" in Muslim-majority societies. I argue for the need to move beyond many common liberal representations and defenses of Muslims as sympathetic or tolerable, including when Muslims face right-wing attack. Countering anti-Muslim racism requires not only challenging their demonization through false accusations and stereotyped representations but also questioning defenses that traffic in variables of assessment, suggesting that Muslims are only tolerable if they abide by very narrow and distinct parameters of acceptability. It also requires interrogating the assumptions about religion, culture, violence, and rationality that undergird variables of assessment, while creatively disrupting the flow of these variables of assessment in the media. The election of Donald Trump and the proliferation of a more explicit anti-Muslim racism corresponded with increased attacks on Muslims, while also exposing the limitations of tolerance talk in creating space for Muslims. Hence this shift suggests the need for a different kind of engagement with "Muslims" as a category, beginning with a deeper, more grounded understanding of the particular political and economic realities that shape the lives, life chances, values, and beliefs of incredibly diverse communities in the United States and societies across the globe.

1. News Stories, Police Profiles, and Opinion Polls

Muslims as a Population of Risk

"These acts of violence against innocents violate the fundamental tenets of the Islamic faith. And it's important for my fellow Americans to understand that," said President George W. Bush at a press conference at the Islamic Center in Washington, D.C., less than a week following the September 11, 2001, attacks. He continued, "The face of terror is not the true faith of Islam. That's not what Islam is all about. Islam is peace. These terrorists don't represent peace. They represent evil and war." Sitting beside him, in a photograph from the press conference published in *Life* magazine, were a number of Muslim American leaders. In the forefront of this group is a light-skinned woman wearing a loose-fitting white head scarf wrapped over her head and shoulders. Next to her sits a man in a blue suit and a tie, with brown skin, a graying beard, and a white skull cap. Bush sits before a microphone, apparently addressing an audience. The somber faces convey some of the mood of the moment, but the president's expression is calm and warm. He takes the role of spokesman for Islam and Muslims, distinguishing "true" Islam from its perversion, and speaks to his "fellow Americans" to advocate interfaith respect and religious tolerance. In this fleeting moment, Bush acts as bridge and interpreter, relying in part on his credentials as an evangelical Christian president, a friend of religion, to offer a defense of Islam and Muslim Americans.

As this image suggests, in the hours, days, and weeks following the

September 11, 2001, attacks in New York City and Washington, D.C., Muslims, Arabs, and those perceived as Muslim or Arab found themselves to be the objects not only of scrutiny and anger but also of interest, curiosity, and sympathy. Even as reports of bias-motivated vandalism, harassment, and violence proliferated,[1] there were also many reports of people reaching out to Muslims and Arabs to make connections and offer support and of people purchasing copies of the Qur'an. In the months that followed, a dual dynamic became clear: the seemingly opposing forces of inclusion and exclusion. Even as President Bush described Islam as a great and peaceful religion, American Muslims as the true practitioners of a religion "hijacked" by the "terrorists," and the United States as on the side of Muslims and against barbarism,[2] he presided over policies that targeted Muslims and Arabs in the United States through surveillance, detention, and deportations. On one hand, the percentage of Americans with favorable views of U.S. Muslims increased from 45 percent six months before the attacks to 59 percent two months after the attack, an increase that was more pronounced among conservative Republicans, going from 35 percent to 64 percent.[3] On the other hand, public acceptance of racial profiling of Arabs—in the form of security checks at airports (58–68 percent support) and even special identification cards (49 percent)—was also widespread and increasing.[4] Bush's discourse served to frame the war in Afghanistan as a war against terrorism, and not against Islam, and helped to distinguish the United States from its enemy, which was understood as hateful and intolerant. Such articulations of tolerance of Muslims also facilitated the disciplining of Muslim Americans into a formulation of religiosity and citizenship closely aligned with patriotism.[5]

In this chapter, I argue that the parameters of inclusion and exclusion for Muslims were articulated not only in policing profiles that sought to identify "terrorists" but also in a more widespread *profiling* of Muslims—in this case, via human interest stories and opinion polls of Muslim Americans—to produce more and less acceptable Muslims and to construct Muslims as a population of risk. Discourses that appear to be in opposition to each other in fact work in tandem as they operate within and reinforce the logics of population racism. Population racism, as explained in the Introduction, builds on preexisting biological and cultural conceptions of difference that manifest through the delineation of one population from another, while ascribing to that population a distinct distribution of characteristics and capacities, measured as *variables of assessment*. These variables become the tools for the measurement and management of that population in the name of the apparently race-neutral goal of mitigation of risk. The post-9/11 debate on racial profiling, along with continued attempts to define and delineate a more effective "terrorist profile," demonstrates a logic of population racism expressed in preemptive policing that is also disseminated to the public via discourses of tolerance. Even as stories and statistics about Muslim Americans are offered as a testament to their tolerability, in their delineation of the terms upon which Muslims can be deemed acceptable, they also offer variables of assessment that align with policing interests and paradigms. As such, these discourses are the corollary to policing discourses, making audiences into citizen-experts and justifying the surveillance and monitoring of individual Muslims.

Aligning with President Bush's call to Americans to tolerate the patriotic Muslims among them was *New York Times* coverage of Muslims and Arabs in the United States, which contributed significantly to an emerging discourse of tolerance. In the six months following the 9/11 attacks, the *Times* published almost five times as many articles about Muslim and Arab Americans than it had in the six months before; these included sixty human interest stories profiling Muslim and Arab communities and individuals in the United States, as compared to just one such article in the period before the attacks. This six-month period was unusual compared to both the pre-9/11 period and the years to come, with much more extensive coverage devoted to Muslim and Arab Americans; coverage in the *Times* and elsewhere during this period was also more in depth and more likely to use Muslims and Arabs as sources.[6] The total number of articles about Muslim or Arab Americans went from 49 articles in the six months before the 9/11 attacks to 241 articles in the six months following the attacks. As Figure 3 indicates, *Times* coverage of Muslim and Arab Americans would decrease in the years to come, assessed in six-month periods in 2003 (ninety-five articles), 2005 (forty-three articles), and 2007 (thirty-seven articles) (I did not distinguish human interest stories during these periods), suggesting the distinctiveness of this post-9/11 period.

As a whole, the post-9/11 *Times* human interest stories present Muslims and Arabs as a diverse population, made up of people of different

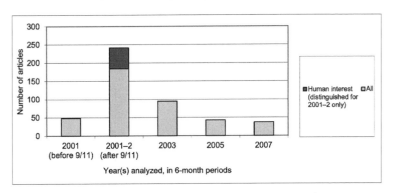

FIGURE 3. *New York Times* articles on Muslim or Arab Americans (in six-month periods).

ethnicities, experiences, and values, often humanizing them through these intimate, emotional portrayals. I place these stories in relation to, on one hand, the racial profiling of Muslims and Arabs as potential terrorists and, on the other hand, opinion surveys of Muslim Americans conducted by the Pew Research Center in 2007 and 2011. These divergent representations of Muslims—the terrorist profile, the human interest story, and survey data—are connected through the framework of statistical thinking, which also underlies population racism.

On the surface, the human interest story and the opinion survey appear to be very different from each other. While survey data most explicitly delineate a statistical understanding of a Muslim population, human interest stories also reference and reinforce such a statistical understanding of a Muslim population. Stories of individuals, families, or communities offer unique, subjective perspectives and experiences, distinct from social scientific research. However, as I show later, representations in these human interest stories regularly make claims to representativeness, placing the portrait of an individual or community in relation to a statistical understanding of a population. These stories are meant to describe patterns of belief and behavior among Muslim and Arab Americans. As a whole, they introduce the *Times* readership to a population that has been ignored, misrepresented, and misunderstood and offer an ostensibly more authentic portrayal grounded in the actual opinions and experiences of this population. The Pew Research Center's surveys of Muslim Americans similarly appear to correct misinformation and offer a more complete portrayal of Muslim Americans, arguing that Muslim Americans are "moderate and mostly mainstream." In addition, they offer demographic data and variable opinions on a range of topics, explicitly painting a statistical portrait of this population.

This shared reference point of Muslims as a population also links these stories and statistics to the policing profile. The profile is a composite figure in theory produced from statistical data to indicate the probability of future outcomes. In policing, a profile points to the behaviors and characteristics that are associated with criminal behavior. As an ostensibly predictive tool, the profile has become especially important in counterterrorism because of the perception that terrorism poses a disproportionate threat to life. Since the terrorist profile, and its derivatives, such as the radicalization pathway theory, distinguish Muslims as uniquely associated with such violence, they never depart from racial profiling. In practice, such frameworks, based on limited data and faulty reasoning, justify sweeping policing and surveillance of Muslims to identify the subtle characteristics that are said to be markers of terroristic potentialities.

Even as the human interest story, the survey, and the terrorist profile can portray Muslims in opposing ways—as patriotic, assimilated Americans or as potential terrorist threats—I argue that each of these presents Muslims as a population that is diverse, yet coherent, and contains within it a distinct threat. They share an assumption of Muslim difference that is conceptualized at the population level but can be operationalized at the individual level through monitoring and assessment of each Muslim. Each also offers tools for distinguishing Muslims by their degree of threat. These tools take the form of profiles portraying types of more or less threatening Muslims or "variables of assessment" in the form of characteristics, opinions, and behaviors that are assumed to be associated with threat.

In what follows, I begin by examining the assumptions and logics that shaped "racial profiling" as a debate and a set of policies and practices that have been used in relation to U.S. Muslims and Arabs for decades. Even with explicit moves away from both racial profiling more broadly and the terrorist profile more specifically, counterterrorism discourses and practices consistently rely on an assumption of a tie between Islam, in some form, and terrorism and seek to delineate methods by which future terrorism can be predicted and preempted. Next, I analyze the human interest stories, first noting the ideological work they do to quell criticism of racial profiling practices and then considering how the stories themselves produce profiles for assessing Muslims and thereby specify, rather than contradict, the crude racial profile. The chapter ends with consideration of the Pew Research Center's 2007 and 2011 surveys of Muslim Americans and how the findings were framed and disseminated by Pew and various media outlets. I argue that because a distinct conception of Muslims' riskiness shaped Pew's survey questions, its findings were open to manipulation such that its claims that Muslims were moderate were easily reversed to prove the existence of a Muslim threat. In shifting between policing and tolerance discourses, and also between stories and statistics about Muslims, I argue that representations of Muslims in each of these arenas are complementary, together painting a portrait of a distinct population and offering tools for assessing individual Muslims in relation to what are deemed the risky attributes of this population.

Much of the early discourses I engage take "Arab" as the relevant identity in the emerging War on Terror discourse; there is evident conflation of Muslim and Arab identities and confusion over whether religion or ethnicity is a more relevant "link" to the terrorists. Critics of the "backlash" against those perceived to be associated with the attacks commonly used the moniker "Muslims and Arabs and those perceived as such" to refer to this group. I use the terminology "Muslim/Arab" to capture the amorphous terrain of this otherization in the period immediately following 9/11. Over the next decade, "Muslim" would emerge as the more salient overarching identity category in this process of racialization—even as it always interacts with other identities, including ethnic, national, class, gender, and sexual ones.

THE TERRORIST, THE PROFILE, AND THE LOGICS OF PREEMPTION

The post-9/11 *New York Times* human interest stories were published at a moment when there was a new anxiety that long-standing law enforcement antiterrorism strategies had failed and that racial and religious profiling, however crude, might provide the only means of protecting the nation against future attack. Such fear was buttressed by reports that information available about the 9/11 hijackers called into question the existing profile of the suicide bomber as a young man facing economic hardship who is quickly indoctrinated into Islamic militancy. Rather, as the *New York Times* noted in a September 15, 2001, article, these hijackers were middle-class, sometimes older men with educations who had spent years in training for their mission, mingled with secular society, and drank alcohol. The tone of the quoted terrorism experts shifts from befuddlement to fear and horror as they describe a possibility of widespread hatred of the West.[7] Despite the shocked and horrified tone of the article, a 1999 report by the Library of Congress on "The Sociology and Psychology of Terrorism" makes clear that there never was a unitary "terrorist profile," even if particular patterns were discernible in particular movements; moreover, Osama bin Laden was believed to be recruiting highly skilled professionals for sophisticated missions.[8] Nevertheless, the notion that the terrorist profile had been disrupted powerfully reverberated with the notion that 9/11 marked a complete break with the past, necessitating a reassessment of the value and validity of racial profiling.

Indeed, racial profiling in policing, which had previously come under enough public scrutiny that President Bush vowed to end it in his first address to Congress, now became defensible with respect to Muslims and Arabs, including among many liberals, who argued it was justifiable as a temporary measure until more targeted security measures could be developed.[9] Many liberal defenses of racial profiling framed terrorism as an exceptional threat and the post-9/11 moment as a state of emergency that required the use of all tools and strategies available. According to an FBI tally, only 6 percent of all terrorist attacks on U.S. soil between 1980 and 2005 were by "Islamic extremists."[10] Nevertheless, antiterrorism measures gave inordinate focus to an "Islamic" threat, and targeted surveillance and policing of Muslims and Arabs did not fade into the background as new security measures were established. While the federal government, under both Bush and Obama, produced guidelines opposing racial profiling in law enforcement, it made an explicit exemption for profiling based on race, religion, and ethnicity to protect national security, particularly at border control and airport security, an exemption that was easily accepted by the U.S. public.[11]

The association of Muslims and Arabs with terrorism, which helps to justify such policies, precedes the September 11 attacks in the realms of both cultural representation and politics. The figure of the terrorist draws from representations of the Muslim/Arab/Oriental other as illogical, backward, and violent, as evident in European Orientalist literature and work since the eighteenth century. As Edward Said's *Orientalism* argues, the division between East and West was produced through a range of cultural products and would be used to justify European colonial exploits.[12] Jack Shaheen has argued that such European cultural representations served to inspire many early representations of Arabs in Hollywood films. Through a survey of more than nine hundred Hollywood films with Arab characters produced over one hundred years, Shaheen shows that Arabs and Muslims were commonly represented as irrational, barbaric villains.[13] The first representations of an Arab terrorist in a Hollywood feature film *(Sirocco)* occurred in 1951. However, the representations of Arab/Muslim terrorists increased greatly in the 1980s and 1990s, with films like *True Lies, Rules of Engagement,* and *The Siege,* which each also represented attacks on the United States. The Arab–Israeli conflict formed a significant political backdrop, as evident in the fact that Palestinians in these films were almost exclusively represented as terrorists. In addition, the 1979 Iranian revolution—which transformed the country from a U.S. ally to an Islamic government—and the taking of the U.S. embassy in the 444-day highly televised hostage crisis provided fodder for seeing Muslims as a direct threat to the United States. In all these cases, "Islam" emerged as the predominant analytical tool for understanding why Muslims resorted to such violence. As Said noted in 1981 in *Covering Islam,*

> much of the most dramatic, usually bad, news of the past decade, including not only Iran but the Arab–Israeli conflict, oil, and Afghanistan, has been news of "Islam." Nowhere was this more evident than in the long Iranian crisis during which the American consumer of news was given a sustained diet of information about a people, a culture, a religion—really no more than a poorly defined and badly misunderstood abstraction— always, in the case of Iran, represented as militant, dangerous, and anti-American.[14]

The Muslim terrorist as a figure helped Americans to interpret divergent acts as indicative of an irrational, religiously based hatred of the West rather than a political tactic used in a context of asymmetrical power.

Recognizing political factors in such acts does not legitimate them, but it does require discussion of the roles of the United States and Israel in these conflicts, which most media outlets preferred to sidestep. It was easier to blame religious fanaticism than to take seriously the Iranians' perspectives on the role of the United States in Iran and their demand that the United States return the deposed Shah so he could stand trial for his crimes against the Iranian people. Similarly, when Lebanese gunmen hijacked the commercial airliner TWA 847 in 1985, their demand that Israel withdraw from southern Lebanon was overshadowed by their Muslim identity as rationale for the act. Ultimately, a caricatured rendition of Arabs and Muslims in both popular culture and the news media served to strengthen the association of Muslims with terrorism, as an irrational and incomprehensible form of violence. The strength of this association was demonstrated when, following the 1995 Oklahoma City bombing by Timothy McVeigh, a White Christian, many in the media quickly argued that Muslim terrorists were to blame and Muslim Americans became victims of bias-motivated attacks.[15]

This association of Muslims with terrorism has been politically useful, giving the U.S. government great leeway in persecuting Muslims and Arabs, especially those supporting causes deemed contrary to U.S. interests. In particular, activism in support of Palestinian liberation movements has long been intensely scrutinized, as evident in the twenty-year case of the LA Eight. Seven Palestinians and one Kenyan were accused in 1987 of raising money for and distributing literature of the Popular Front for the Liberation of Palestine, but not of supporting the group's militant activities. Initially charged under an anticommunist law subsequently deemed unconstitutional, they were then retroactively charged under successive immigration and antiterrorism laws, ultimately being vindicated in 2007.[16] One law used to prosecute the LA Eight was President Clinton's 1996 Antiterrorism and Effective Death Penalty Act, which made support of the humanitarian activities of foreign organizations deemed "terrorist" groups a crime, regardless of intent or knowledge. It also allowed for the use of secret evidence and indefinite detention in particular cases.[17] Even before 2001, secret evidence was used almost exclusively in cases against Arab or Muslim immigrants who were accused only of *associating* with groups the government considered "terrorist."[18] In the weeks following 9/11, the USA PATRIOT Act signed into law further expanded government powers to detain, hold without charges, and deport noncitizens, while also retaining the right to use secret evidence and decreasing procedural protections.[19]

After 9/11, the profiling of Muslims and Arabs expanded in scope and became more explicitly justified. The Bush administration oversaw the detentions of more than twelve hundred primarily Muslim, South Asian, and Middle Eastern noncitizens; the selective application of deportation orders against Muslim and Middle Eastern noncitizens; and investigatory interviews targeting five thousand noncitizens from specific, mostly Muslim-majority countries.[20] However, in this period, profiling occurred through amorphous associations rather than a wholly consistent or unified "terrorist profile." Based on interviews of community leaders who witnessed this targeting, Nadine Naber notes,

> While particular persons were disproportionately targeted by federal government policies (most were Arab or South Asian and most were Muslim), the Bush administration's "terrorist profile" had the potential to single out a wide range of individuals, including Arab and Pakistani Muslims, non-Arab/non-South Asian Muslims; Christians and Jews; aliens, permanent residents, and citizens; and young men in addition to teenagers and the elderly.[21]

Bush also initiated National Security Entry-Exit Registration System (NSEERS), which was not eliminated until the last months of the Obama administration, only to be reestablished under Trump. It required males older than sixteen years from twenty-four Muslim-majority countries, and North Korea, to be registered with fingerprints, photographs, and interviews, suggesting that religion was the key determinant for inclusion on the list. However, political interests also clearly shaped these policies, as the program was initiated by requiring the registration of men from Iran, Iraq, Libya, Sudan, and Syria first, even though none of the 9/11 attackers were nationals of these countries. A very similar short list of "problematic nations" is repeated in Obama's 2015 exclusion of dual-nationals from the visa waiver program and in Trump's 2017 "Muslim ban." While fear of Muslims justified these programs, and nationality was the mechanism of exclusion, it is clear that the lists were often based on the United States' political enmities and alliances in the region.

Such blanket categorical exclusions are commonsensically described as "profiling," given that a specific status of nationality is deemed sufficient to warrant different treatment. However, profiling also evinces a logic where an individual is assessed in relation to a statistical understanding of a population. The profile is the interface between the individual and the population, in the form of an informational composite figure, such as "the drug trafficker" or "the terrorist." As a "practice that incorporates social science theory and statistical methodology into crime solving strategies,"[22] it is based on an assumption that with sufficient data, we can predict future events with some degree of probability. As Wendy Fitzgibbon explains, through a process of preemptive criminalization, police act based on a perception that an individual is statistically likely to commit a crime, often relying on an individual's group identity to determine his riskiness.[23] Race, ethnicity, nationality, and immigration status interact with patterns of behavior to become markers of risk of future criminal or terrorist activity. One obvious problem with this approach is that even a high statistical probability of a certain outcome does not prove that that outcome was imminent; smokers may be at high risk of cancer, but some live healthy lives into old age. Also, preemption is focused on identification of imminent threat and is not aimed at preventing such threats by addressing their causes. Preemption has also shifted into instigation, as evident in numerous entrapment cases. The FBI and New York Police Department (NYPD) has each planted agent provocateurs in mosques who, over the course of months, develop relationships with individuals to encourage and facilitate plans to conduct terrorist attacks.[24] In such cases, a future potentiality that otherwise likely would not have come to fruition is brought into the present to preempt that future. When publicized, these cases assure the public that terrorist threats are real and that domestic counterterrorism operations are effective, even as the circumstances of most cases suggest that no threat was imminent before law enforcement involvement.

NSEERS and other blunt racial profiling tactics have been deemed largely ineffective from a law enforcement perspective. For example, as of 2004, more than 200,000 people were registered under NSEERS, but none were charged with terrorism; nevertheless, 13,400 people were placed in deportation proceedings.[25] Indeed, this form of racial profiling is seen by many in security studies to be an ineffective method of preempting terrorism. Some have sought to better specify the terrorist profile by identifying common characteristics, whether demographic or attitudinal, of terrorists.[26] Marc Sageman, a high-profile government counterterrorism expert, however, has argued that there is no effective terrorist profile. Given how rare terrorism is in any population, whatever characteristics may be deemed more prevalent among terrorists, such as a degree in engineering,[27] do not distinguish terrorists from other members of the population (i.e., most engineers are not terrorists). Sageman and others have argued for the need to shift to analyzing the *process* of becoming a terrorist, referred to as "radicalization."[28] Nevertheless, "radicalization" arguments do not leave behind the profile, particularly the salience of religion, in assessing the potential threat of an individual.

There are distinct problems with the various strains of "radicalization" theory, as Arun Kundnani has shown, in that they fail to take account of the political circumstances and political interpretive frameworks that make the use of violence legitimate in the minds of those who advocate terrorism.[29] As such, they do more to advance the interests of the security institutions than to increase knowledge of the causes of terrorism. Radicalization theories suggest that exposure to specific theological beliefs, sometimes in combination with individual social and psychological processes, is the core mechanism by which individuals become "radicalized." They then argue that radicalization, defined as the adoption of specific conservative theological and anti-Western beliefs, is directly tied to terrorism, without considering that such beliefs could exist in the absence of support for terrorism. As Kundnani shows, the case of Anwar al-Awlaki, the U.S. citizen who was extrajudicially assassinated by the Obama administration while living in Yemen in 2011, does not correspond with radicalization theories. Al-Awaki's initial condemnation of the 9/11 attacks gave way to support for a violent global jihad against the United States, likely due to increasing frustration with U.S. government attacks on Muslims and a perception that civil rights advocacy and antiwar activism were failing. Contrary to radicalization theory, his theological views did not markedly change. Radicalization theory emphasizes variables that can be assessed at the level of the individual and are separated from the political context, failing to account for the fact that terrorist violence is a product of a political conflict in which the United States has a significant role.

Michael German, a former FBI special agent working on counterterrorism, has argued that the entire framework of predictive policing—whether utilizing a terrorist profile or a radicalization theory—is flawed and only serves to provide cover for the surveillance of religious and activist communities.[30] This is demonstrated in the case of the NYPD, which produced its own counterterrorism knowledge to offer tools and justification for the surveillance and management of the Muslim population. In a 2007 guide for identifying terrorists, the NYPD adopted a radicalization pathway theory, arguing that there is no terrorist profile but defining the radicalization pathway such that it only applied to Muslims.[31] Furthermore, in claiming that radicalization behaviors, such as becoming more religious and growing a beard, "make little noise," may seem innocuous, and are almost always legal, the NYPD helped to justify its—at that point, secret—mass surveillance of Muslim communities in New York City, undertaken against individuals and organizations without any demonstration of suspicion.[32]

The NYPD surveillance included the mapping of these communities, suggesting that predictive policing is increasingly depending on a combination of profiling, data collection, and data mining. Indeed, whereas blunt racial profiling tactics of detentions, interviews, and registrations have failed to lead to terrorism-related convictions, they have offered the government an opportunity to collect massive amounts of data that could be subject to analysis.[33] Government interest in such data collection was made explicit in the highly controversial and short-lived 2002 program Total Information Awareness (TIA), which included a proposal for a centralized database of personal information and the creation of data mining software to analyze this material and identify future terrorists. Although officially disbanded, major elements of TIA were secretly moved to the National Security Association.[34] Philosopher Edward Tverdek argues that analysis of deidentified data should produce a *probabilistic* rather than racial or religious profile that would point to traits and patterns associated with terrorism.[35] While Tverdeck raises concerns about civil rights violations—noting that such a policy will inevitably ensnare innocent people—he argues that privacy risks will be evenly distributed over the entire population. However, the collection and mining of data itself may be shaped by the racial profile, for example, if the material analyzed is disproportionately collected from Muslim communities or if the behaviors and characteristic selected for analysis are particular to or more common among Muslims, such as mosque attendance or political activism on specific issues. Such

data collection and analysis procedures could produce "neutrally established" statistical probabilities that mark Muslim communities as risky
populations, while inoculating such interventions from charges of racial
profiling.[36]

Indeed, the logic of racial profiling continued to be central to antiterrorism efforts, including through the facially neutral Countering Violent
Extremism (CVE) initiated in 2014 by the Obama administration in Los
Angeles, Boston, and Minneapolis. While emphasizing partnership between law enforcement and affected communities, the program focused
disproportionately on Muslim communities and created "a gateway for
unwarranted law enforcement surveillance."[37] A CVE-produced guide provides police, social workers, and teachers methods of assessing the threat
of extremism among young people, including ratings on specific measures,
such as "Expressions of Hopelessness, Futility" and "Connection to Group
Identity (Race, Nationality, Religion, Ethnicity)." The CVE guide had service providers rate children, parents, and communities separately, in order
to "plot the scores on a graph to determine what 'interventions could halt
the process of radicalization before it happens.'"[38] CVE makes explicit how
the profile can be mobilized to entwine local law enforcement, community
leaders, teachers, social workers, teens, and their parents into a system of
surveillance and anxiety production.

Over the course of the long War on Terror, and under both Republican and Democratic leadership, racial profiling in the name of national
security went from an "exceptional" policing tactic during a time of emergency to a normalized and widely disseminated component of domestic
and global policing. This intimate engagement with Muslims, the will to
know and assess them, as evident in CVE, bears important resemblance to
the impulses that animate New York Times human interest stories published
in the six months following the 9/11 attacks. These assessment-oriented
and preemptive strategies have not faced widespread critique in part because they fit within a framework of a tolerance discourse that emerged
in the post-9/11 context. The Times human interest stories produce a series of profiles of less or more threatening Muslims, identifying variables
of assessment by which a distinctly Muslim threat needs to be measured.
Through their broad dissemination to the public in a context where all are
deemed responsible for preventing "terrorism"—for example, in the New

York City subway campaign telling riders that "If You See Something, Say Something"—they bring the general population into the task of knowing and monitoring Muslims. These stories on Muslim and Arab Americans not only modeled a tolerant and sympathetic disposition to Muslims and Arabs but also specified and explicated the racial logic at the heart of calls for racial profiling and various surveillance policies. Similarly, polling of Muslim Americans by the Pew Research Center, while representing Muslims as "moderate and mostly mainstream," furthered a portrayal of Muslims as a population of risk that must be assessed along distinct lines of threat.

THE HUMAN INTEREST STORY: PROFILES AND POPULATIONS

In the following sections based on analysis of sixty *New York Times* human interest stories published in the months following the 9/11 attacks, I first describe how these stories go to pains to represent the government practices as primarily protective and tolerant in relation to Muslims and Arabs, thereby undermining critiques of racial profiling policies and practices. Next, I show how these stories answer the question posed by some Americans: "how do you differentiate and figure out which one is the bad one from those who love freedom and our country?"[39] In particular, the stories produced a set of profiles of more and less trustworthy or threatening Muslim and Arab Americans by setting forward a set of interacting variables, especially religion/religiosity, gender/gender norms, and emotional responses to the 9/11 attacks, as a means to assess this population. Together these stories serve a similar function as the law enforcement profile in identifying those presumed to have a higher, or lower, probability of committing terrorism in order to more effectively preempt such threats.

While my analysis is attuned to all these elements, the profiles also must be interpreted in relation to the genre of the human interest story and particularly what role they served in the post-9/11 period. Human interest stories generally report on newsworthy issues from the perspective of individuals or communities to create feelings of emotional and personal connection between reader and subject matter. The stories of Muslim and Arab Americans analyzed here were part of the *Times'* extensive and highly lauded immediate post-9/11 coverage, which would earn the paper a record number of Pulitzer Prizes in 2002.[40] Although not the only venue with a new interest in Muslims and Arabs, the *New York Times* is a widely respected and influential national, New York–based paper. Furthermore, it is considered a center-left news source, as it has a more liberal readership than other high-circulation national dailies, such as *USA Today* and the *Wall Street Journal*.[41] As a result, its extensive post-9/11 coverage of Muslims and Arabs in the United States connects the experiences of Muslims and Arabs to both the local and national experiences of the attacks and is concerned with framing this coverage in relation to such liberal values as cosmopolitanism, multiculturalism, and tolerance.

Of course, it is important to note that these particular stories on Muslims and Arabs were produced in an affectively saturated media milieu of the six months following the September 2001 attacks. The spectacular attacks, resulting in thousands of civilian deaths, were captured in real time and endlessly replayed on television. Targeting major institutions of U.S. global hegemony, they were quickly cast as attacks on "American" and "Western" values by Muslim/Arab enemies willing to die in the service of their cause. A reeling New York City, its downtown area covered in ash, became a source of identification across the country and the globe. While the attacks disrupted the empathy fatigue of audiences immunized to the horrors regularly represented in the media, the media was all the more saturated with emotions, including horror, anger, vengeance, fear, sympathy, camaraderie, love, and pride. Even as sympathy first and foremost focused on those most directly victimized by the attacks, such as families of the victims, Muslims were represented at times also in a sympathetic light as targets of a "backlash," including increased discrimination, scrutiny, and violence. Therefore I track the portrayal and evocation of emotion in these profiles as a means of delineating lines of belonging, which become an element of profiling technology.

As a whole, the human interest stories produce a data set about a distinct and analytically coherent population, despite the fact that this population is alternately defined in relation to a religion (Islam), an ethnicity (Arab), or a geographical region (the Middle East). These stories often take the pairing of Muslim and Arab for granted, not acknowledging that most Muslims are not Arab and that many Arabs, particularly in the United States, are not Muslim. They also do not interrogate where this interest in

Muslims and Arabs has come from, as a result naturalizing the attention that has suddenly fallen on these communities. Earlier pieces especially used the terms "Muslims" and "Arabs" almost interchangeably, even when the terms do not clearly refer to those being profiled.[42] For example, one article, ostensibly about a predominantly Christian Arab American community in Yonkers, New York, includes quotes and images from various South Asian Muslims.[43] Even despite these inconsistencies, these stories together carve out a population of concern distinct from the population at large, one that will be defined most consistently in its relationship to Islam. Furthermore, this sudden unexamined interest in this population demonstrates an assumption that there is a substantive link between them and "the terrorists."

While human interest stories often focus on a small group of people or an individual, they gain their significance through an assumption that these experiences and perspectives can be extrapolated to the larger community or population. In fact, it is clear that portrayals of Muslim/Arab individuals and communities in these human interest stories are always in relation to a conceptualization of a population. In other words, human interest stories are not only *representational* but also *representative,* resting on a social scientific conception of populations, which is most evident in the repeated use of demographic data and statistics to link a specific portrait to a wider population and make a claim about the broader significance of the portrayal. Almost all articles take a moment to position their specific subject matter within a broader population-based understanding to demonstrate a degree of representativeness, most commonly by noting the population of Muslims or Arabs in the specific locality.[44] For example, an article about a mosque in Long Island references the seventy thousand Muslims in Naussau and Suffolk Counties, and another on tensions in a mosque in Queens mentions the twenty thousand Afghans in New York. In other articles, we learn also about racial/ethnic subpopulations of Muslims, including African American Muslims (25–40 percent of all Muslim Americans) and Latino Muslims (10,000–25,000).[45] There are said to be at least 4,000 Muslims in the military, 88,000 Muslim students enrolled in private Islamic schools in the country, and 150,000 households in the United States that receive the Arabic-language news station Al Jazeera.[46] We also learn, based on mosque attendance, that the vast majority of the estimated four to six million Muslims in the United States appear to be secular but that the number of Muslims "vocally distancing themselves from conservative Islam . . . is probably a small minority."[47] This Muslim/ Arab population also takes shape through a mapping of its geographical distribution through these articles, which are always attuned to *where* we find Muslims and Arabs, focusing on cities and neighborhoods with large populations of Arabs and Muslims. The cumulative effect of these statistics is to produce a diverse, yet still coherent, population that is distributed by particular variables, such as geographic concentration, ethnicity, institutional affiliation (military, schools, etc.), and religious affiliation.

Informationally, the *Times* coverage is broad, sweeping, and varied, and for every stereotype that is reinforced repeatedly in these articles, there seems to be at least one article that in some way challenges or adds nuance to the representation. While many pieces focus on South Asian and Arab Muslims, a number of articles portray other Muslim communities, especially African Americans and Latinos, and other Arab communities, such as Christian Arabs. While many articles portray individuals who are parts of "ethnic enclaves," living or working in neighborhoods centered around a mosque or an Arab business district, some portray small, isolated communities, such as in Laramie, Wyoming, or individuals not associated with such enclaves, such as Manhattan-based artists. While many articles focus on apparently traditional and religious Muslims, such as members of a local mosque or students at an Islamic school, one article argues that secular Muslims are the majority of U.S. Muslims. The repeated images of men standing or kneeling in prayer or of women wearing head scarves are counterbalanced by occasional portrayals of secular Muslim men and women who are described in reference to such "secular" practices as yoga and shopping. However, the diversity of Muslims and Arabs presented in these stories is in part in the service of making the overall portrayal *seem* representative. Ultimately, Muslims and Arabs as a whole are represented as strongly religious and tradition-bound communities, while, as I argue in greater depth later, variations among Muslims emerge as variables of assessment by which Muslims/Arabs can be identified as more or less tolerable. Before I turn to how articles represent these distinctions among Muslims, I first examine the ideological work human interest stories do to explain and justify racial profiling of Muslims in the post-9/11 moment.

A Protective and Tolerant State

Although, during the months following the 9/11 attacks, racial profiling was gaining more public supporters and being utilized by the government, the logic of racial profiling is rarely highlighted or critiqued in these human interest stories. Rather, the dominant narratives revolve around a notion that state actions are motivated by a desire to offer protection and to promote tolerance. Whether describing police officers stationed outside mosques, the FBI knocking on people's doors and detaining and deporting individuals not connected to the attacks, the interviewing of Muslim/Arab men, or the experiences of Muslims in the military, state actors are presented as operating in good faith and taking a protective, paternalistic position. While sometimes specific actions are faulted for violating the rights of particular individuals, they are counterbalanced by an articulated need to aggressively pursue terrorists; while particular Muslims and Arabs may experience even great hardships, they are by and large shown as being treated with respect and tolerance by the police, FBI, and military.

Particularly striking is the repeated, yet never critically engaged, image of the police officer stationed outside of a mosque, an Arab shopping strip, or a residential neighborhood.[48] On one hand, the police embody a state discourse of tolerance, protecting Muslim and Arab communities against "isolated" bigots. In one article, a police officer echoed Bush's framing: "No one should feel bad. . . . We are after evil. We are not after your religion. We don't want revenge; we want justice."[49] On the other hand, police officers implicitly serve a double function, not simply protecting but also policing these communities, as is evident in one article's two images: a map of Afghanistan's military targets and an image of a police officer, shown walking down a New York street with people wearing identifiably Islamic dress, who is described as "patrol[ing] . . . one of the city's biggest Arab neighborhoods," creating a parallel between the international and domestic "fronts" of the War on Terror.[50] Reflecting the duality of protection and policing, an Arab deli owner says of a visit by two police officers, "They said there was a threat to blow up the store. Maybe they just wanted to look around and see if we had any bombs here."[51]

Even articles directly dealing with racial profiling offer few questions regarding the legitimacy or logic behind these policies. One piece describing seven experiences of detention of primarily Arab and Muslim noncitizen men brings to life these hardships but suggests their targeting is justified as being a result of "resumes suspiciously like those of the 19 hijackers."[52] The apparent similarities include individuals making flight reservations at Kinko's or visiting a department of motor vehicles at the same time as a hijacker. However, not noted is that these "similarities" were only meaningful because the people involved were Muslim, Arab, or South Asian men. A piece on a man dubbed "Dr. Terror" by the media, and detained for thirteen days simply because he had the same common Saudi last name as one of the hijackers, quotes the man as saying, "What I went through was not fun. But in another country, I might be in jail for four years and nobody would know."[53] While concerns about civil liberties are lightly broached, ultimately the government is presented as a good faith actor that is finding its way during difficult times. A Justice Department spokesperson gets the last word in one piece, saying that although mistakes may have been made, they have "no interest in detaining people who are not a threat to us."[54] The purity of intentions stands as alibi and contrasts with the intention of the terrorists, which is understood to be the slaughter of innocent people.[55]

Finally, most remarkably, in these stories, the military, an institution being mobilized to war with Afghanistan, a country devastated by the long-term effects of Cold War militarism in which the United States is heavily implicated, repeatedly plays a central role in both demonstrating the patriotism of Muslims and Arabs and establishing the tolerance of the state in relation to Muslim and Arab Americans.[56] As such, the military multiculturalism that emerged during the Gulf War now has expanded to include Muslims and Arabs.[57] One cadet compares his experiences in the military favorably to the "icy attitudes and sideways glances" a friend of his received in the quintessential liberal community of Berkeley, California. Three Muslim West Point cadets describe respectful conversations with their peers, who are curious to learn more of their religion and cultures.[58] A Muslim woman is training to become a military chaplain, portraying the military as a place where women have greater access to power.[59] All are supportive of the war in Afghanistan. Through these stories, the *Times* manages to transform the military—an institution built on violent masculinist values and essential to maintaining U.S. global hegemony—into a purveyor of gender equality and religious and ethnic tolerance. The *Times* human interest stories thereby leave the racial profiling practices of the U.S. government unquestioned and present the state as a purveyor of tolerance and religious freedom.

The other mechanism by which these human interest stories promote population racism is through their production of a set of profiles of more and less tolerant Muslims, which aligns with a policing interest in assessing the potential threat of any Muslim. These profiles can be broadly put into two categories: "traditional" Muslims and "modern" Muslims. "Traditional" here refers to a representation that emphasizes being demonstrably religious, being a first-generation immigrant, holding a working-class or immigrant niche job, and associating strongly with a Muslim/Arab community. "Modern" refers to characteristics such as being nonreligious or privatizing one's religious practice, holding an upper-middle-class or "professional" job, and not associating strongly (or uncritically) with a Muslim/Arab community. I do not subscribe to a notion of teleological progression from tradition to modernity, nor a binary opposition between the two categories, but only use them to mark patterns within these representations. I found that most profiles can be placed in one or the other category, and this categorization is helpful in identifying what I argue constitute the profiles of more or less tolerable Muslims/Arabs that emerge in these stories. The specific profiles that I identify and analyze in depth are the fearful traditional woman, the patriotic traditional man, the ambivalent traditional Muslim/Arab, the angry modern woman, and the tolerant modern man.

Fearful Victims and Emphatic Patriots

The photographs of "traditional" women and men that accompany articles on Muslim/Arab communities are telling. Men are very often in the midst of prayer, usually in a collective, while head scarf–wearing women are shown in close-up images that emphasize their facial expressions and emotional states. Each type of image emphasizes religiosity through a mechanism—prayer and the head scarf—and, in the U.S. context, difference over similarity. Islamic religiosity is also represented as gender segregated and unequal, with publicly active men and women who are closed in by the close-up and the head scarf. Men are forever foreign and to some extent unknowable, and while women are also different, the close-up offers

a moment of emotional intimacy not present in photographs of men pray-
ing. The articles, however, suggest another dynamic, as no article focuses
primarily on a single traditional Muslim woman, while there are articles on
specific traditional men and modern women and men. Even as it seems we
want to read emotions on traditional women's faces, traditional men are
the ones we *need* to know.

In a period of targeted detention and deportation of Muslim and Arab
men, and increasing incidents of individual attacks, vandalism, and other
kinds of violence, including the murders of five men—three of whom were
Sikh, not Muslim or Arab—it is tolerance and sympathy for the traditional
Muslim woman that become the articulation of U.S. tolerance.[60] The Muslim woman donning a head scarf emerges as the embodiment of the victimization and fear in these communities as a result of the "backlash" against
Muslims, which is almost entirely referenced as taking the form of vigilante
violence rather than state persecution. By contrast, profiles of "traditional"
Muslim and Arab immigrant men focus not on their fear of victimization
but rather on their patriotism. These stories parallel the sudden proliferation of flags flown in Muslim/Arab neighborhoods mentioned in numerous articles[61] and demonstrate an "imperative patriotism"[62] intended to act
as a shield against scrutiny and suspicion. Gender demarcates which emotional response is appropriate to a traditional Muslim, as victimhood aligns
most clearly with the figure of the Muslim woman, while the Muslim man
must actively demonstrate his lack of terrorist proclivities.

While vulnerability is more acceptable in women in many cultures,
there is a distinct representation of Muslim women, particularly those who
observe hijab, as sympathetic victims because of a perception of the oppression of women in Islam. The head scarf is also a visible sign of Muslim
identity that may make these women more likely targets. These various
dynamics are evident in the following passage from "Trying to Soothe the
Fears Hiding behind the Veil":

> She refuses to remove her scarf.
>
> But Efrah, a Muslim woman who lives in Prospect Heights, Brooklyn,
> is still afraid because she has heard stories of women in hijab (Arabic for
> veil) who have been attacked and called names. It was Efrah's fear that
> made her ask that her last name not be given in this column. She will
> not ride a subway or a bus. And it is a reflection of her fear that where

she works, the Arab-American Family Support Center in Cobble Hill, Brooklyn, has made a list of volunteer escorts for women, like her, who are afraid.[63]

In various articles, women debate staying home, removing their head scarves, or continuing to wear them.[64] Despite this focus on Muslim women's victimization, the strong Muslim woman who emerges is one who chooses to keep her head scarf on. In another article, we see a different emphasis on this question of choice, in a profile of Muslim students who describe college as a context where women are able to find community and develop a stronger religious identity, including in the choice to wear hijab. As one woman says, "you can practice your religion the way you want . . . because nothing is forcing you into it."[65] Even as there is an acknowledgment of anti-Muslim hate crimes that target and delimit the choices of head scarf–wearing women, a notion of the particularity of U.S. religious tolerance is established through the image of the Muslim woman free to choose how she practices her religion.

Fear and victimization do not stick to Muslim/Arab men as easily. Articles describe men as at most "jittery" (at the murder of a store owner),[66] "shaken" (at a bomb threat),[67] or feeling "worry" (about FBI interviews)[68] but nevertheless going on with their daily lives. In fact, there is no sustained focus on their fear. Rather, the focus is often on these men's articulations of a vociferous patriotism, suggesting that this, along with distancing oneself from Muslim communities and politics, is necessary to these men becoming tolerable. However, the passion with which the patriotism is articulated seems also to point to a fundamental irrationalism that produces a kernel of doubt. As such, these men retain an undercurrent of threat that continues to associate them with the terrorist, despite or *because of* their strongly articulated patriotism.

Individual profiles of traditional Muslim men are often of first-generation Arab immigrants who have achieved success in this country, becoming a testament to the notion of the United States as the land of opportunity. One profile focuses on the patriarch of an immigrant family who was a victim of the attacks—he worked in the World Trade Center—and a patriotic American.[69] He feels "blessed" to be an American citizen, has a son in the marines, and "wholeheartedly support[s] the war" in Afghanistan, despite the fact that his support of war has created a rift between him and his family in Egypt. Another profile focuses on the newly elected mayor of Wayne, Michigan, Abdul Haidous, an immigrant from Lebanon who has made a living owning a grocery store and says that he is "living the American dream."[70] The reporter notes that Haidous says "a million clichés," such as "the greatest country on this earth is the United States of America." However, "there is a resonance in his voice and a glint in his eyes that says maybe this guy is the real deal." Even as Haidous's views are "maybe" sincere, the reporter suggests his patriotism is somehow excessive.

Similar themes are repeated and expanded upon in "Terrorist from Central Casting Has Hard Lessons to Teach," which describes how a man achieved his American Dream as an actor playing the roles of terrorists in various Hollywood blockbusters. Nevertheless, in the mid-1990s, he joined his local mosque to find out more about "radical Islamic fundamentalists" but then fell in love with the community and "got a little fanatical for a while."[71] Although "not terrorists," the members of the mosque are presented as susceptible to joining a holy war, and the actor's own love of the community serves to demonstrate the hidden threat that seems to lie within all Muslims. Ultimately, the actor's love finds a more appropriate object: "I love this country because I didn't always have it. . . . Freedom, food, water that is clean, Constitution—these are not things I take for granted."[72] The economic conditions that bring most migrants to the United States, suggested in the references to food and water, are overshadowed by the more familiar tropes of "Freedom" and "Constitution." His patriotic love of the United States is further established in his current project, a documentary he is making on Muslim militants' recruitment efforts in the United States. As such, readers are assured that the transfer of his affection has been complete, and he is no longer a threat.

In these profiles of traditional Muslim/Arab men, excessive patriotism, a patriotism that was in fact demanded of them, seems to indicate a more primordial, emotional, and irrational form of affiliation. This exaggerated patriotism is presented as a product of a need to have a strongly felt identification with a larger community. While in these cases, these men articulated that emotional connection with the United States, an irrationalism seems to be at the heart of the identification producing a potential threat. These men seem like switches that can be flipped, and in the third case is flipped. Their emotionalism is their vulnerability that produces a lack of trustworthiness. Should these men articulate any ambivalence about their relation to the United States, they are easily transformed from patriots to threats.

Ambivalence as Threat

Indeed, in other human interest stories, when individuals deviate from these particular scripts and criticize the international role of the United States or doubt the culpability of the Taliban or Bin Laden in relation to the 9/11 attacks, their ambivalence about the predominant narratives about the War on Terror produces a threat. Although human interest stories are intended to introduce readers to new experiences and perspectives, these moments of questioning or doubt do not become opportunities for exploring the sources of such perspectives, the evidence for or against them, or their implications. Rather, they become markers of the dual loyalty and conflicting attachments of Muslims and Arabs that makes it difficult for them to fully integrate into the United States. In a moment when Ari Fleischer, the White House press secretary, had warned that Americans "need to watch what they say, watch what they do,"[73] the distinction between opinions and actions, between dissent and treason, was intentionally being blurred for all Americans. In such a context, traditional Muslims/Arabs who do not strictly abide by the narratives of victimization and patriotism recounted earlier are cast as likely aligned with "the enemy."

While a number of articles, especially early on, seem to be ambivalent about the loyalties of Muslims and Arabs, as more articles are written, clearer distinctions emerge between the sympathetic patriotic and/or victimized Muslim as opposed to the alarming and likely dangerous Muslim. In an article on a Long Island mosque, a woman interviewed says of the Taliban, "they haven't really proved they are terrorists and all they are doing is following their religion more stringently than the average person does."[74] The woman's perspective is not explored further. Without any deeper examination, and because of an equivalency created between the Taliban and Bin Laden, who was quickly deemed responsible for the attacks, such statements were likely read as support for terrorism. This article generated several concerned letters, the most sympathetic of which opposed the increased scrutiny of Muslims, then critiqued this woman as undermining efforts to "draw a sharp distinction between Muslims and the Taliban" and being unappreciative of the standard of justice that she enjoys in the United States but is denied those living under the Taliban.[75] As this letter indicates, the mosque member is made responsible for perceptions of all Muslims, who must appreciate the U.S. justice system, even as the government is actively targeting Muslims and Arabs.

A profile of an Islamic school in Brooklyn, titled "The 2 Worlds of Muslim American Teenagers," superficially takes the form of a humanistic portrayal of a misunderstood minority but provides little context for understanding the statements of the students. As a result, fears of volatile teenagers, of unassimilated immigrants, and of an Islamic threat come together to create a portrayal of an incipient threat that exists throughout the country. The students are represented as torn and confused by their presumed dual loyalties to Islam and to the United States and as likely aligning themselves with Islam. As the second paragraph says,

> to be young and Muslim in the United States today . . . is to be consumed by causes abroad and removed from politics at home, to feel righteous and also confused, to alternate between gratitude and resentment toward the world outside their classrooms.[76]

Of particular concern seem to be the teens' claims that they might refuse to take up arms against other Muslims but would be willing to follow a true Muslim leader elsewhere. While the article describes these students as "like other immigrants" in being tied to their homelands, these ties are presented as sinister because they have "empathy for the young Muslims around the world who profess hatred for America and Americans." Although they "may not be a scientific sampling of Muslim American youth," the author suggests that their viewpoints are widely shared, making a profile of a single school into a story of the incipient threat of Muslim American teens.

Human interest stories therefore treat Muslim/Arab Americans as part of a broader global population of Muslims and Arabs that is often portrayed as homogenous, anti-American, and dangerous. Moreover, because these articles evince no interest in understanding the *politics* that connect some Muslims and Arabs in the United States to those abroad—including a critique of U.S. support of occupation, militarism, and authoritarianism in South and West Asia and North Africa—pointing to these political views without explanation is particularly damning. As a result, the strength of association with Muslims/Arabs abroad becomes a significant variable for assessing the threat level of Muslims/Arabs in the United States. Articulations of political or religious affiliations that emphasize solidarity with Muslims/Arabs abroad are deemed threatening, unless they are demonstrated to promote U.S. interests and values.

Moderate Exceptions

In contrast to "traditional" Muslims and Arabs, a number of stories profile "modern" and apparently exceptional individuals living independently outside ethnic enclaves (often in Manhattan), having a secular or privatized relationship to religion, and practicing a consumer lifestyle that marks them as well integrated into U.S. society—in essence being good neoliberal subjects. This exceptionality is consistently maintained, despite the fact that one article notes that the majority of Muslims are likely secular.[77] These women and men are able to articulate a more subtle form of patriotism, manifested particularly through their acceptance of a dominant discourse about U.S. tolerance and Islamic intolerance. Women, in particular, are presented as rebels who express anger at both sexism and terroristic violence, which they see as rooted in strains of Islam. Anger, rebellion, and challenge become their predominant emotional modes as they become responsible for reforming their religion. A very small number of men, by contrast, can escape the specificity of their religious and ethnic identity, articulating an empathy and tolerance that crosses such divides and produces a universal humanism. While such exceptional individuals are emotional, they are not excessively tied to their religious, ethnic, or national identities. As such, they seem to take more nuanced positions, neither Islamophobic nor uncritical of the religion, neither excessively patriotic nor unappreciative of U.S. values. While challenging a cultural racism that sees Muslims/Arabs as a homogenous threat, these profiles consistently reinforce a notion that culture or religion, rather than politics, is at the heart of the emerging conflicts.

In "Moderates Start Speaking Out against Islamic Intolerance," "moderate Muslims" are presented as exceptions who probably constitute "a

small minority" of Muslims in the United States and exhibiting very specific characteristics.[78] They are predominantly female, young, assimilated,
and educated and embroiled in a battle against restrictive cultural norms,
especially related to gender. Anger is the central emotional expression:
"outrage, it seems, has helped shatter the silence." And 9/11 is a turning
point: "after years of quietly watching a harsh, puritanical strain of Islam
enter America, many moderate Muslims are speaking out in favor of a more
tolerant form of their faith." This puritanical strain is blamed for the 9/11
attacks and identified through cultural conservatism; as a result, sexist
practices among Muslim American men become signs of alignment with
"terrorism." "Traditionalists" are equated with "extremists" and "Wah-
habists" and deemed responsible, as the closing quote indicates: "your
hands are dirtier than this."

Similar themes are explored in two stories profiling angry women—
oddly, both described as "daughters of Islam"—who counter the twin
threats of Islam: religious conservatism and terrorism. In contrast to "traditional" Muslims, these women are able to engage with Muslims and Arabs
because they become vehicles for the transmittal of "Western" values. In
"Stitch by Stitch, a Daughter of Islam Takes On Taboos," Ghada Amer, an
Egyptian-born artist now living in Manhattan, explains, "What is going on
now politically is like a mirror of what has always gone on in myself, because I am a hybrid of the West and the East. It's a clash between civilizations that of course don't understand each other."[79] Framing the "conflict"
as cultural, the artist holds up cultural hybridity as a solution, although
one that prioritizes Western values. While noting as "ludicrous" Western
clothing styles modified to conform to Islamic concepts of modesty, Amer
describes her own art, which includes images of women lifted from pornography, as appreciated by her "strictly religious" family and hence able to
change the world "a little bit." Cultural hybridity, it becomes clear, is only
valid when "Western" cultural norms are determinant.

The other "Daughter of Islam" profiled by the *Times* is Aasma Khan, a
lawyer and the founder of Muslims against Terrorism.[80] While her formation of Muslims against Terrorism is clearly a "patriotic" act, the emotional
weight of the article lies in its descriptions of the intimate aspects of her
life as an (almost) typical, cosmopolitan Manhattanite. We meet her barefoot and bare-headed in her upper Manhattan apartment that is mostly

empty due to a divorce, where her prayer rug is rolled up in the corner but not used as regularly as she would like. Described as having been a "citified, New Age Muslim who shopped at Ikea, [and] skated in Central Park" before 9/11, she has now become "an angrily articulate advocate intent on" reclaiming her religion from the terrorists. Her anger, evident in her "clenched fist," gives way to other emotions, her eyes welling up with tears as she explains that while she initially feared bigotry from other Americans, now, as someone who dares to speak the truth, she fears becoming the target of Islamic extremists. Despite her emotionalism, her patriotism does not seem to be overly exaggerated but rather is confirmed by a combination of her consumer lifestyle, her secularized/privatized religiosity, and her alignment with a particular War on Terror discourse of opposing intolerance. Much like the other "Daughter of Islam," she is presented as a modern Muslim woman who can be the agent of change in relation to an Islam cast as reactionary and in need of reform.

Finally, one lone article suggests that the exceedingly rare modern, secularized man is the only Muslim/Arab able to fully transcend identity and achieve a universal cosmopolitanism that epitomizes New York City. An article with a headline not referencing religion or ethnicity, "Strains on a Man and the City, Distilled in 10 Minutes," presents a sympathetic portrayal of Moukhtar Kocache, a Lebanese American curator who lost a friend on 9/11 and whose office, formerly in the World Trade Center, is now contained in a purple folder.[81] Kocache is a "typical" Manhattanite who likes yoga and in-line skating and has a conflicted relationship with his therapist. He "barely know[s] the basic principles of Islam" and does not associate much with Arab-identified organizations. The piece focuses on his personal trauma and emotional state, noting that having grown up in war-torn Lebanon, he knows "how to laugh and cry at the same time." On September 12, Kocache had an experience that "is so New York," when he found himself in the presence of a police officer and a middle-aged woman speaking Hebrew to each other. His initial discomfort gave way after he joined in the conversation (remarkably, he speaks Hebrew also), which continued in Arabic and subsequently ended with a hug from the woman and a handshake from the police officer. We do not hear the conversation but can guess that it did not address the conflicts between Israel, Lebanon, and Palestine or the policing of Muslim Americans. For Kocache, this experience was "beautiful" and "is what makes it possible for all of us to live together." Mr. Kocache is never explicitly presented as patriotic, but he is already aligned with American values as secular, individualist, and tolerant. He is able to transcend his religion and ethnicity and to embody both the suffering and the tolerance of the city in a way that no other Muslim/Arab profiled can.

Even as these stories represent Muslims/Arabs as highly diverse, they produce a separation between "us" and "them," reinforcing the assumption that Muslims and Arabs have a unique relationship to the attacks that must be interrogated. The diversity and variation they describe then become a set of variables to which readers must become attuned to assess the degree of threat that various types of Muslims pose. These variables of assessment that are also repeated in other discourses of tolerance include gender, religiosity, strength of association with Muslim communities, political positionality on U.S. foreign policy, and participation in discourses of tolerance. In these stories, these variables come together in specific constellations to depict "traditional" Muslims/Arabs as objects of tolerance, if they are fearful or exhibit patriotism, or intolerance, if they are too strongly associated with Muslims/Arabs abroad. They also depict "modern" Muslims/Arabs as objects of identification and sympathy. These variables of assessment, however, can be reassembled into new constellations, allowing for constructing new profiles, depending on the demands of the particular political moment. Nevertheless, as the Pew Research Center surveys indicate, there is consistency in the frameworks through which Muslims are assessed, which is made explicit not only in policing profiles and human interest stories but also in the questions that are asked of Muslims on opinion polls and how their responses are interpreted.

MUSLIM AMERICAN EXCEPTIONALISM

In contrast to "soft" human interest stories, the Pew Research Center's studies of Muslims seek to portray Muslim Americans by documenting their experiences and opinions through the framework of "hard numbers" or "objective" quantitative data. Over the course of fifty-six pages of text and tables, the 2007 report presents data on Muslim Americans' religiosity and religious tolerance, views on gender and sexuality, and attitudes toward the United States, arguing that they are "largely assimilated, happy with their lives, and moderate with respect to many of the issues that have divided Muslims and Westerners around the world."[82] While this report, along with another similar one released in 2011, appears to be designed to assuage the public's fears about Muslims, the lengthy surveys have also been manipulated to accomplish the opposite. Furthermore, the consistency of Pew's analysis with security studies' counterterrorism efforts is evident in the number of works that draw on the Pew study to develop their analysis.[83] Indeed, a shift in framing from 2007 to 2011 reports makes explicit that the question of susceptibility to terrorism sits below the surface of many of the other questions. The 2011 report—framed in terms of the anniversary of 9/11, concerns about "homegrown Islamic terrorists," and conflicts over building mosques—presents its primary findings of Muslim Americans in the negative, as the *absence* of any indication of "increased alienation or anger" or "rising support for Islamic extremism."[84] Ultimately, the Pew studies bolster an assumption that Muslims compose a population that contains within it a distinct threat that must be assessed and managed, even as they argue that most Muslim Americans are worthy of tolerance.

The Pew studies offer a set of articulated questions that assist in measuring the tolerability or riskiness of Muslim Americans. As is clear from the narrative description, Muslim Americans become worthy of tolerance through a specific immigrant narrative of assimilation, achievement of the "American Dream," and appreciation for such opportunities—a narrative that by and large leaves out African American and other nonimmigrant Muslim communities. The questions that emerge as most significant, through Pew's own framing and through media reports, can be organized into a few thematic areas: religiosity and tolerance (religiosity, practices, views on other religions), gender beliefs and practices (segregation, hijab, women working, and homosexuality), the War on Terror (discrimination, views on War on Terror, beliefs on "extremism"), and relationship to the United States (political beliefs, identity, assimilation, satisfaction). Most of the other questions are demographic, including immigration status/nativity, race/ethnicity, age, gender, income, and education level. Many of the questions in some way speak to whether Muslim Americans are tolerant, modern, and patriotic, which in Pew's framing suggests the status of the "moderate Muslim."

The concept of the moderate Muslim is produced in contrast to other Muslims, particularly those "around the world," both in Europe and in Muslim-majority countries. Muslim Americans are said to "reject Islamic extremism" more than Muslims in Western Europe and to be more concerned with the global rise of "Islamic extremism" than either European Muslims or Muslims in Muslim-majority countries. They are also contrasted to Muslims in Muslim-majority countries as less religiously dogmatic and more supportive of women working outside the home, characteristics that in U.S. discourses have become measures of threat, as is discussed in the next two chapters. As such, these contrasts indicate that Muslim Americans are exceptional relative to Muslims across the world.

Media coverage of the release of the 2007 study highlighted that even though Pew framed its findings in terms of demonstrating Muslim American tolerability, they also could be used to reinforce a notion of a distinctive Muslim threat. News coverage alternated between two possible images of Muslim Americans. Of forty-one news articles and editorials published in daily newspapers within a month of the release of the study, approximately half presented a neutral or positive rendition of the findings, and the other half were alarmist in tone. Some outlets, like the *New York Times*, actually shifted back and forth over the course of the day between these two versions of the story, seemingly unsure of which actually represented the major finding of the study, ultimately settling on "Muslims Assimilate Well in U.S., Survey Finds."[85] While many followed Pew's lead, with headlines like "Survey: U.S. Muslims Assimilated, Opposed to Extremism" or "US Muslims More Assimilated than British," others pointed to something much more nefarious, focusing on a specific question about views on suicide bombings.[86] The *New York Post* headline read "TIME BOMBS IN OUR MIDST—26% OF YOUNG U.S. MUSLIMS BACK KILLINGS." The article further elaborated, "One out of four young U.S. Muslims believe suicide bombings against innocent civilians are OK to defend Islam, a disturbing new poll revealed yesterday."[87] Focusing on responses to a single question, this article and many others pulled out and amplified a finding that seemed to indicate the distinct threat contained in Muslims as a population.

While Pew's report notes that "the overwhelming majority of Muslims in the U.S. (78%) say that the use of suicide bombing against civilian targets to defend Islam from its enemies is never justified," it also reports that 7 percent say it is sometimes justified, 1 percent that it is often justified.[88]

Numerous commentators focused on data on Muslim Americans under thirty years of age and grouped those who said suicide bombings are rarely justified with those who said they were sometimes or often justified to come to this much higher percentage of 25 percent. The *New York Daily News* further exaggerated the finding with the headline " 1 IN 4 MUSLIMS SAY BOMBERS OK," which dropped "young" and "American" to ascribe the statistic to all Muslims.[89] Whether alarmist or dripping in sarcasm, the articles move easily from an expression of a political opinion captured by the survey to the threat of violence, without much concern for the distinction between belief and action: "The first major poll of the U.S. Muslim community finds that 'only' one in four young Muslim Americans would be suicide bombers."[90] Much quoted in these pieces is the declaration of Radwan Masmoudi of the Center for the Study of Islam and Democracy that it is a "hair-raising number."

These polls that apparently capture the tolerability of most Muslims are easily circulated to produce fear and panic, when variation in opinion is transformed into the certainty of threat. This example demonstrates how numbers can become charged and circulate to produce rapid assessments of the tolerability or intolerability of Muslims, assessments that can also differ dramatically from context to context. Kathleen Woodward argues that statistics have come to saturate our everyday lives, producing panic as individuals are made responsible for "avoiding risk in our society of ever-increasing risk."[91] As the citation of statistics has proliferated in daily life, and particularly in reporting, a scientific discourse of probability and distribution produces an everyday experience of insecurity. When the object of fear, in this case, terrorism, is more uncertain or unknown, fear is exacerbated and transformed into panic or anxiety.[92] Statistics as a science of probability and prediction, which does not claim certainty about the future, is particularly apt to produce such feelings. As Woodward notes, "even when the citation of statistics is meant to provide reassurance, it may more often than not produce its opposite: a sense of foreboding and insecurity."[93] Because even small numbers point to possible futures, they can produce anxiety and incite a desire to eliminate all risk, as exhibited in the demand for racial profiling and preemptive action.

In the case of the Pew findings, the numbers are understood as speaking for themselves, transparent, and requiring no contextualization, and the contrary reporting of more liberal sources is dismissed as a result of stifling political correctness. The media does not examine the numbers in terms of the study's margin of error or how to interpret the opinions. Indeed, across the entire spectrum of articles, including those that present the research findings in positive terms, there is little curiosity about how to understand these minority expressions of support for suicide bombing; what are the interpretations people give to these questions? What context of suicide bombing are they considering? What justifications do they provide for them? Within the alarmist reporting, a political opinion on a particular use of violence, perhaps in opposition to the occupations in Iraq and Palestine, is transformed into evidence of a *propensity for* such violence. For example, one article mathematically extrapolates the data to suggest that they indicate that one hundred thousand Muslim Americans are likely homegrown terrorists.[94] While Pew's report emphasizes that the vast majority of respondents said suicide bombings are never justified, their representatives are quoted in articles noting that these numbers indicate "trouble spots" and that "any time you see numbers like that, one has to take notice."[95]

The racialization of Muslims through population racism allows for the weaponization of these data to transform Muslims as a whole into a threatening population, particularly through the framing of the findings in terms of "tiny minority, big problem."[96] Since Muslim racialization is not based solely on a reading of the body but also through a construction of threat based on presumed beliefs and ideologies that can be hidden,[97] any small indicator of nonalignment with U.S. hegemony is actually read as a marker of a much larger threat. As Arjun Appadurai notes, there is also a tension within liberal political theory between sympathy for minorities, when represented in their singularity, and the fear of "small numbers," particularly the fear of "the cell, the spy, the traitor, the dissident, or the revolutionary," threats that are often feared in part because they are hidden.[98] While more liberal sources do not explicitly articulate such fears, their unwillingness to engage these data and contexualize them more broadly perpetuates the notion that Muslims are a population of risk.

Pew's inclusion of the question on suicide bombings in its 2007 and 2011 surveys is also indicative of population racism, because the question is tailored to assess a threat that is already deemed to be unique to a Muslim population. The key controversial question reads, "Can Suicide Bombing of Civilian Targets to Defend Islam Be Justified?" Such a question does not allow for comparability to other populations, given the specificity of the questions and the particular geopolitical role of suicide bombings. By contrast, if the question of suicide bombings were reframed in terms of attacks on civilians, it would have highlighted a comparison with another poll showing that a *majority* of Americans believe that attacks intentionally aimed at civilians are often (5 percent), sometimes (19 percent), or rarely (27 percent) justified; notably, the survey also finds that much higher portions of Iranians (80 percent) than Americans (46 percent) condemn all such attacks.[99] Similarly, sixty years after the use of the atomic bomb killed more than two hundred thousand people in Hiroshima and Nagasaki, the majority (61 percent) of the Americans polled believe it was "the right thing" to do.[100] As this reframing points out by separating one kind of violence against civilians from others, such as U.S.-led drone attacks, bombings, and military occupations, Pew contributed to a construction of violence as a particular problem of the Muslim population. To its credit, Pew dropped the question from its 2017 survey of Muslim Americans, replacing it with a question about support of violence against civilians, to be asked of all U.S. populations.[101]

Nevertheless, such studies do little to challenge a broader context where mass violence against Muslim populations is justified in the name of preventing potential future violence by a small threat seen as residing within that population. Even as Pew establishes that Muslims are "Middle Class and Mostly Mainstream," as the "mostly" in the title subtly indicates, they are also deemed a unique source of a threat of terrorism. Although Pew explicitly says that most Muslim Americans should be tolerated, it suggests that all Muslims must be assessed in relation to this threat of violence against other Americans. As evident in the Pew polls and how they were engaged by the media, what may seem like a positive representation of Muslim Americans does not undermine the racialization of Muslims as a category if it leaves intact variables of assessment as particular to a Muslim population. In this way, the Pew polls actually reinforce the assumptions that undergird anti-Muslim racism by enacting and justifying an assessment orientation toward Muslims, while failing to turn a critical eye to U.S. imperialism and policing. Ultimately, these polls reinforce a U.S. hegemonic framework and make contrary viewpoints expressed by Muslims incomprehensible, except as articulations of support for terrorism.

• • •

The 2011 hearings on "The Extent of Radicalization in the American Muslim Community and That Community's Response," held by Congressman Peter King, further demonstrate how apparently polarized discourses around whether Muslim Americans are deserving of tolerance actually share a set of common assumptions that maintain Muslim Americans as containing within the group a distinct threat.[102] King and his allies emphasized the apparent prevalence of terroristic sympathies among Muslim Americans, manifest in survey data and the work of Muslim American organizations that they sought to discredit. King cited the Pew study to argue that 15 percent of all Muslim Americans were susceptible to al-Qaeda recruitment. Congressman Keith Ellison and other defenders of Muslim Americans, by contrast, argued that the majority of Muslim Americans are "honorable, loyal citizens" who are being scapegoated and stereotyped in the ascription of collective blame for the actions of a few "madmen."[103] On closer analysis, however, it is clear that both sides agree that there are many "good" Muslims, in the words of Melvin Bledsoe, a supporter of Rep. King and the father of the man responsible for the 2009 Little Rock army recruiting office killing—"modern, peaceful, law-abiding people."[104] While Ellison cites the Southern Poverty Law Center's work on the rise of extremism in the United States, including white supremacist organizations, such statements fail to disassociate Muslims as a population from terrorism. Indeed, the idea that Muslims have a special relationship to the problem of terrorism is reinforced in his own testimony emphasizing Muslims' cooperation with law enforcement and the idea that Muslims are part of the solution to the problem of "radicalization." Indeed, the tolerability of some or most Muslims does not challenge the common conception of Muslims as a population of risk that must be constantly surveilled and assessed in terms of its particular threat.

Rather than following a culturally racist logic of seeing Muslims as a homogenous other, these stories and statistics demonstrate an interest in differentiating within this Muslim population, challenging a notion that individuals are locked in a cultural heredity. There is a continuity between the racial profile, the law enforcement profile, the human interest profile, and the opinion poll. More specifically, stories and polling data maintain the logic of risk analysis and preemptive criminalization at the basis of the racial profile and the law enforcement profile. They refine, rather than challenge, the crude and inefficient racial profile that sees all Muslims as potential terrorist threats, producing a set of profiles of Muslims that reinforce specific variables of assessment as particular to Muslims as a population. Even as these profiles might be understood as producing representations of "good" and "bad" Muslims, in fact what they more consistently produce is a set of interacting questions that are necessary to answer in assessing the tolerability of Muslims. In these profiles, emotions interact with variables, such as gender and religiosity, to produce gradients of differentiation among Muslims and mark degrees of rationalism or irrationalism, backwardness or modernity, and trustworthiness or threat. Operating through a logic of multilayered distinctions, they function less through a good–bad binary than through a framework of probability and risk. Such a framework offers more flexibility and fluidity, creating a multiplicity of positions for Muslims, but also producing greater movement and instability. As such, it is useful as both a policing tool that needs a framework through which it can claim to be identifying threats and a managerial tool by which Muslims can be moved from a position of tolerability to intolerability (as evident in chapter 4). As a result, the tolerability of some or most Muslims becomes aligned with a conception of Muslims as a population of risk, with a distinct set of unruly characteristics that manifest at the population level. These dangerous capacities of a Muslim population become particularly stark through liberal discourses of sympathy that are produced in relation to Muslims in Muslim-majority societies, to which I will turn in the next two chapters. As I will argue, representations of Muslims abroad partake in a more binary conceptualization of Muslims as good Muslims and bad Muslims.[105] However, they also interact with conceptions of Muslim Americans by offering an unambiguous vision of what is deemed distinctively problematic and risky about Muslims as a population, thereby providing a clear reference point through which variables of assessment are produced.

2. From Reading Lolita to Reading Malala

Sympathy and Empowering Muslim Women

In the post-9/11 period, the impulse to "know" Muslims and to sympathize with their experiences extended beyond the borders of the United States to the lives of people in Muslim-majority societies. The corollary of discourses of tolerance toward Muslims in the United States was a more affectively intensive discourse of sympathy for Muslims abroad. As the United States waged war in Afghanistan, justified in part to save Afghan women from life under the Taliban, stories of the hardships of women living under Islamic rule found a ready audience. A decade later, these narratives crystalized in the figure of Malala Yousafzai, a Pakistani girl who became an international icon of the struggle for gender equality in Muslim societies when she was shot in the head by the Taliban. Yousafzai had garnered international attention, through an anonymous BBC blog and a *New York Times* documentary, for her advocacy of girls' education in the Swat region of Pakistan when it fell under the control of Tehrik-e-Taliban. However, it was the moment of her victimization, when she was shot, and the subsequent dramatic fight for her life with the help of British doctors, that raised her to the level of global icon. Yousafzai garnered impassioned responses and wishes for recovery from global leaders, celebrities, and publics in Pakistan and across the world and would come to gain a public podium as "the girl who was shot by the Taliban." Her iconic status was fully legitimized when, two years later, having to a remarkable degree recovered and now living in the United Kingdom, Yousafzai was awarded the Nobel Peace Prize. Yousafzai has since dedicated herself to advocacy of girls' education, traveling to conflict zones and refugee camps and meeting with world leaders, while also continuing to pursue her own education.

Through the narratives told about her, Yousafzai has served for millions as an entree into girls' experiences of living in Muslim-majority societies, and especially under the Taliban's imposition of what they described as Islamic law. These narratives reached large audiences through her bestselling memoir, *I Am Malala,* including a youth edition, and a feature-length documentary, *He Named Me Malala,* by Davis Guggenheim and narrated by Yousafzai.[1] The memoir describes Yousafzai becoming an activist, in her father's footsteps, when the Pakistan Taliban entered the Swat Valley. In 2007 to 2009 the Taliban gained direct control of Swat, violently imposing their strict norms and rules on the entire population through public floggings and the spectacular display of executed bodies. Among the Taliban's targets was education, which it made known through bombings and attacks on schools for boys and girls, and later a command that all girls' schools be closed. Yousafzai's father, Ziauddin Yousafzai, who ran several schools in Swat, and Yousafzai became vocal opponents of the Taliban and defenders of girls' right to education, garnering regular death threats. At the point of the 2012 shooting, the Taliban were no longer in control of the region, having been pushed out by the Pakistani army in 2009, yet they sent an individual to meet Yousafzai on her school bus and shoot her at point-blank distance.

Yousafzai's story, in a more distilled form, has also been told through countless interviews, speeches, news programs, articles, children's books,[2] blog posts, tweets, and memes. Through this mass of circulating material one can see the distillation of Yousafzai's narrative to the core elements that make it particularly appealing to audiences in the Global North. Khoja-Moolji has commented on this dynamic, as a process in which "radically specific forms of violence are assimilated into preestablished maps of meaning, where brown and black girls are articulated as perennial victims of angry black and brown men and backward cultures and traditions."[3] While this dynamic is evident, there is still a retention of enough specificity and nuance in the retelling of Yousafzai's narrative, including points that counter dominant stereotypes of Muslims, that makes the narrative feel compelling and authentic. While her story fits a narrative of Muslim

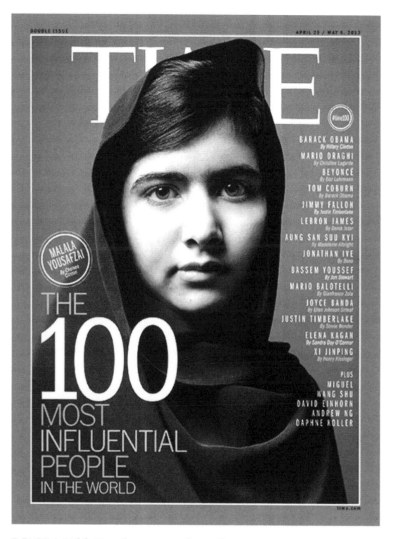

FIGURE 4. Malala Yousafzai was named one of *Time* magazine's 100 Most Influential People in the World in 2013, after being shot by the Taliban, but prior to her receipt of the Nobel Peace Prize.

women's oppression that has served as a core element of Orientalist construction of Muslim societies since the colonial period, it also disrupts an image of Muslim women as silent, passive victims and creates a space for recognizing Muslim women's voice and agency.

This chapter examines how, in the telling and retelling of Yousafzai's story, a potentially complex portrayal of the humanity of Muslims, and the sources of violence in one Muslim-majority society, is distilled into a neo-Orientalist reformulation of civilizational divides, which I will argue serve to link cultural racism with population racism. This neo-Orientalist framework was articulated almost a decade earlier through the highly lauded and influential memoir by Azar Nafisi, *Reading Lolita in Tehran.* My analysis of Nafisi's memoir and its reception shows how in the early period of the War on Terror, a need emerged to challenge a simplistic civilizational binary between Islam and the West and to show that many Muslims in fact shared the values and desires of their Western counterparts. The memoir and the discourses surrounding it nevertheless produced a neo-Orientalist opposition that depended on gender and religiosity to delineate "good" from "bad" Muslims, moving Muslims to different sides of a redrawn civilizational divide, a dynamic which is also evident in the circulation of Yousafzai's narrative.

Azar Nafisi's *Reading Lolita in Tehran: A Memoir in Books* was released in March 2003, as the United States initiated its second war in Iraq—a highly televised bombing campaign intended to garner a quick victory through "shock and awe," leading to sixty-seven hundred civilian deaths in the first three weeks of war.[4] Remarkably, as a book focused on a highly politicized subject during a time of strong liberal and leftist opposition to the Iraq War, it was widely lauded by commentators across the political spectrum—from outspoken feminist critics of the Bush regime to neoconservative advocates of war. The book was both a critical success and extremely popular—a *New York Times* best seller for 113 weeks, selling close to a million copies, and read regularly in book clubs and colleges.[5] In a context of very little cultural representation of Iran, and a dearth of interest in translated works of Persian literature,[6] *Reading Lolita* had an outsized role in constructing perceptions of Iran, producing an authoritative account of "women in Islam" in the post-9/11 context. *Reading Lolita* also made Nafisi a public persona, a woman lauded for her courage and asked to speak in the media and public forums on topics as variable as arts and literature, humanism and empathy, women's status and human rights under Islam, and U.S. foreign policy. The memoir traverses the period of 1979 to 1997, portraying Nafisi's experiences as a professor of English literature in Tehran in the period of the Iranian revolution; the subsequent Iran–Iraq war, and her later experience leading a book group of women who were former students. It tells a narrative about Muslim women oppressed by authoritarian Muslim men in the context of the rise of an Islamic regime. The twist is that the agents of emancipation are the great works of Anglophone "Western" literature. Iranian women gain reprieve from their oppressive conditions through these works of fiction, while crossing cultural divides and testifying to the universalism of "Western" culture and values, thereby joining "us" on the right side of history.

What gave both Nafisi's and Yousafzai's narratives so much power was that even as each narrative was taken up in ways that reinforced neo-Orientalist assumptions about the differences between "Islam" and the "West," they did so in ways that could feel fresh and challenging. These representations aligned with what Evelyn Alsultany has described as "simplified complex representations" where stereotypes of Muslims are reinforced even as audiences are invited to "*feel* for a certain character type—a person who formerly was not seen as deserving of human feeling," and "the growth of this affect in turn comes to symbolize multicultural progress."[7] As she notes, Muslim women especially have come to figure as sympathetic in part due to the perception of misogyny and terrorism as having the same roots. Muslim women are seen as akin to Western victims of "Islamic" violence, in that terrorist men are seen as acting out their frustrated sexualities through both sexist and political violence.[8] It is worth noting that by contrast, militarism and sexism in the U.S. context are rarely viewed as linked, except in the scholarship of feminists who examine how both express masculinity, domination, and violence.[9] What is distinct about the cases of Nafisi and Yousafzai is that in their respective time periods, they marked a new frontier of liberal and sympathetic discourses about Muslims, contrasting with other prominent secularist (ex-)Muslim women, such as Ayaan Hirsi Ali, who vociferously critiqued Islam as a fundamentally flawed religion. Nafisi and Yousafzai describe the root of oppression not as religion or culture but rather as a distinct ideology; both present Islam in a positive light.

However, in failing to account for this ideology meaningfully, neither undermines the connection between violent men and their religion/culture. By offering no framework for understanding other than a fundamental irrationalism, their analyses easily fall into Orientalist binary logics. In essence, this chapter tracks how increasing amounts of "complexity" can be brought into representations of sympathetic Muslim women, while maintaining a kernel of difference that establishes Muslim riskiness and justifies domestic and global War on Terror policies.

While both Nafisi and Yousafzai faced critiques of being tools of U.S. imperialism, particularly by scholars and laypeople of their own nationalities, these arguments could not gain popular traction because they lacked superficial plausibility, given that both were seen as telling their own stories and resisting stereotyping. One such critique was articulated by the scholar Hamid Dabashi, who wrote that Nafisi's work serves to corroborate Samuel Huntington's clash of civilization thesis, thereby legitimizing "neoconservative ideology in the American empire."[10] Nafisi directly contradicted this claim, saying she sought to demonstrate commonalities across borders and that through reading fiction, we can see that "we all, essentially, as human beings, want the same things."[11] In my view, it is the truth in both of these claims that speaks to the particular appeal of Nafisi's vision—and of Yousafzai's story—which both challenge and reformulate an Orientalist divide between "us" and "them," demonstrating the connection between cultural racism and population racism. Cultural racism is the construction of racial categories based on notions of inherent, inherited, and unbridgeable cultural differences, whereas population racism constructs races as populations that can be internally diverse, yet exhibit higher probabilities of specific characteristics and capabilities when analyzed as a population.

Huntington's "clash of civilizations" thesis is a clear example of a cultural racist framework, taking an essentialized notion of "culture" as producing the most fundamental divisions of humankind. Envisioning the world as divided into civilizations, Huntington argues that differences based on "history, language, culture, tradition and, most important, religion" are exceedingly difficult to change.[12] An advocate of the superiority of Western civilization, Huntington argues that the "ideas of individualism, liberalism, constitutionalism, human rights, equality, liberty, the rule of law, democracy, free markets, the separation of church and state, often have little resonance" in other cultures.[13] While in his view, such differences do not necessarily lead to violent clashes, Islamic civilization is particularly prone to violence, in his words "Islam has bloody borders."[14] Huntington in effect declared Islam as the new global enemy of the West following the end of the Cold War. Although Huntington's thesis is an important marker of this historical shift, as Mamdani has noted, Orientalist scholar Bernard Lewis was much more influential in offering justification for the Bush-led wars by arguing that the United States would bring to Muslims a democracy that they themselves desired.[15] Lewis also portrayed Islamism as a vast totalitarian movement posing a threat comparable to that of Nazism in pre–World War II Europe, thereby producing a new binary framework of good pro-democracy Muslims and bad Islamist/terrorist Muslims, which maps directly onto Nafisi's representation of Iran.[16]

In the case of *Reading Lolita,* gender and religiosity interact to distinguish good, pro-modern Iranians from bad, antimodern Iranians, but ultimately, like Huntington's and Lewis's analyses, her representation maintains the "flexible positional superiority" of the West, which is indicative of Orientalist thought.[17] This analysis also builds on Melani McAlister's analysis of U.S. Orientalism, as distinct from the European version. McAlister argues that the domestic politics of gender and race in the United States have shaped perceptions of Muslim-majority societies, such that "the meanings of the Middle East in the United States have been far more mobile, flexible and rich than the Orientalism binary would allow."[18] It does so by identifying barbaric violence as particular to Muslim-majority societies and framing only Western cultural sources as offering resources for resistance and change. Therefore this chapter demonstrates the appeal of liberal discourses that challenge cultural racism, such as Huntington's clash of civilizations theory, while contributing to population racism by circulating an image of Muslims as associated with a distinct threat. Population racism, or a racism that draws from statistical thinking to attribute certain capacities, characteristics, and risks to a population, is reinforced through an association of irrational misogynist and terrorist violence with Muslims as a population.

In Nafisi's work, this dynamic is produced through disregarding continuities between secular and religiously identified violence. Although Yousafzai's narrative, as told in her memoir, is more complex than Nafisi's, identifying a range of sources of violence and explaining connections between different political actors, in the repetition and circulation of Yousafzai's narrative, it is evident that the most resonant elements align with Nafisi's neo-Orientalist formulation. In both cases, a distinct horror is attributed to violence associated with Islam or Islamism, which rarely attaches to the violence of secular states. At the same time, these stories become high-profile narratives of not only Muslim women's oppression and resistance but also an idea that these women are culturally aligned with "us," in part because the West is assumed to be associated with gender equality and liberation. In both cases, the renditions of their narratives hinge on the same analytical points, namely, that (1) Nafisi and Yousafzai can appropriately represent the desires of other Muslim women, even as they are recognized as exceptional to these women; (2) political Islam— referred to as "Islamism" by Nafisi and as "terrorism" by Yousafzai—is a unique global threat to freedom particular to Muslim societies; (3) a main project in this conflict is the liberation of Muslim women from religious and fanatical Muslim men who are the purveyors of political Islam; and (4) the liberation of Muslim women takes the form of individual rather than collective transformation, marked externally through "unveiling" practices and internally through women's moral development into liberal autonomous self-actualized subjects.

In each of the following sections, my analysis begins with Nafisi's work and its reception in Western media sources, then shifts to consideration of Yousafzai's self-presentation and representation in a range of media. The two cases are not parallel: in Nafisi's case, the memoir itself was central, and Nafisi's profile grew out of that, whereas in the case of Yousafzai, the memoir was secondary, supplementing her rise to the status of international icon of an entirely different scale than Nafisi. As a result, my analyses are not entirely parallel, in the case of Nafisi focusing primarily on the memoir and the reviews of the book, whereas in relation to Yousafzai, I consider the memoir, reviews, and also a broader range of media representations, including the documentary *He Named Me Malala,* speeches, and television interviews.[19] In both cases, I am tracking how each one's story—which is most elaborated in the memoirs—is retold and distilled, thereby identifying the elements of these narratives that are distinctly resonant to their audiences in the English-speaking Global North, especially the United States and the United Kingdom.

GESTURING TOWARD AUTHENTICITY

Nafisi and Yousafzai are very different figures in terms of their identities and accomplishments: an elite secular Iranian university professor of English literature and a Pashtun Pakistani Muslim schoolgirl activist–turned–Nobel laureate. Yet they are both insider-outsiders relative to the communities they are made to represent and speak for, and their status as outsiders could be a threat to the authenticity of the arguments they make. In both cases, the authentication of their messages happens explicitly through their positioning of themselves relative to other, more "average" Iranian women or Pakistani girls, in what I term as gestures toward authenticity; but authentication more fundamentally emerges from the fact that they both offer stories that ring true to their audiences, with only minor challenges to prevailing understandings of Muslim-majority societies. In considering transcultural texts, Mary Louise Pratt speaks of how colonized subjects may "undertake to represent themselves in ways that *engage with* the colonizer's own terms," involving "partly collaborating with and appropriating the idioms of the conqueror," but also being potentially inventive and dialogical, posing challenges to dominant conceptions.[20] While both Nafisi and Yousafzai, along with coauthor British journalist Christina Lamb, seek to make their stories accessible to audiences unfamiliar with their societies' histories and cultures, they tend to do so in ways that align with prevailing expectations, even as small revelations can offer audiences a feeling of having gained a more complex insider account. As David Butz and Kenneth MacDonald argue, authenticity is attributed to the native informant who is perceived as an appropriate and authoritative source and tells "the appropriate story in a way that sounds authentic to a Western ear."[21]

Of the two, Nafisi's background makes her more exceptional to "average" Iranian women. However, this difference does not render her account inauthentic; rather, it renders her as one who can bridge "West" and "East" for both her readers and students.[22] Nafisi came from an elite background—her father was mayor of Tehran, her mother a member of parliament—and left Iran at thirteen, studying in Europe and the United States, and returning as a professor following the 1979 revolution. However, Nafisi describes her female book group students as a diverse cross section of Iranian society, although they are all university educated and proficient in English. She describes herself as having access to their intimate feelings and perspectives in the "fairy-tale atmosphere" of her living room, where all were "free to discuss our pains and joys, our personal hang ups and weaknesses."[23] Reviewers similarly see Nafisi as a "secular cosmopolitan teacher"[24] who can reveal "what life was like for women under this regime"[25] through the experiences of her "diverse" students, who belong "to different classes and social backgrounds"[26] and who share their secrets and reveal themselves in Nafisi's book group.[27]

These claims of telling the intimate stories of average Iranian women combine with Nafisi's focus on the theme of empathy to evoke a feeling that readers should empathize with the women portrayed and that such empathy will lead them to see similarities across borders. Just as she tells her students that "empathy is at the heart of the novel,"[28] Nafisi explains that a goal of the memoir is for readers to

> empathize with women in Iran because when they read about women living in Iran, they realize that those women are not very different from the women living in the States—they both dream about a future for themselves and for people around them; they fall in love, are jealous, are betrayed, love music, love poetry, love to hold hands.[29]

Nafisi here emphasizes her memoir as a path toward what Melamed has described as the "self-care of elites," whereby "literature has something to do with antiracism and being a good person" and allows one to "learn to see themselves as part of a multinational group of enlightened multicultural global citizens and to uphold certain standards as (neoliberal) multicultural universals."[30] Nafisi emphasizes empathy as one of these universals that allows us to see "our common humanity." However, the passage suggests that empathy here actually rests not simply on commonality but rather on a production of similarity. As R. Shareah Taleghani has noted in analyzing Iranian American memoirs, reviewers evince a preference for a narrator who has an "'American voice,' via its fluency in U.S. popular cultural references" and, within the memoirs, "the translations of Iran rescript it as recognizable, Americanized (instead of demonized) terrain."[31] Indeed, Nafisi erases elements of Iranian culture that suggest important social and affective differences, such as that poetry is much more valued and integrated into daily life in Iran than in the United States or that holding hands is a common nonromantic act between two women or two men, not as easily practiced in the United States. Rather, difference is only attached to negative, oppressive elements of life in Iran, not to the meaningful ways people of a different culture construct their values, norms, and rituals.

Even as Nafisi claims to tell her students' stories, these are always brief and fragmentary, as she never immerses readers in her students' lives. Because I was often struck by the difference between how people I knew described the memoir as difficult to read and engage and the glowing reviews that it received in the press, I decided to analyze reviews written by Amazon users, focusing on the thirty reviews rated "Most Helpful" by other users, to consider the lay experience of reading the memoir.[32] While a number of the top-rated Amazon reviewers offer similar accolades as other reviewers, a significant portion of the reviews indicate dissatisfaction, saying, "The characters are one-dimensional. . . . I never came to care for any of the group's members as they were portrayed" and "I wanted to see more of the unveiling and the metamorphosis fiction has upon the women Nafisi gathered together."[33] Nevertheless, even these critics did not question the validity of the central claims of the book, suggesting that the substantive authentication of Nafisi's account actually comes from how its analysis of Iran rings true to most of her readers.

Nafisi's possible failure to generate true empathy for her students' lives contrasts with the widespread and apparently sincere emotions many felt for Yousafzai's dramatic story. The fact that Yousafzai's experiences were conveyed to audiences not only through her memoir but also through interviews, photographs, and video footage of her before and after the attack meant that an immediate feeling of connection with her was more effectively produced. In videos of her before the attack, Yousafzai's appeal is apparent in her youthful, attractive face, strong command of English, and willingness to stand up to a dangerous and violent Taliban, conveying her message for girls' education passionately. After the attacks, journalists regularly express deep awe and reverence for Yousafzai, holding her at a distance as someone capable of acting with exceptional fearlessness and love and putting her in a category with great political and spiritual leaders like Martin Luther King Jr. and Mahatma Gandhi. This distance is visually reinforced in countless interviews where tall, thin, heavily made-up women reporters interview a diminutive Yousafzai, her hair pulled back and covered in a light shawl, her face free of make-up and still exhibiting signs of the injury she endured. As a young brown woman, Yousafzai is also subject to expressions of paternalism, allowing Jon Stewart to shift from reverence to exclaiming that he wished to adopt her.[34]

Even as most news reporters prefer to focus on the singularity of Yousafzai and that, as Nicholas Kristof said in a *20/20* interview, "at times we can find leadership in the most unexpected quarters," Yousafzai seeks to represent herself and her story as conveying the experiences and desires of countless other girls. Yousafzai's self-branding through her first name and the role her name plays in the memoir speaks directly to her positioning as both unique and universal, speaking for herself and for other girls in Pakistan and across the world. While Yousafzai is presented as an exceptionally brave girl, her desires and political campaign are presented as rooted in the lives of ordinary girls. The memoir and film describe how she was named by her father after a Pashtun warrior woman who fearlessly led her people into battle and died in the service of her cause. The name marks her as both connected to a history of strong Pashtun women and different from other Pashtun girls around her, in that she was unfettered by her father and able to become a full individual. Her father's choice to give her this name aligns with his own claim, repeated in many interviews, that the main way in which he encouraged her activism was to "not clip her wings." She is extraordinary only because she is free. At the same time, Yousafzai suggests that in fact there were other girls like her; for example, when she and a number of girls from her school went to Islamabad to attend workshops, the host exclaimed, "It's a room full of Malalas!" and Yousafzai explains, "I think Shiza was surprised how strong-willed and vocal we all were."[35] The flip side of this image is clear in an interview in the documentary in which Yousafzai is asked what her life would be if she were an ordinary girl from Swat Valley; she says, "I am still an ordinary girl. But if I had an ordinary father and ordinary mother and a conservative family, then I would have two children now. This would have been my future. You would have seen Malala with two babies."[36] Rather than mention friends who were continuing their education, she recognizes ordinary to indicate unfree, and evoking the image of child marriages, she implies a destiny her culture demands for girls. In using her own name, she asks that the viewer see her as that girl, her advocacy as in the name of that girl.

The branding of "Malala" through titles of books and the documentary; through her NGO, the Malala Fund; and repeated on T-shirts and in hashtags, such as #IamMalala, confirms her star power as someone identifiable by first name alone. Through frequent third-person references to her first name, Yousafzai not only brands herself but takes the broad appeal in her story and transfers it to her campaign for education, broadening her experiences and desires. As she says, the Taliban "wanted to silence one Malala, but instead now thousands and millions of Malalas are speaking."[37] Yousafzai takes the affinity for her story and recasts it in the name of all girls denied an education, as she did in her Nobel Peace Prize acceptance speech: "I tell my story, not because it is unique, but because it is not. It is the story of many girls. . . . I am Malala. But I am also Shazia. I am Kainat. I am Kainat Soomro. I am Mezon. I am Amina. I am those 66 million girls who are deprived of education. And today I am not raising my voice, it is the voice of those 66 million girls."[38]

Nevertheless, when reviewers and commentators in U.S. and British media speak of Yousafzai, they are less likely to connect her to other girls in her home country than they are to people in the West. Rather than having Yousafzai represent all those other girls, they present her as "our Malala," reinforcing what her father says: "She's a daughter of the world." In reviews on the memoir, Yousafzai's bravery is described through comparison to Anne Frank or Joan of Arc, and her ordinariness is established in relation to a presumably typical U.S./European teen. For example, one review says, "It is the memoir of a 16-year-old girl who is both a normal child—fighting with her brother, endlessly styling her hair, worrying that she'll never be tall enough—and, at the same time, possibly the most inspiring teenager in the world."[39] References to Yousafzai's consumption of Western pop culture, such as Justin Bieber, *Twilight,* and *Ugly Betty,* and her concern for her appearance, including her hair, her height, and having lighter skin, are much more frequent in reviews than in the book.[40] Yousafzai's rise to iconic status is marked by her support from celebrities like Angelina Jolie and Bono, and audiences are encouraged to interpret these experiences through the lens of how a U.S. teen might feel about them. In an interview, Yousafzai lightly pushes against yet another question about being a Justin Bieber fan, noting that she and her friends preferred to sing Urdu songs; this comment, however, does not garner a follow-up question.[41] In these ways, Yousafzai is subtly moved from her own cultural context to being part of a Western "global" cultural milieu, one that includes the world but centers individuals and cultural values that are seen as Western in origin. In line with a viral campaign to stand with Malala, where people from across the world posted video clips of groups calling out the phrase "I am Malala," former British prime minister Gordon Brown described "friends of Malala, who are wearing 'I am Malala' T-shirts across Asia and in the west. Malala is being adopted as every child's sister and every parent's daughter."[42] In this rendition, Yousafzai is part of a global cosmopolitan arena where civilization resides, opposed to the Taliban and all "traditionalist" forces that oppress girls, as the line between "us" and "them" is redrawn between those who support freedom for girls and those who don't.

Nafisi's call for empathy becomes, in relation to Yousafzai, a more intensive enactment of identification, as Yousafzai supporters tweet #IamMalala, and Yousafzai claims to speak for all girls seeking an education. Even as Yousafzai presents herself as similar to other Muslim girls, or girls of the Global South, the media presents her as recognizable as an ordinary (Western) teenager, as like "us," even if she is better and more morally upright. Her Muslimness is not erased but also not engaged in a serious manner; rather, it is rendered a private matter or a curious cultural remnant, as demonstrated in Diane Sawyer's lengthy *20/20* profile of Yousafzai in which the only question regarding Yousafzai's religion was on why she covers her head. The fact that Yousafzai, a devout Muslim girl raised in a conservative community, can seem to embody the desires of children the world over suggests that her Muslimness does not create an unbridgeable divide. At the same time, the selection of her story of bravery and victimization as iconic speaks to the desire to find and hold up Muslim women opposing Islamic barbarity. Much like Nafisi's narrative, the authenticity lies less in Yousafzai's presumed similarity to Pakistani girls—she is in fact regularly separated from them—but rather on the fact that her story comes to exemplify an interpretation of a problem that rings true to her audiences in the Global North.

TELLING HISTORY, DEPOLITICIZING POLITICAL ISLAMIC MOVEMENTS

While neither Nafisi nor Yousafzai is a historian and so should not be judged as such, each offers an interpretive framework for understanding the sources of violence in Muslim-majority societies. This violence, often rendered "barbarism" or "terrorism," has in turn been used to justify and shift attention away from other violence, especially by the United States and its allies. Furthermore, these interpretations of violence contribute to population racism by constructing Muslims as a population with a distinct set of risks and capacities. Sayres Rudy points to this dynamic in his critique of the "misapprehension of Islamism," where potentially legitimate grievances are seen as resulting in disproportionate and irrational responses from Muslims, if only a small minority of them, who then demonstrate a uniquely antimodern element of Islam.[43] As Rudy notes, complexity, historicism, and contextualization are allowed to enter an analysis of Muslim-majority societies but are not allowed to undermine a coherent conception of the "Islamist" threat.[44] As a result, "irrational" and "disproportionate" violences become a peculiar problem of Muslims as a population, even if not all Muslims are guilty of them, a dynamic that becomes especially clear when comparing to representations of U.S.-initiated violence.

This framework manifests in a tendency to separate violence seen as linked to Islam from violence seen as secular in origin, a dynamic that is also extensively discussed in the next chapter. Nafisi and Yousafzai each tells stories of relatively liberal or idyllic societies wrenched backward by power-seeking individuals and organizations that use their interpretations of Islamic beliefs to justify their actions. While each separates the violence she describes from "Islam," their stories are used to reinforce a notion that a distinct worldview originating in an interpretation of Islam is the central cause of that violence. In Yousafzai's case, there is a greater attention to the role of political dynamics and state powers, including Pakistan and the United States, but this web of interconnections and complicities is often lost as the Taliban's rigid worldview becomes the cause of the transformation, separated from the geopolitical context. Ultimately, the transformations in each society, Iran and the Swat region of Pakistan, are rendered fundamentally inexplicable, and the psychology or cultural ideas of power-hungry, sadistic men abusing religion emerge as the most obvious explanations. By contrast, violence from secular sources is rarely rendered in such personal terms but rather comes to comprise more or less justifiable actions of dispassionate state actors.

The story of the Iranian revolution, as Nafisi tells it, is one of a modernizing prerevolution Iran that is dragged into the past by unpopular, anti-West, antimodern leaders. In telling the story of the Iranian revolution,

Nafisi ignores the continuities between the Shah regime and the Islamic Republic in their highly repressive policies, presenting the actions of the revolutionary regime as solely an expression of politicized Islam, rather than in any way a reaction to, or continuation of, the Shah's authoritarian state-making project. Nafisi strikingly does not describe any substantive grievances she or others had with the Pahlavi regime, only saying that people were seeking more freedom. Lacking are references to the Shah's highly repressive and corrupt government; his ostentatious lifestyle; or the high rates of illiteracy, poor rural infrastructure, and the trauma of mass rural–urban migration.[45] Similarly lacking are references to U.S. support of the Shah, who was a major regional ally and supplier of oil and in turn garnered CIA funding and training for the secret police and the ability to purchase from the United States an enormous supply of weaponry.[46] Most surprising is the lack of reference to the 1953 CIA-backed coup of the democratically elected nationalist prime minister Mossadegh. Nafisi's association of democracy with Western literature furthers this effacement of the antidemocratic role of the United States in Iran, which continued after the revolution with U.S. involvement in the Iran–Iraq War, initially as both a supporter of Saddam Hussein and a surreptitious provider of arms to Iran, through the Iran–Contra Affair. Rather than describing undemocratic policies and actions of the United States, the Shah, and the Islamic Republic, Nafisi seeks to create a stark contrast such that political Islam becomes the distinctive source of repression in Iran. This contrast is most starkly established by the apparent opposition in women's status before and after the revolution.

Nafisi does not give a sense of the incredible breadth of support the revolution had among the Iranian people, a cross section of society who subscribed to various secular and religious political frameworks. Nafisi presents the only legitimate framework of resistance as her own individualistic rebellion and assertion of autonomy, suggesting that collective political action is always necessarily corrupted. She also does not examine the views of Ayatollah Khomeini's supporters, only saying that the Islamic Republic came "in the name of the past" and yet lacked any cultural foundations, imposing "its relentless fictions on us."[47] In contrast, Samira Haj has argued that Khomeini's appeal must be understood in how he engaged with a dynamic Islamic tradition of inquiry that had resonance in the broader society; rather than "cynically manipulating the past," his arguments were about "relating the tradition to the present."[48] Furthermore, as Minoo Moallem has described, Islamic fundamentalists in Iran are best understood as responding to modern conditions and concerns in relation to identity construction and gender.[49] Indeed, the twentieth-century project of modernization/Westernization of Iran included the coercive "unveiling" of women, and the revolutionaries reacted with an alternative model of modernization, including an Islamic revolutionary version of femininity.

Without such context, reviewers are left with a feeling of the incomprehensibility of the revolution itself, and even more so of life under the Islamic Republic. As one says, "the lot of women under sharia law mystifies us in the liberated West. It seems so terrifyingly and illogically restrictive."[50] Ascribing irrationality to public religion, and ignoring the role of religion in politics in the United States, Nafisi's representations come across as confirmation that political manifestations of Islam necessarily produce irrational and arbitrary violence not attributable to secular and/or Western governments. Iranian theocracy is understood as the polar opposite of the United States, which, despite the power of the Christian Right, is described by a reviewer as a place "where private faith hasn't been hijacked for political means, and where private life isn't subordinated to public policy."[51] Rather, Nafisi's depiction of Iranian history, which deemphasizes violence done in the name of secular modernization by both the Shah and the U.S. government, results in an understanding of political Islam or Islamism as *the* major determinant of the oppression in Iran, and perhaps globally.

By contrast, Yousafzai's memoir provides examples that demonstrate that the relationship between Islam and politics is multidimensional, rather than singular. As Saadia Toor explains, in modern Pakistani history, there have been multiple formulations of the relationship between Islam and politics, including Muhammad Ali Jinnah's modernist Muslim nationalism, Zulfikar Ali Bhutto's Islamic socialism, and Muhammad Zia-ul-Haq's Sunni radicalism.[52] Yousafzai's telling notes some of this diversity, arguing that the Pakistani government moved away from the ideals of tolerance and religious freedom advocated by Jinnah, who helped found the country as a "Muslim homeland." Although Toor critiques how the concept of "Muslim homeland" makes a parallel between Pakistan and Israel, noting that Pakistan was never imagined as a state for all Muslims of the world, the concept does make legible a secular Muslim nationalism as foundational to the formation of Pakistan. In contrast to this Muslim national identification, Yousafzai notes that when Zia came to power via a coup in 1978, he initiated an Islamization campaign to shore up his legitimacy, resulting in muftis being empowered; conservative religious schools being opened; and interpretations of Islam being used to regulate women's sexuality, labor, and mobility.[53] By historically positioning such misogynistic outcomes within Zia's Islamization project, Yousafzai suggests that this is not an inevitable outcome of the political uses of Islam; rather, as she shows, political Islam is more diverse than the antidemocratic and authoritarian versions that garner attention.

Yousafzai also contextualizes the rise of the Taliban within regional Cold War politics, where the conflict between the Soviet Union and the United States over Afghanistan helped to produce militancy in Afghanistan, which then laid the groundwork for the emergence of the Taliban. She describes how, following the 1979 invasion of Afghanistan by the Soviet Union, the Pakistani military intelligence service, ISI, began training Afghan mujahedeen. In this time period, Yousafzai notes that many Pakistani Pashtuns felt solidarity with Pashtuns across the border in Afghanistan and went to fight against the Russians. Religious leaders who had been empowered under Zia were, Yousafzai notes, "condemning the Russians as infidels and urging people to join the jihad," and Yousafzai's father was among those who considered joining the fight.[54] Later, in 2001, Pervez Musharraf came into power via a coup and yet was perceived as "Westernized" owing to his advocacy of a policy of "enlightened moderation." He nevertheless continued support for the Taliban in Afghanistan, although more surreptitiously after 9/11 because of the U.S. alliance with Pakistan. Yousafzai places the greatest blame on Pakistani leadership, both Presidents Zia and Musharraf, but also critiques U.S. support of these leaders, emphasizing the absence of democratic processes, rather than secularism, as a key obstacle to obtaining security.

While Yousafzai's historical framing notes the political nature of these conflicts, the element of Yousafzai's argument that is repeated most in reviews is her description of how her father considered joining the Afghan mujahedeen, a story that even in the memoir seems packaged for Western consumption. What Yousafzai initially described as motivated by Pashtun solidarity and commitment to self-determination becomes a process of religious indoctrination into "jihad," which Yousafzai calls "a kind of brain-washing." Of her father, she says, "for a while his Muslim identity seemed more important than anything else in his life." This story of Yousafzai's father's brief "flirtation" with "jihad" is often repeated in articles, suggesting that even exceedingly moderate Muslims are susceptible to radicalization, hence pointing to a threat that is contained in Muslims as a population. Furthermore, in Yousafzai's rendition, when her father is later drawn to secular nationalist and anticapitalist politics, she concludes, "He found himself torn between two extremes, secularism and socialism on one side and militant Islam on the other. I guess he ended up somewhere in the middle."[55] Rather than explaining and discriminating between the contents of these different political perspectives, Yousafzai, like Nafisi, dismisses the rich history of Pakistani leftist thought and activism, which has been documented by Toor. Instead, she falls in line with a view that the thread of continuity between the Cold War and the War on Terror is that both were fights against "extremism," and liberalism and neoliberalism are marked as rational and good "centrist" perspectives.

More broadly, in the retelling of Yousafzai's narrative, the memoir's historical contextualization of the rise of the Taliban falls away as a simple story of a paradise destroyed by power-hungry men abusing religion. As Yousafzai describes, the Taliban "are cruel people who are misusing the name of Islam. They are enemies of Islam." The Taliban is primarily represented through images that convey their barbarism and their difference from other Pakistanis. Violence comes to stick to the Taliban through their physical appearance. In the memoir, Yousafzai notes their short pants, black masks, turbans, and beards, describing them as "so dark and dirty that my father's friend described them as 'people deprived of baths and barbers.'"[56] This image notably resonates with the memoir's repeated references to preference for lighter skin, for example, in describing Yousafzai's mother as fair skinned and beautiful. It is also common in other media representations, as in Diane Sawyer's *20/20* special, which repeatedly references shadows and darkness in relation to the Taliban and its associates, while showing images of the Taliban as men with black guns, dark turbans, and bearded or covered faces.[57] In the memoir, the Taliban are also subtly conflated with all brown-skinned men, as Yousafzai describes how, after moving to the United Kingdom, she flinches every time she sees an

"Asian-looking" man coming close.[58] This is remarkable not only because she had previously separated the Taliban in appearance from other Pakistanis but also because it implies that such an affective response to South Asian men is natural and perhaps warranted. This slippage between the Taliban and other South Asian men becomes most evident in how the Taliban's gender-based persecution, although quite distinct from sexism of the local culture, is often rendered as on a continuum with that culture, as I discuss in the next section.

While Yousafzai is critical of U.S. involvement in Pakistan, and particularly the use of drone attacks, which have regularly killed civilians,[59] her critique does not demonstrate the extent of devastation caused by such attacks but rather stays within the frame of counterterrorism discourses to suggest that drone attacks are ineffective at achieving their stated goals. In the memoir, she describes the early uses of unmanned drones by the United States, aimed at killing local militants and bin Laden associates but leading to many additional deaths. She notes a 2006 attack resulting in eighty deaths, including members of the family of the future leader of the Taliban in Swat, but does not mention that sixty-nine of those dead were children.[60] When referencing Obama's increased number of drone killings of civilians, Yousafzai notes their role in increasing anti-U.S. sentiment: "Where once we used to blame our old enemy India for everything, now it was the United States. Everyone complained about the drone attacks which were happening in FATA almost every week. We heard lots of civilians were being killed."[61] The book's critiques of drone warfare do not focus on the loss of life but on their illegality and ineffectiveness.

Not present in the memoir are detailed accounts of drone attacks, even as there is documentation of this sort from human rights groups. For example, a 2012 joint Stanford and NYU Law Schools clinic report included an account of a 2011 attack under Obama's leadership. A group of men, including tribal leaders, respected community elders, and four members of the Taliban, gathered for a government-sanctioned mediation of a local dispute. Ignoring the drones flying overhead on the assumption that they were not targets, these men were nevertheless hit by several missiles, leading to the deaths of at least forty-two people. These deaths had devastating ripple effects on their community in part because the men were both community leaders and the providers of their families.[62] In contrast, in Yousafzai's telling, drone warfare becomes one of a litany of sources of violence, naturalized through association with other aspects of living in Pakistan: "It's not just the Taliban killing children. Sometimes it's drone attacks, sometimes it's wars, sometimes it's hunger. And sometimes it's their own families."[63] Such a sweeping statement that suggests a general lack of valuing life trivializes the anger and resentment caused by drone warfare, fitting Yousafzai's critique within a counterterrorism discourse, while sidestepping the question of whether these attacks themselves constituted terrorism.

Media accounts similarly rarely address this question substantively, including in the sparse coverage of Yousafzai's meeting with President Obama, in which she spoke to him of drone warfare, as described in the introduction of the memoir.[64] In a notable exception, on CBS This Morning, Yousafzai was asked about her message to Obama; she responded, "It is true that when there's a drone attack the terrorists are killed, it's true. But 500 and 5,000 more people rise against it and more terrorism occurs, and more, more bomb blasts occur." Yousafzai does not mention innocent victims, suggesting that those who rise up may be acting irrationally. The interviewer then pivots, "And you said that to President Obama?" to which Yousafzai answers, "Yes, of course," and the topic is dropped.[65] Deftly moving away from the suggestions of U.S. complicity in a cycle of violence, the reporter returns to the overarching narrative of a remarkably brave girl raising her voice to those in power.

The absence of moral outrage at killings ordered by the U.S. president, actualized at a comfortable distance via the technology of drones, reflects a view that the United States simply could not cause reprehensible violence. Violence done in the name of a modern secular democratic imperial superpower—even as it can have far greater reach and consequences—is treated as being of a completely different moral order than violence done in the name of the Taliban. Even when civilian casualties have been well documented, drone warfare has been implicitly rationalized through an assumption that U.S. actions are based on secular, rational, and ultimately moral motives. Violence against Pakistanis only comes to matter when it can be put within the War on Terror framework of seeing Islamism/terrorism as a unique threat.

THE GENDER LITMUS TEST: POLITICS THROUGH
THE LENS OF CULTURE

In both Nafisi's and Yousafzai's accounts, gender-based violence and misogyny emerge as the central realm of conflict. Ultimately, what makes both of their accounts so compelling is that they operate within a familiar yet modified Orientalist binary of East–West, doing so through their personal accounts, where sexism and misogyny become the key manifestations of an assertion of political power by Islamist/terrorist leaders. While Nafisi challenges an absolutist East–West binary, she reconfigures this Orientalist dichotomy into antimodern and promodern Iranians, which maps onto gender and religiosity/secularism. Women are constructed as overwhelmingly the victims of religious state violence and oppression and thereby are inherently more open to the ideals of liberal democracy and freedom. Religious men are constructed as supporters and beneficiaries of these policies, and secular men as the passive witnesses, only secondarily affected through women. Yousafzai's rendition of the Taliban in the memoir does not immediately fall into such neat gender divisions, presenting the Taliban as a fringe movement that was opposed by many men but also had some support from women. However, as Yousafzai's narrative is circulated, it is consistently distilled into one about a fundamental cultural conflict over the role of women and girls in a traditional society. As a result, women and girls become the main victims of the Taliban and those most receptive to the enlightening power of education that would oppose the Taliban. The line between the Taliban and other Pakistani men, one that is sometimes articulated very strongly, becomes more and more blurry as the question of gender relations emerges as the fundamental litmus test for one's alignment with the side of "humanity." The effect is that a regional, political conflict in which the United States has been deeply involved since the Cold War is explained as a cultural, gendered conflict internal to one society that is best solved by education.

Culture and religion have often been seen as the direct causes of women's status in Muslim-majority societies, even as anthropologists advise that cultures are hybrid and dynamic and are more appropriately seen as that which requires interpretation and explanation, rather than that which explains.[66] Mahmood Mamdani notes that when it comes to Muslim-majority societies, "culture talk" predominates as the analytical frame within which social problems and conflict are understood.[67] Joseph Massad similarly finds that while most area studies disciplines were explaining regional differences between the Global North and Global South in terms of differences in economic and political power, that in Middle East studies culture has persisted as a primary explanatory framework for understanding differences in societies. Since at least the nineteenth century, European travelers and colonists have seen gender roles as indicative of what was distinctly different, and problematic, about Islam and Muslim societies. Muslim women, Massad notes, served as a foil for early European feminists, such as Mary Wollstonecraft, who critiqued European sexism by analogy to the treatment of Muslim women while ignoring that Muslim women had the right to own property centuries before European women.[68] In addition, liberal feminists often, and increasingly, see themselves as the agents of change, freeing Third World, including Muslim, women from patriarchal traditions imposed by Third World men.[69] The result of bringing together these three discursive threads—that Muslim-majority societies are inordinately shaped by their culture/religion; that Islam exhibits its cultural differences through its treatment of women; and that Western feminists are relatively free in comparison to Third World women in need of rescue—is that in Muslim-majority societies, many political issues, including terrorism and authoritarianism, have been framed through the lens of culture and gender, offering Western-aligned feminists a unique platform. Even as Nafisi and Yousafzai move away from blaming "Islam," they support an understanding of Muslims as having a distinct problem with gender, which becomes a tolerability litmus test that must be applied to all Muslim men. Sexist Muslim men become aligned with irrational violence in a way that sexist White men do not.

Nafisi holds up women's rights as the barometer of freedom, as she says, in the "Reader's Guide" of the 2008 edition of the memoir, "Women have now become the canaries in the mine in Iran, as well as in many Muslim majority societies," adding that "gays, minorities" can also serve this function.[70] Indeed, the memoir's condemnation of the Islamic Republic happens primarily through a description of a litany of horrors women experience. However, Nafisi's conception of the essential components of women's rights is highly selective, giving the greatest attention to the policing of dress and behavior in public and some attention to the repression of political activism. By contrast, Nafisi does not consider socioeconomic concerns, giving little information about how her adult students are meeting their educational and occupational goals or making ends meet. She also gives little context for understanding where legal restrictions come from, to distinguish enforcements of widely accepted, and contested, social norms and more purely arbitrary expressions of state power. Rather, Nafisi describes these incursions as the invasion of the "personal realm" and the destruction of individuality. Iranian society is depicted as oppressive at all levels from the state on down to family relations and the construction of the self. The streets are a "war zone" where women can be harassed or arrested at any moment. Nafisi imagines a student leaving her home and walking outside: "She doesn't walk upright, but bends her head toward the ground and doesn't look at passersby. She walks quickly and with a sense of determination."[71] Her representation presumes the universality of the experience of being a woman in a woman's body projecting her own perceptions onto others. In a passage repeated frequently by reviewers,[72] Nafisi exclaims, "Living in the Islamic republic is like having sex with a man you loathe. . . . You make your mind blank—you pretend to be somewhere else, you tend to forget your body, you hate your body," playing into the idea of Middle Eastern societies as fundamentally, and uniquely, centered around men's sexual control of women's bodies.[73] While the title of the book, referencing Nabakov's novel of a man's obsessive sexual fantasies and control of a "flirtatious" young girl, and its cover image of two head scarf–wearing girls looking down (see Figure 5) evoke Orientalist fantasies of lifting the veil or peeking into the harem, within the book, Nafisi depicts this "harem" as a space of women so deeply traumatized that they must separate themselves from their reality.

Reviewers follow Nafisi's lead, focusing on regulations that are deemed particular to political Islam, most frequently referencing regulations on dress and appearance, followed by the regulation of women's public behaviors, state violence against women, and changes in the family law affecting women. In the writing, these restrictions are often made even more incomprehensible and horrifying. For example, one reviewer writes,

> Here, young women are often rounded up for humiliating virginity checks at local clinics. Girls can be married off at the age of 9, and in the rare case of a divorce, men always get custody of the children. . . . The Revolutionary Guard . . . routinely reprimand and arrest women for

FIGURE 5. The cover of Azar Nafisi's *Reading Lolita in Tehran*.

eating fruit "too suggestively," or laughing in public, or wearing bright-colored socks.[74]

Each of the examples has a connection to the memoir, yet in this decontextualized form, they appear even more senseless and horrifying. The reviewer has generalized specific stories—of a student and her friends being arrested and given virginity tests and of students being reprimanded, not arrested, for the way they ate their apples—into patterns that, using the present tense, appear to have persisted over decades. He also has robbed these incidents of their emotional content, the former of which was told through tears and the latter with fits of laughter. These descriptions also efface a more complex and dynamic situation for women in Iran. For example, while the legal age of marriage did decrease under Ayatollah Khomeini, the actual proportion of women under twenty marrying decreased to less than 20 percent, as opposed to the majority of women a few decades before.[75] Remarkably, many reviewers also make claims that are not grounded in the memoir itself, seeming to confirm that the memoir can act as a foil for their own preconceived notions, including that "all endured regular strip searches," that women outside their homes were required to be escorted by a male relative, and that some of Nafisi's students experienced "forced arranged marriages."[76] Through this repetition, reviewers confirm a prevailing view that religious Muslim men are motivated by a singular desire to oppress women.

Although *Reading Lolita* spans an almost twenty-year time frame, the situation of women from the time after the entrenchment of the regime to the conclusion of the memoir is presented as fundamentally unchanged and marked by persistent, pervasive hopelessness. The revolution did quickly produce significant legal, political, and social setbacks for women, felt most strongly among urban upper- and middle-class women. In the immediate aftermath of the revolution, the state pushed women out of workplaces and educational institutions, imposed strict rules on gender segregation and modesty in public, and reversed the legal gains women had made, especially in the realm of family law. However, the state gradually reversed course on many of these changes both as a result of significant resistance and also because of larger social and economic forces that had already led to women's entry into many aspects of public life; because of the need to include women in public roles, for example, as doctors and teachers, to enforce gender segregation; and owing to the important role of revolutionary women who moved up the ranks of the government and legitimated their roles within an Islamic discourse.[77] Furthermore, even as Nafisi seems to adopt Western standards of progress, she ignores improvements in postrevolution Iran in line with conventional development metrics. From the time of the revolution to the publishing of the memoir, there was a "massive government investment in public education," a significant increase in the literacy rate to 75.6 percent for females over age six in 2001 and 80.4 percent for everyone over age six, and a university population that was more than half female.[78] There were also dramatic decreases in fertility, maternal mortality, and infant mortality rates; significant increases in life expectancy; and women's continued presence in the political and economic realms, as members of parliament, and in administrative, professional, and technical jobs.[79] Nafisi's analysis cannot make sense of these discordant facts. Contrary to a sociological understanding of gender norms and structures as being rooted in various interconnected socioeconomic, political, and cultural factors,[80] she follows a reductive cultural understanding of gender relations that sees the status of women in Muslim-majority societies as primarily rooted in Islamic/Islamist beliefs.

Nafisi's gender divide is further articulated through a litmus test of appreciation for Western literature and the ability to feel empathy for characters. This gender divide becomes expressive of a civilizational divide through her representations of her classroom where enlightened women are contrasted to religious, revolutionary men who obstinately oppose the works they are reading. Two female students who defend the literature they are reading, and are presented as individualistic and rebellious, are the heroes of the classroom. While the revolutionary female students' views are never presented, a later encounter with one such student in which she expresses how much she enjoyed *The Great Gatsby* suggests these women are open to change. However, male Iranian revolutionaries are unable to engage in "true dialogue" and are incapable of "tolerance, self-reflection and empathy."[81] As outspoken defenders of a simplistic prorevolutionary position, including an opposition to their readings, they are given to "strident objections" and "childish outbursts," having "discovered an absolutist refuge called Islam."[82] Only two secular and highly educated men, one Nafisi's student, the other a reclusive former professor, are portrayed in positive terms in the memoir. Therefore, while religious women and women who supported the revolution can apparently be "enlightened" through Western literature, the same does not hold for revolutionary men. Through a depoliticized discourse about the importance of empathy, gender and religiosity interact to demarcate a new civilizational divide between promodern Iranians and antimodern Iranians. Religious men's alleged inability to feel empathy places them on the other side of this divide, even as Nafisi's lack of serious interest in their perspectives demonstrates a similar lack of empathy, but one that they apparently do not deserve.

Representations of Yousafzai's story follow a similar pattern: the Taliban's oppression is represented primarily in gendered terms, often as a kind of pathological fear of strong or educated girls and women, and girls emerge as those who are motivated and able to traverse cultural and civilizational divides and pose a real threat to the Taliban. While the memoir strongly distinguishes the Taliban from other Pakistanis, including Pakistani men, in reviews and other media renditions, a focus on the Taliban as primarily motivated by misogyny places it within Pashtun and Islamic cultures, which are similarly represented as distinctly oppressive to girls and women. As such, a narrative Yousafzai provides of a terrorist organization vying for state power morphs into a narrative of particularly sexist Muslim men attempting to violently impose their views. What this narrative framing misses is that the Taliban's political project encompassed much more than the subjugation of women, and the Taliban's sexism was not a simple extension of the sexism that existed in Pakistani, Pashtun, or Islamic culture. Similarly, the Taliban's targeting of Yousafzai was not simply because she was a girl seeking an education but also because she was an anti-Taliban activist. The somewhat complex and nuanced rendition of the relationship between sexism and violence in the memoir is distilled, in the retelling of Yousafzai's story, to a simple association of Muslim misogyny with terrorism.

The memoir demonstrates that the Taliban were separate from and opposed by most people, including men, in Swat and Pakistan. It represents the Taliban as a fringe political movement seeking state power that misuses and manipulates cultural and religious beliefs to establish its legitimacy. Yousafzai says, "The Taliban targeted not only politicians, MPs and the police, but also people who were not observing purdah, wearing the wrong length beard, or the wrong kind of shalwar kamiz."[83] Both men and women were targeted, including in relation to strict dress and morality codes, although these were different based on gender. Both boys' and girls' schools were bombed, although ultimately the ban on schools only applied to girls' schools. This ban was met by opposition throughout the country, and locally a group of male elders organized opposition to the Taliban. Through this process, Yousafzai's father emerged as an anti-Taliban spokesperson, and Yousafzai also became a prominent critic of the Taliban.

In the memoir, the narrative of the Taliban-led violence is embedded in, yet kept distinct from, a broader narrative about growing up as a girl in a Pashtun community in the Swat Valley. Sexism is presented as rooted not only in Pashtun culture and some interpretations of Islam but also in structural forces that shape girls' opportunities. The reader sees that women's status in Pakistan varies based on family, social class, and region. Although child marriages, "honor killings," and using girls as bargaining chips in tribal feuds are noted as problems, stories of unilateral gender oppression do not dominate. Rather, we hear more complicated narratives, for example, of Yousafzai's mother, who was given the option of going to school but, upon seeing that she was the only girl in her class, decided not to continue, without any objection from her family. Yousafzai's school is full of girls seeking an education; she also describes how cultural taboos, early marriages, and poverty keep other girls from getting an education. Yousafzai writes extensively about her distress at learning that some children must work to survive and cannot afford school tuitions. Furthermore, the figure of Prime Minister Benazir Bhutto as a brave and strong Pakistani woman and a role model for Yousafzai reigns large. Nevertheless, the notion that Muslim-majority societies are uniquely oppressive to women is at times reinforced, for example, in Yousafzai's repeated argument that Pashtun women were very strong, and yet not free, while "across the water were lands where women were free."[84] Nevertheless, the status of women in Pakistani society is never reduced to sexism in Islam—Yousafzai notes that the Prophet Mohammad's first wife was a businesswoman—and the Taliban's impositions contradict the diversity and flexibility evident in broader Pakistani society.[85]

The Taliban as an organization is also shown to change over time. Maulana Fazlullah, the "Radio Mullah" who advocates Islamic piety and later aligns with the Taliban, is initially broadly popular, including among women. In the face of a failing Pakistani justice system, his audience sees a call to institute Islamic law to settle disputes as reasonable. Yousafzai also describes active women supporters of the Taliban, including members of the Bin Laden–supporting Red Mosque in Islamabad, which until 9/11 had strong links to the Pakistani military. In mid-2007, the military, now concerned with stemming the growing power of the Red Mosque, surrounded and ambushed the mosque, killing one hundred people, including girls and women. This event is described as a turning point that increased the use of violence in Swat by Fazlullah and the Taliban. It also demonstrates that men were not the only political actors supportive of the Taliban. Yousafzai does not examine the politics beneath this support but rather frames it in terms of the Taliban's hypocrisy: "when it suits the Taliban, women can be vocal and visible."[86] Despite opening up questions about where the appeal of the Taliban came from, ultimately, the memoir reduces such views to indoctrination. Therefore, even as the memoir offers a more nuanced rendition of the relationship between various Pakistani women and the Taliban, the overall narrative that emerges to explain women's sympathy for or support of the Taliban becomes a case of false consciousness, or lack of "true" education, an argument that is amplified by Yousafzai's claims that education is the best way to prevent terrorism. This notion transforms a political conflict into an ideological one between the enlightened and unenlightened.

In the reviews, the element of Yousafzai's story that becomes most salient is the idea that gender oppression was the primary form of oppression to shape her life, and Muslim-majority societies are portrayed as particularly focused on gender subjugation. A number of reviewers note Yousafzai's birth story as indicative of this problem: "In their part of northern Pakistan . . . rifle shots ring out in celebration of a baby boy's arrival. But there is no such fanfare for females: their destiny is to cook and clean, to be neither seen nor heard."[87] Reviewers note that Yousafzai's father, Ziauddin Yousafzai, nevertheless celebrated her birth. As another reviewer notes more succinctly, "in a land that esteems boys and commiserates with the family when a girl is born, Ziauddin was the exception."[88] His exceptionalism is further established by the fact that he married Yousafzai's mother out of love and treats her as an equal in the family. He emerges not as a member of a community under siege who, along with other men, takes a stand against the Taliban but as someone who was always exceptional in the context of his own community. This narrative suggests that other Pakistani men may in fact be not that different than the Taliban.

Even as Yousafzai tells of the many different forms and targets of Taliban violence, these are distilled as gender-based violence, as noted in one review: "The recurring theme of her tale is the assaults on the rights of women and girls. Every chapter sheds a glaring light on women's subordination."[89] Furthermore, decontextualized examples of gender subjugation are offered as indicative of Pakistani culture in general, such as this one: "The treatment of young village girls perturbed Malala. 'Our prisons,' she says, 'were full of cases like that of a 13-year-old girl who was raped and became pregnant and was sent to prison for adultery because she couldn't produce four male witnesses to prove it was a crime.'"[90] While Yousafzai is describing President Zia's Islamization campaign mentioned earlier, without that context, it becomes indicative of Pakistani society in general. This singular focus on gender subjugation as the distinct characteristic of both Pakistani society and the Taliban presents the Taliban as in continuity with the traditional and religious practices of the community, rather than as an aberration, as Yousafzai argues. Yousafzai becomes a lone brave girl who, with her exceptional father's support, stands up for herself in a society that does not value girls' contributions and is suffering under the rule of the most extreme version of that view in the form of the Taliban.

A similar slippage between the Taliban and other Pakistani men is evident in a *20/20* news special titled "Unbreakable: One Girl Changing the World," which aired a year after Yousafzai was shot. Diane Sawyer adopts a good Muslim/bad Muslim framework that initially starkly separates the Taliban from other Muslims: "and remember, worldwide, there are more than a billion Muslims, 1% in the shadows, the 1% who are dangerous, implacable when it comes to the education of women."[91] However, when seeking to explain why the Taliban emerged, there is no historical or political context but only a culturalist argument presented by *New York Times* journalist Nicholas Kristof, one that connects the Taliban to Pakistani men in general:

> There is this perception that they are under assault. And particularly, the notion of honor of their women is kind of emblematic of that. And they

see girls' education as a road toward women controlling their fertility and having fewer children, listening less to their husband, wanting to go work, kind of symbolizing the end of that way of life.[92]

As Kristof references an ambiguous "they," but one that appears to reference traditional Muslim men in general, the program alternates shots of his face with images not of the Taliban but of brown-skinned men, some with beards and some without, apparently regular Pakistani men. In presenting this ahistorical and cultural explanation for Taliban violence, the program implies that all conservative Muslim men are on a continuum with the Taliban. In a span of a few minutes, this 1 percent seems to transform into the majority of Pakistani and perhaps Muslim men, whose presumed patriarchal attitudes are seen as linked to terrorism. The broader message becomes that Islam's unique sexism connects it with the Taliban, becoming both a litmus test of tolerability and a way to understand the sources of terrorism in religious beliefs.

LIBERATION THROUGH TRANSFORMATION

Part of the appeal of both Nafisi's and Yousafzai's narratives about the emancipation of Muslim women lies in how they can be made to fit within a notion of the civilizing role of the "West" in Muslim-majority societies. Resistance takes particular individualized forms that are valued in liberalism, including self-expression and self-transformation, while grassroots collective resistance is represented as absent or ineffective. Western culture and political institutions become the major sources of social transformation that occur through the empowerment of women via education. By focusing on individual transformation, the geopolitical factors and global economic conditions that undermine the establishment of democratic institutions are sidelined. Rather, it seems that the fundamental problem is a lack of a democratic spirit in a people who need to be brought out of their state of backwardness and ignorance through the enlightenment of Western literature and education. The United States, the United Nations, the World Bank, and other international bodies can then be progressive forces through their funding of educational projects, even as the United States continues to maintain regional alliances, enforce economic sanctions, and use military force in ways that create widespread social insecurities and undermine democratic movements.

Neither Nafisi nor Yousafzai considers collective action as a means to liberation; rather, they argue that lifting of the fetters of sexist cultures and ideologies—through unveiling, through reading Anglophone literature, and through education—offers liberation by allowing women to become fully actualized and autonomous individuals. Their frameworks align with a liberal development discourse that has, since the 1990s, promoted the education of girls as a panacea to a range of social ills in the Global South. As Khoja-Moolji has described:

> this promise of education is grounded in liberal humanist sensibilities that see schooling as one of the key practices that can equalize the playing field, give individuals the ability to enact freedom, increase their productivity, and enhance their competitiveness in the global market. In the context of the global South, where access to formal schooling, especially for girls, is limited in some areas, improving such access is posited as the solution to problems as wide-ranging as poverty, corruption, terrorism, and environmental degradation.[93]

Moeller has analyzed this development discourse, noting that it has been taken up by corporate philanthropic entities, such as Nike, which sought to distract from critiques of its exploitative labor practices by promoting the "Girl Effect." She explains the reasoning of this campaign:

> Once [girls] are educated, they are expected to generate a multi-indicator, multi-scalar ripple effect across multiple development indicators from the scale of the family to the world. The theoretical basis of this logic assumes that the combination of their unpaid social reproductive labor, anticipated paid professional or entrepreneurial labor, and increased consumption practices will underpin future capitalist growth and development.[94]

However, such analyses ignore the systemic nature of labor exploitation and gender-based oppression.[95] Furthermore, the economic effects of girls' education are not actually established; as Caron and Margolin argue, scholarship "is inconclusive about the relationship between education, employment and empowerment, and stresses that the size and composition of the labour market are an important factor for women's employment . . . and thereby structure what kind of job is available for the taking."[96] The same holds true of arguments for girls' education as a countermeasure to terrorism or political violence, ones that Yousafzai frequently makes. These types of arguments divert attention from the role of much more significant political and economic powers, such as states, corporations, and global institutions, in producing and exacerbating these conflicts and depoliticize the demands of social movements that advocate systemic changes. Rather, they place the burden of change onto the shoulders of individual girls, particularly "poor, racialized girls and women in the Global South."[97]

While Nafisi does not purport to offer any wholesale solution to antidemocratic and authoritarian elements of the Iranian regime, she does offer women's individual transformation as the realm within which freedom can be attained. Nafisi's female students' mundane activity of taking off their outerwear when they enter her home becomes an essential step toward achievement of selfhood, and Nafisi's line that the women "shed their mandatory veils and robes and burst into color" is frequently repeated by reviewers.[98] Nafisi associates the hijab with uniformity and lack of enlightenment and its removal with individuality and humanity. Such association of unveiling with enlightenment perpetuates the politicization of women's veiled or unveiled status, offering a mirror image of religious fundamentalists' imposition of veiling by ascribing a unitary meaning to the practice.[99] Similarly, while the Islamic Republic is represented as invading women's personal sphere, the Western novel serves as a means of escapism, consciousness raising, and education in a democratic disposition of empathy. Reviewers understand the memoir as about the "universality" and "power of western literature to cultivate democratic change and openmindedness," and Nafisi's study group becomes a *unique* opportunity to achieve freedom from oppression, "an air pocket in the suffocating atmosphere of the Islamic revolution."[100]

Such a polarized notion of Western versus Iranian culture is further perpetuated through a focus on Anglophone literature as a primary mechanism for Iranians to feel empathy, which suggests that the absence of democracy in Iran is due to a deficit within Iran that must be addressed through Western cultural or political intervention. Nafisi casts the antidemocratic element of the Iranian state in cultural terms, when she follows a claim about the "democratic nature" of the novel with the disputable assertion that "the realistic novel was never truly successful in our country."[101] Indeed, rather than consider any modern Persian novels, or the creative works of many women writers, such as Simin Daneshvar, Shahrnush

Parsipur, and Moniru Ravanipur, only one Persian work is discussed in the memoir, *A Thousand and One Nights,* which is understood as "an allegory about the trapped situation of women."[102] In fact, in describing the regime's censorship policies, Nafisi says, "We lived in a culture that denied any merit to literary works," a shocking statement, given the centrality of poetry to the daily lives of Iranians across classes.[103] Culture of any value, and particularly culture that is conducive to democracy, is understood as Western culture. As a corollary to this argument, Nafisi represents the postrevolution period as monolithically oppressive, being dismissive of the reform movement that arose in the 1990s and of "Islamic feminists" as "a contradictory notion," despite the fact that activists made some important legal gains, such as a 1992 divorce law that entitled women to payment for housework, and partook in lively debates on women's rights, particularly through an active women's press.[104] Nafisi also fails to note other political activism by Iranian women, both secular and religious, although she does make reference to historical and postrevolution Iranian feminists in a 2000 interview.[105] Despite this later acknowledgment, the memoir gives the impression of no possibilities for positive change and no reason to participate in grassroots activism or other kinds of resistance. Rather, moments of liberation only come in the form of reading the Western novel.

Yousafzai's memoir does not fall as easily into the tropes of liberation through unveiling and Western literature, offering a more nuanced understanding of her relationship to her community's traditions and why and how she resisted oppressive forces of the Taliban. However, as her story is disseminated and distilled, it increasingly becomes a story of a girl who is liberated through education that is signified through unveiling and access to Western culture. Furthermore, as her message has broadened to position her as a global advocate of education, she has taken up the "Girl Effect" discourse described earlier, emphasizing both a development and a counterterrorism frame. Both the "Girl Effect" framing and a notion that education is manifest through access to Western culture are referenced in the opening of one review:

> Ask social scientists how to end global poverty, and they will tell you: Educate girls. . . . Nowhere is that lesson more evident than in the story of Malala Yousafzai, a Pashtun girl from Pakistan's Swat Valley who was born of an illiterate mother, grew up in her father's school, read Stephen

Hawking's 'A Brief History of Time' by age 11 and has a gift for stirring oratory.[106]

Indeed, these few lines quickly bring together the specific image of Yousafzai produced in the reviews as a girl for whom education is about escaping her tradition and gaining enlightenment through Western literature. Even as Yousafzai herself values and draws from her tradition in explicit ways in the memoir, representations of her evince a preference for fitting her within a notion that education and access to Western culture have been key to her self-advocacy and liberation.

While Yousafzai never presents unveiling as a necessary step for the liberation of girls and women, noting that women can be "modern" and keep their culture,[107] the idea that showing one's face and/or hair is an indicator of one's relative freedom is repeated frequently in representations of her. Yousafzai's coauthor, Christina Lamb, in an article on her year working with Yousafzai, writes in a vein similar to Nafisi's representation when describing a visit to a girls' school: "To my amusement the girls arrive in rickshaws with their heads covered, then the moment they are through the door they throw them off."[108] Lamb also describes her consternation at the possibility that Yousafzai's mother would not allow herself to appear in the book. Lamb convinces Yousafzai to pressure her mother, who eventually acquiesces, with little concern for whether this is coercive. Conversely, when Yousafzai expresses surprise at the standards of dress for women in the United Kingdom, she is not seen as offering a meaningful cross-cultural critique. The judgmental gaze only operates in one direction, as evident in the fact that so many media accounts portray Yousafzai as relatively "unveiled," by frequently noting that unlike other girls in her school, she did not cover her face. Therefore, despite Yousafzai's insistence that women should have the choice to veil or not, unveiling is used by many who tell her story to signify a step toward liberation that sets Yousafzai apart from other Pakistan girls.

Yousafzai's activism, as represented in the memoir and through her work with the Malala Fund, emphasizes the importance of education for liberation. In the memoir, Yousafzai's activism for education is presented as a very personal fight rooted in her family's experience and her personal desire to learn. However, the broader framing of her activism is more consistent with a "Girl Effect" frame, whereby education becomes the primary means to the liberation of girls and the entire society. Yousafzai notes, "When I speak for education, it's for all those children who are suffering from terrorism, from child labor, from child trafficking; they are also victims of the cultural norms and taboos that are against their rights."[109] One reviewer notes of Yousafzai's father, "He believed that lack of education was the root of all Pakistan's problems."[110] Yousafzai's messages to government officials, the United Nations, and President Obama have consistently been that the way to fight terrorism is not through military solutions but rather through education. A meme posted on Twitter effectively captures this, showing Yousafzai sitting in a classroom before a blackboard, appearing calm and beautiful, with white capital letters that read, "WITH GUNS, YOU CAN KILL TERRORISTS, WITH EDUCATION YOU CAN KILL TERRORISM." In contrast to the common framing of the madrassas as the breeding grounds of terrorism through brainwashing and indoctrination, education becomes that which produces rational, disciplined, and productive members of society.

While Yousafzai frames her project as compatible with indigenous cultures and values, these are not emphasized in the reviews. Yousafzai declares herself a proud Pashtun, referencing cultural practices, works of literature, and mythology that have enriched her life, even as she also describes elements of Pashtun culture she does not value. While she critiques patriarchal and tribal practices—such as child marriages and revenge—she also notes that a deep commitment to hospitality saved people's lives when they were internally displaced due to the Pakistani military battle with the Taliban.[111] This multidimensional relationship to her culture highlights the fact that all cultures are complex and contested. Yousafzai presents education as consistent with the culture and religion of Pakistanis, noting that almost everyone in Pakistan was outraged at the closure of schools by the Taliban. She makes a point of justifying education within indigenous frames, noting that Islam gives girls and boys a right and duty to gain an education and more broadly explains the importance of advocating for education in ways that account for local conditions.[112]

However, the broader presentation of Yousafzai's educational attainments suggests a valuing of an American liberal arts education that ironically is under attack in the United States. The content of Yousafzai's education is often specified only in relation to her books, for example, the treasured books she was forced to leave behind when her family had to flee Swat Valley. While these books may well have been science or history textbooks, they are evoked in a nonspecific way that suggests that Yousafzai was an avid reader of literature. In a 2014 *New York Times* piece, "Malala Yousafzai: By the Book," Yousafzai is asked a total of eighteen questions about her favorite books, and for book recommendations, to which Yousafzai provides about twelve book titles. At one point she notes that with a curriculum focusing on history, science, and math, and a lack of access to literature, "I read eight or nine books in Swat, and I was considered to be a bookish girl! Here [in Birmingham, England] girls have read hundreds of books." Nevertheless, reviewers frequently reference the few Anglophone titles that Yousafzai notes in the memoir, such as *The Wonderful Wizard of Oz*, the Twilight novels, and Stephen Hawking's *A Brief History of Time*. Although the last is not a work of literature, it attests to Yousafzai's interest in secular science, understood as contrary to religious fundamentalism. These few titles are made to attest to the fact that the education Yousafzai received and advocates aligns with Western values.

By contrast, distinct elements of Yousafzai's education are tied to her own cultural heritage but are not highlighted outside of her memoir. Yousafzai describes the importance of crafting her public speaking abilities and how they tied her to her father and grandfather. The memoir recounts Yousafzai's father's struggles to overcome a stutter and become a powerful speaker, following in the footsteps of his father, an imam who would draw large crowds for his "mesmerizing" sermons.[113] Yousafzai's grandfather is presented as a multifaceted man: he was an imam who sent his son to a government high school rather than a religious school; he was a patriarch committed to tribal traditions and also a cosmopolitan man who spoke Persian and Arabic and read the great classical poets of those traditions. However, Yousafzai's willingness to take up a microphone and speak out at a young age is rarely highlighted as a product of her own cultural upbringing and form of education but rather is referenced as a natural "gift" or "talent." This focus on the development of one's voice also presents activism through an individualistic framework, rather than effectuated through tradition, community, and collective action.

Excluded from distillations of Yousafzai's story is that humanity is experienced collectively, as Khoja-Moolji describes in her ethnography of Pakistani girls: "participants experienced their humanity in relational terms; that they viewed themselves as embedded in different systems of living, including nonhuman ones; and that they emphasized a heightened sense of complementarity and interdependency to achieve individual as well as collective well-being."[114] Yousafzai's mother, Tor Pekai, is represented in the memoir as a woman with a full life in Swat—someone who was an important and active member of the community, who frequently offered charity by feeding and hosting people in her home. However, this rich life is ignored in reviews that prefer to describe her as illiterate. The representation of activism connected to Malala's work is one that centers the singular girl who raises her voice and speaks out, acting independently, separated from her culture and community. "Breaking the silence" and "raising her voice," she partakes in a break from her tradition, rather than actively drawing strength from traditions inculcated through her own community, such as those of public speaking and hospitality. The educated girl who rejects restrictive tradition becomes the front line against the Taliban.

Despite the differences in Nafisi's and Yousafzai's representations of liberation, their narratives are both made to fit a view of Western cultures as offering liberating potentialities for Muslim women that are absent in their own cultures. In Nafisi's case, the (Anglophone) novel, and in Yousafzai's case, education become the means of rescuing women and changing culture and society. While Yousafzai insists that education is not grounded in Euro-American cultures and is required in Islam, the telling of her story emphasizes liberal and neoliberal values of individuality, entrepreneurialism, and self-expression over those cultural values that Yousafzai associates with her own Pashtun and Islamic cultures. Even as Yousafzai's cultural differences are sometimes noted, ultimately, her campaign for global girls' education easily aligns with development and corporate philanthropic discourses of girl empowerment that posit individual girls as change makers while deemphasizing the role of economic, political, and social structural factors that delimit the life chances of girls and others.

The narratives formed around Nafisi and Yousafzai have important similarities: Muslim women's victimization, but also agency; the distinct threat of political Islam that seeks to transform a society from the inside out; and the centrality of education for the betterment and resistance of girls and women in Muslim societies. However, an apparently self-correcting dynamic is also evident in the shift between these narratives, as a more starkly binary conception of us–them is replaced by a representation that offers a more nuanced and layered understanding of various elements of these societies. Whereas Nafisi is an elite, highly educated, and secular individual, Malala is closer to an "average" Muslim girl, who is religious, comes from an economically struggling family, and hails from a smaller city far from the centers of power in her country. Nafisi's starkly gendered divisions between promodern Iranian women and antimodern (religious) Iranian men are challenged by Yousafzai's centering of her father's role in the fight for girls' education and her references in her memoir to other men critical of the Taliban. Nafisi's reductive rendition of Iranian history, which paints the U.S.-backed Shah regime in relatively positive light and omits mention of the negative role of the United States in Iranian politics, can be contrasted to Yousafzai's positioning of the Taliban's seizure of power in the Swat Valley as in part a product of the actions of the Pakistani and U.S. governments. Finally, in comparison to Nafisi's secularist ambivalence about religion, Yousafzai unequivocally defends Islam and identifies the Taliban as comprising power-hungry terrorists exploiting and perverting the religion.

Nevertheless, there are important continuities between how Nafisi's and Yousafzai's narratives function in the broader media context. As Yousafzai's story is distilled and circulated, we see that the core resonant narrative has much in common with Nafisi's neo-Orientalist frame. Whereas empathy and identification operate to mark some Muslims as civilized "like us," others are pushed further into the categories of not simply uncivilized but also incomprehensible, inhuman, and monstrous. As Khoja-Moolji observes, "within the doctrine of humanism, only particular kinds of subjects are recognizable as human, and all else is constituted as the other or the repressed other through practices of racialization, sexualization, and naturalization."[115] The "flexible positional superiority" of the West is reproduced especially in the portrayal of violence in Muslim-majority societies as irrational and inexplicable.[116] Distinctly "bad Muslims" who draw from their "culture" negative traits are seen as a major source of conflict. The horror attached to these other Muslims is not primarily a response to violence—of a child being shot, a shockingly common occurrence in the United States—but to the meanings attached to that violence and its association with Islam, a process that is intrinsic to the racialization of Muslims. Even as a narrowly defined "true" Islam may be redeemed as a peaceful religion and a source of comfort for many, Islam more broadly is still uniquely associated with a distinctly horrifying violence. This association is made possible through a simplification of the histories that have produced diverse Islamist movements and a rationalization of violence that is committed by the United States and its allies. Horror does not attach as readily to some forms of violence as others, reflecting both the differential valuing of life and the marking of "Islamic" violence as lacking the rationality of Western violence. Through this formulation, the only acceptable Islam is a pacifist one, where Islam can only be defended through the claim made repeatedly by Yousafzai, and many others, that "Islam is peace." Furthermore, both Nafisi's and Yousafzai's narratives present a solution that offers a primary role to Euro-American culture in transforming Muslim women inside and out to make them the agents of change in their own societies.

Therefore these discourses produced by and about Nafisi and Yousafzai reconfigure the oppositional conception of us–them articulated in cultural racism, by redrawing the boundaries of who can appreciate Western culture. Even as these narratives challenge pure cultural racism, they contribute to population racism by reinforcing a particular set of conceptions about how to determine who are the more and less threatening Muslims. While these figures and their memoirs undercut a notion that *all* Muslims are backward and threatening, they depict violence and oppression in Muslim-majority countries as irrational and incomprehensible. The threat of irrational violence becomes uniquely associated with Muslims as a population, because other forms of violence are not highlighted. Nafisi says on her Dialogue Project website that "Islamism has become the biggest threat to the development and survival of democracy in the world today."[117] In this light, both *Reading Lolita in Tehran* and the story of the girl who was shot by the Taliban become warnings to the rest of the world about the potential consequences of a threat unique to a Muslim population, one that is cloaked in a message about identifying and sympathizing with Muslim women, who share the same desires and values that "we" have. A threatening group that is identified as a small minority in one context can be transformed into a much larger threat in another, and potentially the majority of Muslims in still another. Therefore, whereas culture is presented as not necessarily determinant or inescapable at the level of the individual, at the level of the population, Islam seems to lead to predictable problems.

3. "Iran, Stop Killing Gays"

Queer Identifications and Secular Distinctions

In July 2005, news and images of the public hangings of two teens, Ayaz Marhoni and Mahmoud Asgari, in the city of Mashhad, Iran, spread via the internet with a report that they were executed for homosexuality. The disturbing images quickly circulated among lesbian, gay, bisexual, transgender, and queer[1] (LGBTQ) activists in the United States and Europe, who responded with statements of protest. Soon, however, it became clear that the claim of homophobic persecution was based on a faulty translation and that the youths had been charged with the rape of a thirteen-year-old boy. A fierce debate ensued among a small group of activists as some remained adamant that the youths were likely executed for being "gay," while others argued that the deaths should be protested upon grounds of opposition to the torture and execution of juvenile offenders. Despite this controversy, the interpretation of the executions as state-sanctioned homophobic violence seemed only to gain in power as the images circulated, LGBTQ activists organized international protests, and expressions of sympathy proliferated.

Why does the suffering of some become cause for outrage and protest, while the suffering of others is ignored? Why do some victims become objects of sympathy and remembrance, while others remain unknown? In the context of the War on Terror, responses among "Western"[2] audiences to the suffering of those perceived as "Muslims" have been highly differentiated, exemplifying both ends of this spectrum of possibilities. I consider this case where the pain and suffering of two Iranian youths elicited a dramatic outpouring of protest and remembrance among a group of Western activists to interrogate a liberal, secular politics of sympathy that has been productive in the racialization of Muslims. I am less interested in assessing the evidence for or against the notion that the youths were executed for consensual homosexual acts than I am in understanding how an apparent consensus that they were gay developed despite significant reasons for doubt. To be clear, I deem these and all executions reprehensible and worthy of being opposed, all the more so in the case of executions of youths. I also would note, as some activists did, that Iran since 1990 has been a signatory to the Convention on the Rights of the Child, which forbids the use of capital punishment for crimes committed while younger than eighteen years of age.[3] Hence activists could have critiqued Iran for violating its own international treaties. Nevertheless, activists chose to frame the executions as antigay persecution.

I argue that to understand how this consensus developed, we need to consider how the images, in combination with an interpretation of antigay persecution, resonated emotionally with the secular sensibilities of activists. As Saba Mahmood has argued, "while it is common to ascribe passion to religion, it would behoove us to pay attention to the thick texture of affinities, prejudices, and attachments that tie us . . . to . . . a secular worldview."[4] Similarly, Ann Pellegrini has called for analyzing "secularism as a structure of feeling that constructs and privileges particular subjectivity, social belonging and social knowledge."[5] Although secularism sees itself as cerebral and reasoned, it has an emotional and affective dimension that is important in shaping responses to suffering.

The executions, when interpreted as homophobic persecution, resonated with a secular imagination that sees an opposition between the secular and the religious and affirms a liberal conception of the individual as an autonomous subject that can and ought to choose its culture and religion. This secular imagination has become complicit with an anti-Muslim racism that sees Islam as antisecular and illiberal and therefore prone to uniquely irrational and antimodern violence. When framed as a case of homophobic persecution, as Islamic repressiveness versus Western freedom, this case positions LGBTQ activists as aligned with the values of properly secularized "Western civilization." This framing integrates LGBTQ activists into the story of clashing civilizations at the heart of the War on Terror, affirming their patriotism, even while many of them maintained their liberal antiwar stance and affirmed their liberal sentiment of sympathy for "Muslim" victims, seeing "Muslim" as a reference not to the professed identities of the individuals but rather to their racialization into the category of "Muslim." Through a story of homophobic persecution, these sympathetic victims became paradoxically an example of commonality, in the form of a universal LGBTQ experience, and of difference, in the form of an essentialized "civilizational" (i.e., cultural and religious) divide between a violently intolerant "Islam" and a progressively more tolerant "West." This opposition is at the basis of anti-Muslim cultural racism, which sees those perceived as "Muslims," regardless of their own identification, as determined by an immutable cultural heredity that is essentially incompatible with "the West."

In the years following the 9/11 attacks, a range of political projects and interests on the left converged in an increasingly impassioned defense of secularism. While LGBTQ activists and liberals have long advocated separation of church and state in their political battles with the Christian right, an interpretation of the War on Terror as a "clash of fundamentalisms" represented secularization as necessary for global coexistence.[6] Furthermore, a secularist opposition between the secular and religious has increasingly been articulated as an opposition between "the West" and "Islam," a religion presented as highly resistant to modernizing and secularizing forces.[7] In a secularist worldview, while religions viewed as confined to the private realm are often deemed acceptable, nonsecularized religions are seen as communitarian, bound to the past, resistant to reason, and maintained through violence and a threat to individual self-determination. Therefore some secularists claim to have no problem with Islam per se, if properly secularized and privatized, but simply oppose expressions of Islam in politics. Liberal secularists reserve a particular abhorrence to what is deemed religious violence, while violence in the name of secular ends, which is often more far-reaching and devastating, rarely elicits similar responses. As a result, they fail to recognize the linkages and continuities between "secular" and "religious" violence, even when both are expressions of the modern centralized state.[8]

An interpretation of the executions as antigay violence built on a view that differences between Islamic and Western "civilizations" are often expressed in views on gender and sexuality. Historically, this perspective has been evident in Western scrutiny of such practices as veiling, gender segregation, homosociality, and same-sex sexuality in various Muslim-majority countries.[9] As discussed in the previous chapter, Western liberal feminists have mobilized in the name of global sisterhood to address the "plight" of Muslim women, in the process constituting themselves as already-liberated women. In the context of the War on Terror, some neoconservative advocates of military intervention argued that the most significant differences between "Western" and "Islamic" civilizations are not with regard to politics but center around norms of gender and sexuality.[10] The Mashhad case, when interpreted as a case of homophobic persecution, constitutes Western LGBTQ activists as not only liberators of Iranian victims but also protectors of Western civilization, resonating with a liberal secularist and civilizational concept of Islamic difference. As such, this dynamic is part of the process of incorporation of a normative patriotic queerness that is bound with racist imperialist projects as expressed through what Jasbir Puar terms "homonationalism," sifting among populations in favor of normative *Western* LGBTQ subjects.[11] While some queer lives are fostered, and some queer deaths are grieved, "others are targeted for killing or left to die."[12] Sima Shakhsari has argued that the representability of the executions in Mashhad must be understood in relation to the unrepresentability of other deaths, including the death of an Iranian transgender refugee who took her own life in Canada upon being asked to vacate her subsidized housing.[13]

While identification with these executed boys in some respects cuts against cultural racism, insisting that these "gay" youths are like "us," representations of their victimization were nevertheless mobilized to reinforce a notion of essential cultural difference at the basis of cultural racism, but one that also feeds into population racism. While cultural racism defines a racialized other as determined by its cultural heredity, population racism conceives the racialized other as a diverse population that nevertheless exhibits a distinctive distribution of characteristics and capacities, in this case, a higher propensity to irrational homophobic violence. While cultural racism separates "us" from "them," population racism uses stereotypes as assessment tools in analyzing who is more or less acceptable within the racialized population. When identified as "gay" victims of Islamic homophobia, the youths become objects of sympathy, but a sympathy that is articulated through both an identification of the youths as "like us" and differentiation of them as victims of an irrational and backward religion and culture. These youths are "like us" not as a result of their choice to adopt Western culture but rather because of their ascribed "gay" identity, which is cast as an unchosen, natural, and universal identity. Presenting gay identity simply as a variation of "human nature," Western LGBTQ rights discourses often frame Islam as incompatible with natural human diversity, in contrast to tolerant and even accepting Western liberalism and secularism. Such a framing of support for LGBTQ rights as a measure of one's civilizational status has been mobilized by the Israeli government in a "pinkwashing" public relations campaign to frame Israel as the protector of liberal values and sexual freedom in the Middle East, even as Israel brutally oppresses Palestinians, in stark violation of human rights and international law.[14] Therefore cases of LGBTQ persecution in Muslim-majority contexts strongly resonate with a binary conception of civilizational difference at the basis of cultural racism, while also circulating a variable of assessment in relation to Muslim populations, where homophobia of any sort becomes a measure of broader threat.

Indeed, views on homosexuality have become a variable of assessment within population racism, which circulates much more broadly in discourses on global Muslim populations. For example, in the Netherlands, a video produced by the Ministry of Alien Affairs and Integration includes images of gay men kissing as part of a message to potential immigrants that the Netherlands is a "free society" where "violence," "female circumcision," and "honour killing" are forbidden.[15] In a similar vein, in 2016, presidential candidate Donald Trump seemed to soften his call for an across-the-board ban on Muslims entering the United States by suggesting a system of "extreme vetting" whereby Muslims would be assessed in terms of their positions on various issues, including whether they support the execution of gays.[16] Such targeting of Muslim immigrants—whether in the service of acculturation or of exclusion—defines Muslims as a population that contains a higher tendency toward "barbaric" violence. Views on homosexuality can become a litmus test raised against any Muslim to determine his acceptability, no matter how irrelevant it is to the specific issue at hand, as I discuss in the next chapter in relation to the Park51/Ground Zero Mosque controversy. Therefore, while analysis in this chapter emphasizes the representation of the Mashhad executions as productive of a stark civilizational divide, this execution also entered a wider field of circulation, contributing to views on homosexuality becoming variables of assessment particular to Muslims as a population.

In what follows, I begin with an overview of the initial controversy among LGBTQ activists regarding how to respond to the news and images of the executions and the emerging broader consensus. I also consider how this case has come to overwhelm a more nuanced understanding of the social and legal regulation of sexuality in the Iranian context, coming to stand in for the experience of being "gay" in Iran. I then provide a theoretical framing for considering how emotions and affects shaped responses to produce a particular interpretation of the executions that resonated with activists' secular imagination. Next, I analyze the specific processes by which a particular interpretation emerged in relation to three emotions: love, fear, and disgust. Finally, I conclude with a consideration of the broader implications of my argument for the question of complicity of liberal/left secularist politics with anti-Muslim racism.

EXECUTIONS, IMAGES, AND CONSTRUCTING "GAY IRANIANS"

The executions of Marhoni and Asgari would not have gained the attention they did without the devastating photographs that accompanied the release of the story. The initial Farsi-language report of the executions from Iranian Students' News Agency included three photographs, showing (1) the two youths being interviewed by journalists; (2) one of the two youths, blindfolded, being escorted by a guard and an executioner; and (3) two hooded executioners placing nooses around the youths' necks. Other circulated photographs showed the teens hanging from the nooses and images of the crowd gathered to watch. The teens had been detained fourteen months earlier; they had received a sentence of 228 lashes for drinking alcohol, disturbing the peace, and theft and a sentence of death for a crime that would become the center of controversy. At least one and probably both of the youths were under eighteen years of age at the time of their arrest, and their executions were protested in Iran on the grounds of opposition to the death penalty for minors by Nobel Peace Prize winner Shirin Ebadi.[17] Notably, the ban on executing individuals for crimes committed under the age of eighteen has been deemed by the Inter-American Commission on Human Rights to be so widely accepted as to be "a norm from which no derogation is permitted."[18]

As Richard Kim describes in his analysis of the initial spread of news of the executions, a core group of LGBTQ activists was quickly divided over the precise meaning of the photographs.[19] OutRage!, a British LGBTQ rights group, posted the initial, much-circulated report that the youths were executed "for the 'crime' of homosexuality."[20] However, Human Rights Watch (HRW) and the International Gay and Lesbian Human Rights Commission soon raised questions, noting that the original Farsi-language article named the crime "Lavat beh Onf," or "homosexual act by coercion," which a Mashhad newspaper described as the rape of a thirteen-year-old boy at knifepoint. OutRage! responded that the rape charges were fabricated, citing unnamed or discredited sources, such as the National Council of Resistance of Iran.[21] Doug Ireland, blogger and journalist for the New York City weekly paper *Gay City News,* also continued to call the executions instances of antigay persecution through extensive reporting. He cited Afdhere Jama, editor of a U.S.-based queer Muslim e-zine, who claimed his informants in Iran said that the youths were lovers, arrested following an incident of sexual relations with several boys. HRW's LGBT Rights Program director, Scott Long, in turn argued that no one had been able to verify Jama's claims and advocated focusing on the well-documented violations of human rights, including torture (for the lashings), execution of minors, and the death penalty more broadly.[22]

Despite this yearlong, murky, and at times personally charged debate,[23] a growing consensus emerged among a broader group of LGBTQ activists that Marhoni and Asgari were executed for their homosexuality. On the one-year anniversary of the executions in July 2006, events to protest the hangings of "two gay teenagers" were held in approximately twenty-seven cities around the world.[24] The protests were endorsed by international organizations, including the International Lesbian and Gay Association; by local and national organizations in the United States, Europe, and Latin America; and by many prominent LGBTQ activists, academics, and artists in the United States.[25] This consensus was also evidenced by a range of creative responses that presented the youths as gay teens, including a 2006 album dedication by the Pet Shop Boys; several YouTube videos (including one that has garnered more than two hundred thousand views); an award-winning opera entitled *Edalat Square* performed in Houston, Texas, in 2008 and 2009; and a play entitled *Haram Iran* performed in Chicago in 2008, Los Angeles in 2010, and New York in 2017.[26] When in 2017 the television show *The Handmaid's Tale* included shots of people wearing hoods with pink triangles, hanged to death for homosexuality, many saw this as a reference to Iranian executions, particularly these in Mashhad.[27] As one early and astute journalistic analysis of the protests said, "the force of the images, for many gay people, has cut through any doubt about their particular meaning."[28] Such an interpretation also became prevalent in the non-LGBTQ press;[29] the *New York Times*, which in 2005 had described the executed youths as "two young men convicted of sexually assaulting a 13-year-old boy," in 2007 called them "two gay teenagers."[30]

While, for many, these executions were clearly a case of persecuting two "boys in love," for other activists, doubts about this specific case were overridden by a feeling of certainty that others have been executed for consensual same-gender relations in Iran. Indeed, there have long been isolated reports from Iran of executions of men on charges of sodomy. The numbers of such executions are wildly divergent, with many activists referencing an estimate attributed to Homan, a Los Angeles–based Iranian LGBTQ organization, of four thousand executions of homosexuals since the Iranian revolution, while the International Lesbian and Gay Association has estimated eight hundred executions for sodomy in the period between 1979 to 1997, although noting that most of these also involved other charges, such as pedophilia or murder.[31] Despite difficulties in documenting such cases, activists can point to Iran's legal code, which makes sodomy a crime punishable by death. The law requires either confession or the eyewitness testimony of four men, a standard that former president Khatami deemed so stringent as to argue that such executions should be almost impossible. However, human rights organizations report that in practice, this standard is overridden either by a coerced confession or a standard "the knowledge of the judge," where a judge may deductively arrive at a ruling based on existing evidence.[32] Therefore, while there are doubts about the facts of this case, the Iranian government can treat cases of consensual sodomy extremely harshly, including through application of capital punishment. Not as clear is whether the death penalty has been used as part of a concerted campaign against consensual same-gender sexual relations.

Furthermore, the place of same-gender sexual relations in Iranian society cannot be reduced to such laws or reported executions. Even a cursory review of scholarly literature points to a more complicated situation. Indeed, gender segregation and a strong tradition of homosociality appear to have created a postrevolutionary context in which same-gender sexual relations are at times deemed safer than extramarital heterosexual relations, are often tolerated, and do not necessarily translate into a "gay" or "lesbian" identity.[33] Among some subcultures of urban middle- and upper-class youth, same-gender sexual relations are one among many illegal sexual activities in which individuals partake and are not viewed as determinant of a sexual identity.[34] Social expectations, especially the pressure to marry, are much more present in individuals' lives than a fear of criminality, placing restrictions on same-gender relationships.[35] Finally, even an Iranian organization that supported protests of the Mashhad executions, when asked about the "atmosphere of constant fear" Iranian "gays" face in a 2005 interview, responded with a nuanced and historicized description:

> The GLBT situation in Iran has changed over the past 26 years. The regime does not systematically persecute gays anymore, there are still some gay websites, there are some parks and cinemas where everyone knows that these places are meeting places for gays. . . . Having said that, the Islamic law, according to which gays [sic] punishment is death is still in force but it is thought not much followed by the regime nowadays.[36]

Arguing that lack of information about sexuality was the biggest challenge for their constituents, this organization presents a more complex picture of life for sexual minorities in Iran than is represented by Western LGBTQ activists. Furthermore, this broader analysis challenges the universal application of a Western identitarian model of sexuality, even if some Iranian activists do adopt the language of gay or lesbian identity, and of a politics of visibility and recognition, both of which were central to Western LGBTQ activist responses to the case.

The Mashhad case is not the only one to have garnered Western activist outrage at the apparent executions of sexual minorities by the Iranian state.[37] However, I have chosen to focus on this particular case because of the broad resonance of the images and narratives associated with the case. Indeed, the many creative responses—including highly personalized narrative renditions in the form of written stories, YouTube videos, and theatrical pieces—demonstrate how the seeds of this story opened up to an imaginative realm. These responses in turn have produced material ripe for analysis, offering an opportunity to interrogate how such stories resonate among Western audiences. Furthermore, the images of these executions have continued to circulate broadly in the years since the executions, often serving as a shorthand visual representation of what it means to be "gay" in Iran. For example, a Google images search for the term "gay Iran" conducted six years after the executions, on September 22, 2011, resulted in images of these executions appearing as eleven of the top fifteen results and also as 29 percent of the top 163 images; the next most common images were depictions of Ahmadinejad (12 percent) and of nooses or hangings (10 percent). As such, this case offers an opportunity to analyze the production of *both* an elaborated, personalized story of persecution of same-gender love and an affective "fact" of the execution of "gays" in Iran that circulates in part via the images.

Finally, because my interest is in a *Western* liberal secular imagination, I have not given significant attention to diasporic Iranian LGBTQ activists whose responses were shaped by a somewhat different terrain: not only their experiences in Iran but also the problem of legibility in relation to Western asylum regimes and Western LGBTQ activists. For similar reasons, I do not focus on the responses of activists in Iran, which are often distilled and circulated by Western sources. Rather, I focus on the emotional and affective responses of Western LGBTQ activists to demonstrate that the power and durability of the predominant interpretation of the executions emerged from the way in which it resonated with their liberal secular imagination. Responses to these executions also present an opportunity to interrogate how a liberal secular imagination, circulating in a highly affective media milieu, has contributed to the racialization of Muslims via its contribution to a conception of Muslims as uniquely and violently homophobic.

EMOTIONAL IMAGININGS, AFFECTIVE MEDIA

To analyze the process by which a particular interpretation of the executions took hold and moved activists to action, I explore the interplay of emotions and affects in producing a resonance with a predominant liberal secular imagination. Emotions refer to narratively and linguistically structured responses to an interpretation of a situation, whereas affects are unstructured and felt as intensities of the body.[38] Furthermore, emotional responses to this case must be understood as products of histories and "investments in social norms," building on a history of highly differentiating sympathetic responses to colonized "Others," while resonating with particular liberal secular norms.[39] Furthermore, the primary medium of engagement with the case, the internet, operates through affective means, attuning to, inciting, intensifying, and speeding the circulation of emotions. While emotional narratives expressing love, fear, and disgust were integral to producing a feeling of sympathy for the executed boys, the internet facilitated a swift and affective circulation of the images and sound bites about the executions, which further reinforced this interpretation as a "felt truth."

As also noted in the Introduction, sympathy has shifted from being an expression of a feeling *with* another to an expression of feeling *for* another, who is marked off as the sufferer.[40] Therefore there is a dynamic tension in expressions of sympathy that tends to create both identification and differentiation between sympathizer and victim.[41] In the Mashhad case, activist sympathy for the two youths demonstrated such a tension between identification and differentiation. Many LGBTQ activists saw the executions as an opportunity to expand the perimeter of their identification and the frontier of activism against homophobia. However, this identification was also marked by a differentiation, as the Islamic character of the Iranian state was deemed the source of murderous homophobia, while Western contexts were assumed to be consistently less homophobic. As such, the emotions evoked by a narrative of homophobic persecution reflected secular assumptions about the threat of nonprivatized religion and also a view that "Islam" and "the West" are inherently conflicting "civilizations."

The process by which the youths were produced as sympathetic Muslims was also shaped by how emotional responses circulated via the medium of the internet. Sara Ahmed describes objects as becoming "sticky," accumulating associations, meanings, and emotions through their circulation, a

process that is much more discernable in today's media milieu.[42] In particular, the internet has an affective power that perpetuates a doing that feels
good in itself, regardless of meaning or effect. Puar has argued that "mobility, motility, speed and performance function as primary erotic and addic-
tive charges of modernity. Clicking the 'send' button is the ultimate release
of productivity and consumption, and dissemination, the ultimate form of
territorial coverage and conquest."[43] LGBTQ audiences faced with the horrifying images and story via an internet that facilitated rapid responses felt
a sense of urgency and responsibility to act. They could quickly "forward"
an email, cut and paste a form letter, or post a response on a blog or a You-
Tube video. The sympathetic response also absolves the actor of further responsibility to question or contemplate, placing the onus on the recipient.
As such, internet activism has an affective agency that feeds itself through
movement, points of connection, and repetition. In this case, it was this
entire process by which the story and photographs circulated, resonated
emotionally, and moved people to action that made it exceedingly difficult
to unstick the story of antigay persecution from the images.

While I understand the strength, persistence, and continuing production of this response as intimately connected to the forms of circulation
that the internet facilitates, the rest of my analysis will focus primarily on
the emotional responses to the case. In particular, I focus on the resonance
between three types of emotional responses and a predominant liberal
secular imagination about gay identity, Islam, and violence. These were
(1) *love,* or feelings of identification with the "gay"—and therefore presumably innocent—victims seen as expressing their individuality against
religious mores; (2) *fear,* or feelings of sympathetic terror for what the
youths experienced at the hands of religion, resonating with many other
fears articulated in both Western LGBTQ experience and the War on Terror; and (3) *disgust,* or feelings of revulsion at violence that could be seen
as religious in source and therefore wholly distinct from Western secular
forms of violence. Through these three emotional responses, identification and differentiation with the sympathetic victims were produced in a
manner that resonated with a liberal secular imagination that has come to
undergird cultural racism that sees an essential civilizational difference as
marking off "Muslims" from "Westerners."

LOVE AND (NONTRADITIONAL) COMMUNITY

An image posted on Andrew Sullivan's blog in July 2006 shows a young man at a demonstration in New York City on the one-year anniversary of the executions, holding up a large black-and-white drawing of Marhoni and Asgari.[44] The two are standing side by side with their eyes covered by blindfolds, as in the images of their executions; however, rather than nooses around their necks, a flower arrangement is draped across their chests. Above them are the words "We Remember You." In this image of this young man with a sign, just as in many other responses to the executions, two forms of love, the love of the romantic couple and the love of an LGBTQ community, are articulated to produce a feeling of commonality between the sympathizers and the victims. As two boys in love, the youths are made innocent, therefore sympathetic victims, and gay, therefore part of a "global" LGBTQ community. However, this interpretation of the two youths as executed for a gay love affair was not simply a product of the identity politics of LGBTQ activists but also resonated more broadly with a liberal secularist imagination about how romantic love that violates traditional religious norms is one of the purest expressions of individualism and freedom.

The notion that the boys were lovers, originating from an unverified report of a U.S.-based journalist, acts as an alibi, attesting to their innocence and making them sympathetic victims. By contrast, the story of the execution of two teenagers charged with the crime of raping a thirteen-year-old boy was not emotionally compelling because their possible guilt muddies the viewer's sympathy. Indeed, in the United States, there is much antipathy for juvenile offenders, who can be tried as adults and are serving life sentences at increasing rates.[45] The contrast was apparent in statements, for example, that they were "two fun loving teenage kids who were in love and who had never harmed anybody"[46] or "these boys were not pedophiles. . . . They were kids who found love. . . . They were victims of a hate crime and of state-sanctioned murder."[47] Pairing the claims that the youths were in love and that they were innocent implies that these are mutually exclusive—that one could not both be in love and participate in a rape. In a YouTube video entitled "To Mahmoud Asgari and Ayaz Marhoni with sorrow," which received more than sixteen thousand views and emphasizes the viewers' identification with the boys, their presumed love and innocence are central to creating that identification.[48] The text (somewhat awkwardly) explains that the two youths were executed "for the reason they had made bold to love each other." Then, as a seeming acknowledgment to the doubts raised about this interpretation, it asks, "if you had been them," would it matter "for what purpose" you/they were executed? However, the lack of mention of the rape charges clarifies that it does matter. Their status as two boys in love assures their innocence and the possibility for identification, potentially far beyond LGBTQ audiences. Therefore sympathy appears to be reserved for victims with whom one can identify, and identification depends on the victims' innocence, which is established by describing the teens as in love.

The focus on Marhoni and Asgari as two boys in love, rather than as two boys convicted of particular sexual acts, resonates with an increasingly normative conception of the Western gay subject that emphasizes romantic love and coupledom, rather than sexual expression and sexual liberation. This is part of a broader shift in the goals of Western LGBTQ activism toward a politics of normalization, particularly through the legitimation of the love of the romantic couple in same-gender marriage rights. This notion that the two boys were in love, originating from the reports of a single U.S.-based reporter who said they had been seen attending "gay" parties as a couple, was reinforced by the narrative power of such a Romeo and Juliet story of young, forbidden, and fatal love. Although all versions of the alleged crime involved at least one other boy, the repeated reference to the youths as "gay teen lovers" implied that their purported relationship to each other, and not to the other boy, was the reason for their execution. The simple fact that *two* youths, pictured standing side by side at the gallows, were executed has been crucial in reinforcing this narrative. The photographs function to remove the third boy from the frame of the story and, in combination with reports that they were "gay," quickly evoke a narrative about what happens when gay love is exposed in a place like Iran.

These two spatially and culturally distant people were made familiar via statements of protesters and reconstructions of their lives. As Ahmed notes, love produces the feeling of identification and the character of likeness, and for activists, the youths' presumable gay identity overcomes the obstacle of their difference.[49] Long argues that identification with the youths was a key component of LGBTQ responses to this case, saying,

"The most important thing 'we' saw in 'them' was that they were 'gay': they were like *us.* . . . [They] wanted what 'we' wanted and did what 'we' did; they were part of the family."[50] Indeed, narratives about them mix in details that seem to emphasize how ordinary and recognizable they were, for example, that they had expensive taste in clothing and that one of them was a fan of Michael Jackson.[51] Likewise, in explaining why he wrote an opera about the youths, R. Timothy Brady emphasized his similarity with them, saying, "I'm gay—that could happen to me. It doesn't matter that they're Iranian or they're half way across the world, it still really hit home."[52] As such, Western LGBTQ activists present themselves as expressing a love for their persecuted brethren whom they welcome into the fold of the community. This love further serves as an alibi for the activists, attesting to their purity of intention and disassociating them from the racism of the War on Terror discourse that they nevertheless were reinforcing.

Cases of persecution of "gay love" have powerful resonance in liberal secular imagination beyond LGBTQ identity politics, as activists set themselves apart from "traditional" communities in that they claim to create a liberating space in which youths can escape the restrictions of religious and cultural communities. As such, this discourse has become central to the reiteration of a civilizational difference between the "liberal" West and "tradition-bound" Muslim-majority societies. Liberals see their societies as organized around love, rather than "lust, tribalism, race, kinship, or religion," where "love creates a higher civilizational form even though it happens only between two people."[53] This conception of the West as uniquely appreciative of love has been central to responses to other practices perceived as emanating from Islamic cultures, such as violence against women dubbed "honor crimes." As Lila Abu-Lughod has demonstrated, much of the Western discourse on "honor crimes" presents expressions of romantic love and sexual transgression as epitomizing liberal values of individualism, autonomy, and freedom.[54] Furthermore, when the persecuted relationship is perceived to violate additional cultural norms—Abu-Lughod notes interreligious love, and I would add same-gender love—it provides an opportunity for additional condemnation of "tribalism and intolerance" seen as emanating from Islamic cultures.[55]

Indeed, in a liberal secularist imagination, individual agency and freedom are expressed in large part through the rejection of the restrictions of "tradition." Romantic love, especially when an expression of individual desire against cultural or religious norms, is seen as both a challenge to the social structures and a pinnacle of self-determination. Therefore, expressions of same-gender love can be seen as an all-the-more-powerful challenge to "traditional" societies. As Abu-Lughod notes, this discourse's attribution to the West of a "superior" romantic love not only obfuscates a more complex relationship to romantic love in Arab (and, we might add, Iranian) culture but also disregards illiberal values and practices in the West, such as "chastity, religious moralism, intolerance, racism, incarceration, economic exploitation, or inequality, gendered or otherwise."[56] In this way, such narratives of persecuted love falsely oppose a Western culture, as fostering individual freedom, to an Islamic culture, as violently restricting human expression. Therefore this narrative of the Mashhad executions as the persecution of two boys in love resonates broadly with a liberal secular imagination of both LGBTQ and other Western audiences, thereby affirming Western LGBTQ identities as central to the uniqueness of Western civilization.

THEIR FEAR, OUR FEAR

Those walking down the street in the Washington, D.C., gay neighborhood of Dupont Circle in July 2006 were likely to come across a very disturbing

FIGURE 6. Signs displayed at a July 9, 2006, Washington, D.C., protest on the one-year anniversary of the executions. Photograph by Elvert Barnes.

set of images. On the eve of the one-year anniversary of the executions, in preparation for demonstrations being held in cities across the country and the world, Lambda Rising, an LGBTQ bookstore, placed two large reproductions of the images of the executions in its store window, under the banner "Iran stop killing gays." These large posters were also present at a protest held in Dupont Circle, pictured in Figure 6, which I have decided to include here with some hesitation—particularly due to the difficult content—because it conveys how love and fear circulated through these acts of remembrance, including through these posters. The first poster showed Marhoni and Asgari standing side by side as the nooses were placed around their necks, and the second image showed them, dying or dead, as their bodies were swinging by the ropes. Also posted was a large sign with a quote by "'Mashi,' a 24-year-old gay activist in Iran" that read, "Isn't it time that all homosexuals around the world rise up and come to our defense?" These images of executions were made part of the urban landscape, where one walking down the street comes face-to-face with two young men facing their imminent deaths. What kinds of feelings does this evoke in the viewer? How does this experience reverberate and resonate with other experiences, histories, and associations?

While the emotion of love serves to create sameness and identification with the youths, fear powerfully connects and differentiates the Iranian and U.S. contexts, as the story circulates different types of fear for different bodies. The narrative power of the images in creating a sympathetic fear in the audience and evoking associated fears is of central importance to the power of this story. Indeed, if the photographs had not existed, doubts about the cause of the executions likely would have led many to cease to be interested in the story. The photographs provided powerful material for depicting violent and barbaric "antigay" persecution that many assumed must be occurring in Iran. The fear of Marhoni and Asgari is palpable in the sequence of three photographs initially released with the story, in part because their faces are visible and emotionally communicative. In the first photograph, they are crying and distressed as they speak with the journalist. This allows for a "sympathetic communication"[57] where their tears might elicit the tears of a viewer. Furthermore, as Ahmed notes, fear "involves an *anticipation* of hurt or injury" in the future, and the anticipation of the two teens' imminent deaths is captured with gut-wrenching clarity in these photographs.[58] The fear amplifies as they are blindfolded and walked toward the gallows (in the second photograph) and becomes overwhelming as the nooses are slid over their heads and around their necks (in the third photograph). This fear, although a private experience of terror not fully imaginable by the viewer, "opens up past histories of association."[59] The viewer projects her own fears onto these youths' experiences: fear of death, fear of homophobic persecution, fear of religious homophobia, or fear of the threat of Islam. These fears also resonate with the secularist perspective that when religion is not confined to the private realm, it will necessarily become a source of oppressive conformity and irrational violence.

The photographs circulating in relation to these executions have inspired many narrative renditions of the executions, including at least two theatrical pieces, a number of YouTube videos, and various written pieces. Combining them with narrative, music, and other images, activists were able to maximize sympathy for the cause. It is striking that a number of these renditions also include photographs from September 29, 2002, public hangings of men convicted of abducting, raping, and robbing women.[60] A lengthy examination of the case by Simon Forbes of Outrage!, which extensively narrativized the experiences of the executions, included a photograph from 2002 of the young man in the audience, weeping as an older man looks at him with concern, suggesting that he is Asgari's brother (Forbes writes, "Many cheer while others look on silently in fear. A brother of Mahmoud begins screaming").[61] This image was also used in two YouTube videos, one of which added another image from the same 2002 hanging, showing a ruggedly handsome blue-eyed convict awaiting execution, implying that he, too, was executed for being gay.[62] While such embellishments to this powerful visual narrative hardly seem necessary, they point to an interest in depicting fear and terror of the executions in ways that can be vicariously experienced, through the experience of anticipation and the pain of viewership. A YouTube video paying homage to Marhoni and Asgari further demonstrates how images, especially of the human face, along with music, work to intensify and modulate emotional responses.[63] With a soundtrack of mournful string instruments, it uses simple black screens with white text, interspersed with photographs from the executions and elsewhere. It begins by evoking the viewer's perspective and life experience, specifically as a young person: "Remember . . . / when you were fourteen years old / when you were 16." Then transposing Marhoni and Asgari into the frame and walking the viewer through their executions, the video seeks to make the viewer feel the terror they felt, using the photographs to re-create the executions. The youths' terror is dramatically heightened through mournful music that turns shrill at the moment of the executions. The viewer feels sick to the stomach.

The fear that Marhoni and Asgari experienced as they faced their deaths was at times attributed to all Iranians, described by Peter Tatchell as living in "a gigantic prison," but more commonly linked to the presumed all-encompassing fear defining the lives of Iranian sexual minorities.[64] In the period following the executions, Ireland reported extensively on arrests and violence against men seeking sexual relationships with other men in Iran, especially via internet-based entrapments, saying that the fear he perceived "surpasses by far anything encountered covering dissident movements behind the Iron Curtain."[65] His accounts are detailed and horrifying, portraying a police state that is singularly focused on setting traps for men and then arresting, abusing, and, in some cases, raping them. He describes the resulting community fear as leading individuals to take unusual measures to go about simple tasks, for example, describing a man seeking to communicate with Western journalists as dressing in full facial veil and traveling for a day to an internet café, where he communicated via a newly created instant messaging account. He concludes, "It is that scary. People are rightfully scared for their lives."[66] While Ireland's accounts of internet-based police entrapment are plausible, they are not linked to the larger context of police surveillance that has waxed and waned in Iran over the past many decades and has targeted many different categories of people. They also fail to note that police entrapment and abuse of LGBTQ people is not a phenomenon unique to Iran but also has been practiced in many Western contexts. Finally, an account of Iran as a totalitarian society ruled by fear obfuscates a much more complicated situation in Iran, where people have struggled against and often found ways of evading such surveillance, policing, and abuse. As such, there is an explicit disassociation from the Iranian context, which is presented as wholly oppressive, without opportunities for resistance.

Despite this explicit disassociation between the Western and Iranian contexts, there is an implicit resonance articulated in a fear of homophobic violence that is perceived to cross various borders. Even as the West is represented as progressively more tolerant, the executions evoke another past, one that is written into the consciousness of Western LGBTQ people who have feared being "outed," having their livelihoods taken away from them, or being victims of homophobic violence. One protest organizer said, "For gay people, I think all of us have a fear of being killed, and of being killed for who we are," and that he sees Marhoni and Asgari as being "executed for something you see in yourself."[67] As such, these photographs touched on an "emotional memory" many LGBTQ viewers seemed to have, striking them as a possibility that they had been spared.[68] Furthermore, this case had some parallels to reactions to the 1998 murder of Matthew Shepard, a White gay college student, in Laramie, Wyoming. Beth Loffreda, analyzing responses to the Shepard murder, notes that many outside LGBTQ activists felt a need to speak on behalf of Shepard, expressing a "sense of ownership" about the case. These responses likewise alternated between highlighting the commonality between sympathizer and victim and constructing the context and source of the violence as vastly different and other, and not a reflection of the United States more broadly.[69] Therefore reactions to the Mashhad executions built, in various ways, on responses to other cases of anti-LGBTQ violence that have been documented in the United States.

Finally, the fear encapsulated in the photographs was also generalized and amplified to be a fear experienced by all Americans, or Westerners, in the face of what is deemed an Islamic threat. The War on Terror, which, as Pellegrini points out, is said to be waged against a *feeling*, terror, is also invested in producing fear, making it a "war *of* terror."[70] Ahmed notes that fear is exacerbated when the object of fear is lost, which leads to the entire world becoming fearsome, saying, "The loss of the object of fear renders the world itself a space of potential danger."[71] In the War on Terror, a war where, until the 2011 killing of Osama Bin Laden, the presumed leader of the September 11 attacks was said to have absconded in the mountains of Afghanistan and the source of the attacks was said to be a slippery set of worldviews, fear's object was lost and generalized. By contrast, the fear felt by Marhoni and Asgari was tangible, comprehensible, and clear. There were villains and accomplices: the executioners stood behind them, the government administrators escorted them, the journalists compliantly interviewed them, and the crowd watched. These two were incredibly alone, vulnerable, and helpless. This story concretized the object of fear and gave a form to the floating generalized fear circulating in the War on Terror, thereby making it temporarily more manageable.

This fear of Islam, a fear that seems to be shared by so many different categories of people and not simply LGBTQ individuals, is also palpable in the photographs because these individuals seem to embody this conflict in their physical appearances, which associated the villains more strongly with racial stereotypes of Muslims. The two youthful, clean-shaven, and clean-cut boys, whose eyes are covered but whose faces are otherwise visible, contrast starkly with the men who surround them, with their thick brows and facial hair or with scarves and masks covering their faces and heads. The guards and executioners seem to manifest the irrational, intolerant, and murderous Muslims responsible for the "Islamic terror" also being unleashed on the "West." By contrast, we rarely see images of executioners in the United States—or their victims' corpses—so that images of executions in Iran create a stark difference between "here," where the death penalty is an abstract concept to be debated, and "there," where the terror that such executions perpetuate on individuals and broader populations is vicariously experienced.

However, this fear does not stay concrete long but is again mobilized to feed the free-floating fears of the War on Terror, where some manifestation of "Islam" is associated with an amorphous and shadowy threat that has led to the entire world becoming fearsome. For example, in a sweeping statement, Lawrence D. Mass, cofounder of the Gay Men's Health Crisis, argues that "fanatical Islam," "that blew up the great Buddhist statues of Afghanistan," is the greatest threat to gay people; that "Iran has truly become an evil empire"; and that Ahmadinejad, like Hitler, "must be stopped by any means necessary."[72] Mark Green, candidate for New York State attorney general, speaking at a protest, similarly placed the executions at the center of an age-old Manichean struggle: "History is an eternal contest between hate and hope. Right now hate is winning in the Middle East."[73] Such associations are also implicit in the numerous references of activists to Iran as an Islamo-fascist state.[74] This type of rhetoric generates a malleable fear that quickly moves from referent to referent, from Iranian gays to Western gays, from Buddhists to Jews, and from the Middle East to the

United States and beyond. As such, the photographs come to stand in for a stark Islamic difference that produces a wide range of intolerances, hatreds, and barbaric forms of violence. Fear produces an amorphous and malleable "enemy" that is highly productive in a context of a war waged on many international and domestic fronts, through both policing and military techniques. The fear of these two boys becomes the fear of anyone who sees herself on the other side of this supposed battle against Islamic intolerance, one that is further articulated in disgust at a violence deemed particularly "Islamic."

OUR MORAL DISGUST

A 2006 *Washington Post* article describes the effects of these images on a local D.C. activist, a self-described antiwar leftist who helped organize a local protest of the executions:

> When the images of the hangings went up last year on the Internet, he printed them out and put them up near his desk. He says that all the friends he's shown the pictures to have had "a shift in consciousness," a realization that they live sheltered lives, that evil exists in the world and that despite the vast cultural difference between Iran and the United States, there have to be moral absolutes. And killing children for homosexuality is one thing that is absolutely wrong.[75]

In contrast to the emotions of love and fear, disgust acts primarily to create a line of differentiation and separation. Whereas anger at the status quo is basic to the work of many social justice movements, disgust indicates a revulsion, a recoiling, but one that works in tandem with desire. One moves toward an object only to be revolted and recoil from it; one is both intrigued, and must see it, but cannot look too long. Disgust at the photographs may be in response to the mutilation of human bodies, but it more often takes the form of a moral response to what is seen as a form of depravity. Although the photographs lack what are often deemed particularly gruesome qualities—visibly broken, bloodied, or disfigured bodies—they remain very disturbing. This may be because they remind us of the frailty of the human body and how easily life can be taken from it. However, the narrative interpretation of the photographs was also key in producing a strongly articulated moral disgust, as demonstrated in the preceding passage. This activist's fascination with the photographs, which he says he printed, posted by his desk, and showed to his friends, is linked to his moral disgust at what he sees as "killing children for homosexuality." This disgust made the photographs objects of fascination and horror and kept them circulating; it also created an absolutist response to Iran as "evil," disallowing contemplation about the sources of this state violence. Furthermore, in many responses, a secularist disgust was expressed toward what was seen as "barbaric" and "uncivilized" violence, deemed a "result of religious prejudice and hatred,"[76] a case of "religious puritanism gone mad,"[77] or indicative of "the new medievalism that is modern Iran, where the barbarism of Sharia law holds sway."[78] In their responses, LGBTQ activists imagined a uniquely barbaric Iran doling out religiously rooted violence to gays and lesbians.

In a secularist worldview, barbarity is usually ascribed to societies of the past where violence is believed to be uncontrolled, gratuitous, spectacular, and public. In modern societies, by contrast, violence is supposed to be centralized in the state; calibrated precisely to a purpose; avoiding unnecessary physical pain; and kept out of public view. This contrast emerges from the shift Michel Foucault identified from premodern sovereign power, which depends on the theatrical displays of the tortured or executed body, to modern disciplinary power, which depends on normalization of the body via pervasive everyday practices.[79] However, torture, suffering, and violence do not necessarily diminish in modern societies but rather must be hidden and/or justified by a calculus of means–ends proportionality.[80] Darius Rejali demonstrates that in fact the use of torture and executions by the Islamic Republic of Iran cannot be explained as primarily a result of a reinstatement of the Islamic penal codes but rather is continuous with the practices of torture and execution of the secular and modernizing regime before it.[81] While punishments identified with Islam do at times serve to legitimate the state, they constitute a very small proportion of state violence.[82]

Nevertheless, informed by a liberal secularist imagination that focused on the presumed "Islamic" difference, activists focused on aspects of this case that set Iran apart. As such, activists ignored the fact that Iran, along with the United States, China, and Saudi Arabia, accounted for 95 percent of executions worldwide in 2005 and that until 2005, the death penalty could be applied to juvenile offenders in the United States.[83]

Rather, disgust at this case was in part articulated as a response to the theatrical and public nature of the executions, "executions staged as enter-
tainment,"[84] and the use of "gratuitous" pain that does not seem calibrated
to the ends: Marhoni and Asgari were reportedly executed by a slow and
painful hanging by strangulation and had already received severe corporal
punishment. Therefore, even without the claim that Marhoni and Asgari
were executed for being gay, the photographs disturbed secular sensibilities about violence. However, the gratuitous character of the violence was
even more pronounced when the executions were seen as instances of
"killing children for homosexuality,"[85] thereby appearing in the minds of
activists to be a perfect case of "barbarity" that was absolutely reprehensible and could be completely separated—temporally, culturally, politically,
and emotionally—from most modern forms of violence.

In addition, when understood as instances of antigay violence con-
doned by the onlooking crowd, the executions evoked a U.S. history of
"irrational" mob violence and bigotry: the lynching of African Americans, particularly in the South, often documented in photographs that reinforced white supremacy. Indeed, the noose has become such a symbol
of anti-Black racial hatred that its display may be deemed a hate crime. As
such, it is striking that the noose and images of hangings were strongly associated with conceptions of what it means to be "gay" in Iran, including
in Ireland's choice of image accompanying his stories on Iran—a picture of
the country's map with a noose hanging over it. Racism and homophobia
are recognized to be characteristics of many modern societies. However,
when Iran is explicitly brought into modernity, it is through analogies to
fascism and communism rather than to the United States and its well-
documented history of state-sanctioned anti-Black violence. This is apparent in the description of Ahmadinejad as a present-day Hitler, references
to an antigay "pogrom," and the repeated descriptor for the Iranian state as
"clerical-fascist" or "Islamo-fascist."[86] The concept of *Islamo-fascism* in particular was a flexible label connecting a vast array of apparent threats from
the "Islamic" world, as various as Iran, Syria, Hezbollah, Hamas, and al-
Qaeda. Although the term implies that the source of violence is not Islam
per se, it reinforces a notion that ideology and belief alone, originating in
some form of Islam, are at the root of conflicts with these threats, failing
to account for the actions and grievances of each state or organization in
terms of its specific historical and geopolitical contexts.

By contrast, the U.S. state–perpetrated violence at the Abu Ghraib prison in Iraq, well documented through photographs publicly released in 2004, which was also deemed "disgusting" by many in the West, received a different set of responses within the LGBTQ press. LGBTQ activists were very critical of the torture of Iraqi prisoners, but their criticism carefully delineated who was responsible and accounted for the circumstances of their actions. While the Bush administration argued that the guards involved in the "abuses" were a few "bad apples," LGBTQ activists specified the Bush administration, its occupation of Iraq, and the homophobia of the military as causes of the sexualized torture.[87] They rarely connected the Abu Ghraib torture to the use of torture in U.S. history predating the Bush administration, as perpetrated by the CIA-run School of Americas, or to similar abuses in U.S. prisons today.[88] Indicative of such amnesia is Faisal Alam's statement that "the sexual humiliation of Iraqi detainees represents the worst moral and ethical crime in US military history post–World War II."[89] For many LGBTQ activists faced with the violence at Abu Ghraib, the Bush administration itself became the exceptional "bad apple" in U.S. history.

Furthermore, the types of personalized sympathy and acts of remembrance that Marhoni and Asgari elicited were virtually absent in responses to the suffering of Abu Ghraib victims. Sympathy for Abu Ghraib victims almost never began from the position of imagining oneself in their place but rather emphasized the victims' difference, including their presumed homophobia that was said to make the torture all the more unbearable. The many reasons for this lack of identification are too complex to consider here but certainly include the hypersexualized degradation of the presumably heterosexual Abu Ghraib victims, as opposed to the desexualization of the presumably gay Mashhad victims. Indeed, whereas Marhoni and Asgari were normalized into a particular Western gay identity as the young gay couple in love, the Abu Ghraib victims were racialized and pathologized into an Arab homophobic heterosexual masculinity. The Abu Ghraib victims were never made one of "us" but rather came to indicate the shameful actions of "our" fellow countrymen who needed disciplining and disavowal to reassert the legitimacy of the Western position. Therefore sympathies were often identified with the United States, as commentators carefully positioned themselves as patriotic, supportive of most soldiers in the U.S. military, and distressed that the U.S. cause in the War on Terror may have suffered.[90]

While both the Abu Ghraib torture scandal and the Mashhad executions elicited disgust, this disgust associated differently with conceptions
of the United States and Iran. Violence emerging from modern democratic
states, even when condemned, is rarely seen as reflecting an essential attribute of secular state power. By contrast, the executions of Marhoni and
Asgari, because they violated particular secular sensibilities, resulted in a
moral disgust that requires complete rejection and separation. While re-
sponders to Abu Ghraib were focused on determining responsibility and
causality, the reasons for the executions in Mashhad were seen as transparent, perpetrated by a unitary Iranian government, motivated simply by
religious homophobia.

In a particularly introspective article, the feminist columnist Katha Pollitt
made some interesting observations about the place of Islam in the liberal
secular imagination. Describing her initial outrage at the news that Harvard University had allotted women-only gym hours at the request of a
group of Muslim women students, she then considers why this relatively
innocuous accommodation had garnered such a passionate response from
her. Noting that she had reacted to the associations she has with Islam as
"violent, oppressive, sexist," she remarks, "That is what living in our time
does to you: intelligent people go in a flash from 'Art history major wants
to work out in peace' to 'What about those gays they executed in Iran?'"
Pollitt, in describing her own experience with the affective processes I have
been exploring, inadvertently highlights the place of the figure of the executed "gay Iranians" in the post-9/11 Western secular imagination. Such
"terrible crimes against women, gays and secularists" are for Pollitt the
unquestionable instances where outrage at a "violent, oppressive, sexist"
Islam is completely justified.[91] Indeed, the question of tolerance of homosexuality has become a highly flexible means of marking Muslims as
backward, threatening, and unworthy of sympathy or tolerance. However,
I have argued that even when it comes to such apparently obvious cases, we
need to consider how secular assumptions and sensibilities delimit perceptions of and responses to them.

In this case, LGBTQ activists insisted on presenting the executions
as instances of homophobic persecution by an Islamically motivated state,
and organized protests focused on identifying the youths as gay lovers, and

homosexuality in Iran as an issue requiring more visibility. This response foreclosed other possibilities for activism and social change. For one thing, suggestions such as Scott Long's, that in the Iranian context the rights of sexual minorities would be more effectively protected through "struggles for privacy, women's rights, and an end to executions," fell on deaf ears.[92] In addition, the broader problem of the use of the death penalty in Iran faded into the background. Although there was a dramatic spike in executions in Iran—their numbers almost doubling to 177 in 2006 and reaching close to 300 in 2007—when President Ahmadinejad spoke at Columbia University in September 2007, he was questioned only about the execution of homosexuals.[93] Also, many commentators spoke at length about Ahmadinejad's denial of the existence of homosexuality in Iran, but few noted that his response included a lengthy defense of Iran's use of the death penalty. This dramatic expansion of the death penalty certainly cannot be explained in terms of the persecution of same-gender sexuality or the Islamic character of the state. However, secularists' focus on rooting out what they perceive as religious violence meant that they overlooked this larger story, one that in fact connected the Iranian and U.S. contexts.

In looking for state violence rooted in Islam per se, liberal secularists are led astray when they do not consider that Iranian state violence is often rooted in secular concerns around perceived threats to security and sovereignty. It is not to say that religion is never used to justify state violence in Iran or elsewhere or that the religious legitimacy of the state is never a factor in its persecution of individuals. However, to read state violence as primarily religious in origin is to misunderstand the role of the state, which is in large part to guard its own sovereignty. As such, even if Marhoni and Asgari were executed for consensual sexual relations, this tells us little about *why* exactly it happened. A deeper understanding of the specific context around which the case arose is necessary to understanding and effectively responding to it. In particular, we need to understand what worldly problems, what perceived threats to security, are being addressed by the executions of these two boys. As a result, it becomes necessary to think of their executions in relation to the specificity of the Iranian repressive state apparatus.

The assertion of a "gay" identity that needs protection is a projection of a Western model of liberation that is not at all attuned to such specificities. The emphasis on sameness, while a powerful method of moving Western LGBTQ audiences and therefore maybe an attractive tool for Iranian activists as well, is not strategically tailored to the goal of improving the lives of sexual minorities or eliminating the death penalty, or simply its biased application, in Iran. It focuses primarily on increasing visibility and recognition of these youth as persecuted "gay lovers," while ignoring that visibility and "outness" are not universally shared barometers of equality in struggles for sexual freedom.[94] Furthermore, liberal secularists are wrong to see Islamic traditions as devoid of rationality while presenting liberal secularism as a culturally neutral expression of a universal rationality. Both liberal secularism and various forms of Islam are cultural traditions, which are products of particular histories, and both traditions include processes of inquiry that emphasize the use of reason to engage with authoritative texts, for example, the Constitution, the Qur'an, in different historical contexts in order to reassess predominant values, beliefs, and practices.[95] Similarly, an assertion that this is an example of Islamically rooted intolerance of same-gender sexuality is not only ahistorical but fails to recognize that, in practice, it is through the overriding of Islamic standards of evidence that the prosecution of such individuals occurs, for example, via forced confessions and the standard of deductive reasoning of the judge. Furthermore, the assumption of Islam's inherent incompatibility with same-gender sexuality leads to a politics of rescue that sees "escape" via asylum claims as the only viable option. A more effective approach would connect the legal status of same-gender sexuality and the daily experiences of sexual minorities with other struggles and movements against social bias, oppressive laws, and state violence that are drawing on a combination of liberal and Islamic discourses in ways that resonate with Iranian political traditions.[96] While the strength of the repressive Iranian state apparatus is undeniable, even more so after the squelching of the 2009 election protests, it is through building on movements that aim to protect social freedoms, women's rights, privacy, and due process rights that a space for the expression of same-gender sexuality is most likely to be protected.

While liberal Western politics presumes itself to be secular and therefore rooted in rational argument rather than emotions, LGBTQ activist responses to the Mashhad case demonstrate otherwise. While emotion and reason work in tandem to move people to political action, the internet, an indispensable activist tool that facilitates the rapid circulation of information, also proliferates emotional and affective responses that can overwhelm more reasoned debate. As such, an ascendant internet technology, a construction of an Islamic threat, and a secularism that has become defensive in the face of religion's resurgence in the public sphere have led to the profound influence of secular emotions and attachments in liberal and left politics today. More specifically, uninterrogated liberal secular sensibilities can blind us to complexities and make for responses that are both intellectually deficient and politically ineffective. In this case, the clearest practical effect of Western LGBTQ activism was not to expand the space in which same-gender sexuality could be expressed in Iran—indeed, the effect might have been the opposite—but rather to further legitimize a Western LGBTQ identitarian politics through its resonance with a liberal secular imaginary and War on Terror discourse of "a clash of civilizations." As such, this discourse has mobilized Western LGBTQ rights in the service of producing a stronger distinction between a presumably tolerant, modern, secularized West and a presumably intolerant, antimodern, and religious East, at the basis of both cultural racism and population racism.

4. Defamed and Defended

The Precarity of the "Moderate" Muslim American

As the previous two chapters have demonstrated, sympathetic representations of Muslims in Muslim-majority societies circulating in the United
States reiterate a stereotype of Islamic societies as culturally backward,
violently intolerant, and antimodern, even as they present some Muslims
as enlightened, resisting oppression, or in other ways just like "us." Muslim American public figures, judged in relation to these representations
of Muslims abroad, have in turn presented themselves as peacemakers,
tolerance promoters, and interfaith/intercultural healers to make claims
to acceptability. This approach has failed to protect these public figures
from harsh media-generated attacks, which have tarnished their images as
widely acclaimed "moderate Muslims," often swiftly transforming them in
the eyes of the public into potential threats. While this chapter focuses primarily on a local New York City controversy surrounding plans to create an
Arabic–English dual-language public school, I begin with discussion of the
later national controversy surrounding the building of an Islamic cultural
center in lower Manhattan. Modifying Rey Chow's argument that protest
is the socially and economically viable vocation of the "ethnic," these cases
demonstrate that the promotion of tolerance became the means by which
one could be deemed an acceptable Muslim American.[1] Nevertheless, this
space of acceptability was narrow and treacherous. In participating in such
discourses of tolerance, these public figures and their liberal defenders reinforced their opponents' position that intolerance is a particularly Muslim

problem. As a result, this tolerance discourse could be swiftly turned back on them when their exceptional status was called into question through the same set of standards that were used to defend them. The exceptionally tolerable Muslim, the moderate and the patriot, through media manipulations of variables of assessment, can suddenly find himself transformed into a potential threat. These cases suggest that all Muslims, no matter how much they seem to align with the parameters of acceptability, are susceptible to being recast as unacceptable because of their continued association with a racialized population.

The 2010 uproar surrounding the creation of an Islamic cultural center marked one of the most intense national controversies to date regarding the role of Muslim Americans in the United States. Although the center was initially named Cordoba House to evoke a period of peaceful coexistence and cultural exchange among Muslims, Jews, and Christians in Andalucía, when this name was recast by opponents as a reference to an Islamic conquest of Spain, planners renamed the center Park51. Nevertheless, it was dubbed by opponents the "Ground Zero Mosque," although it was neither at Ground Zero nor primarily a mosque. Located two city blocks north of the World Trade Center site, it was modeled on multipurpose, religiously affiliated institutions such as YMCAs and Jewish community centers, like the Ninety-Second Street Y. Park51 was envisioned as a fifteen-story community center to serve residents of all faiths through a variety of services, including a Muslim prayer space. It was also presented as a space of interfaith and intercultural engagement and dialogue that would heal the divides created by 9/11. Park51 passed all legal hurdles and was passionately defended by New York City mayor Michael Bloomberg, who framed the issue in terms of the rights of religious freedom and private property and the values of diversity and tolerance. Nevertheless, the plan produced a national media outcry that demonstrated not only the broad acceptance of the notion that Muslims in general are culpable for the 9/11 attacks but the malleability of discourses of tolerance that were used by both defenders and opponents of the center.

Much of the discussion about Park51 focused on the central planners, especially Imam Feisal Abdul Rauf, the key religious leader associated with the plan. Although branded an Islamist and a radical by right-wing critics, Abdul Rauf in fact embodied many of the attributes necessary to be deemed a tolerable "moderate Muslim" by U.S. liberals, a fact that he emphasized by frequently referring to himself as a "man of peace." His supporters demonstrated Abdul Rauf's moderate status by pointing to many of his specific qualities as (1) a Sufi, a presumably more spiritually oriented and peaceful Islamic sect; (2) a supporter of women's rights, leading a gender-integrated mosque; (3) an advocate of religious tolerance who has presided over interfaith marriages and worked in interfaith contexts; (4) a patriot working for U.S. interests who served as an international spokesperson for the State Department and worked with the FBI; and (5) a supporter of the state of Israel. His book *What's Right with Islam* describes the United States as a country whose values make it an ideal place in which to practice Islam, which he describes as compatible with secularism and capitalism.

This portrayal of Abdul Rauf as a "bridge builder" and "man of peace," and Park51 as a space of interfaith and intercultural healing, seems to directly counter some of the worst stereotypes of Muslims as violent and intolerant. However, this portrayal did not prevent critics from representing the center as a "victory mosque" where future terrorists would be trained or Islam as an inherently violent religion, for example, in one mass-produced sign present in a New York City protest, in which "Sharia" was written in red, bloodlike letters. More subtly, many critics were able to harness a notion implicit in Abdul Rauf's self-portrayal—that Muslims hold some special responsibility for the problem of intolerance in the world—against the center. As other demonstration signs show, Muslims were cast as having a particular problem with religious intolerance ("Show True Tolerance: Build Churches in Saudi Arabia") and overstepping the bounds of U.S. tolerance ("Eat Pray Love No Problem, Just Not in This Zipcode!"). Other opponents more explicitly engaged a discourse of tolerance, arguing that Muslims can be moderate and peace loving but need to prove themselves as such; many argued that if Abdul Rauf were the moderate he says he is, he would move the center in the interest of promoting peace and reconciliation. Along these lines, Sarah Palin, former governor of Alaska and vice presidential candidate, tweeted on July 18, 2010, "Peace-seeking Muslims, pls understand, Ground Zero mosque is UNNECESSARY provocation; it stabs hearts. Pls reject it in interest of healing."[2] Another common line of argument focused on a need to be sensitive to the pain of the families of the victims of 9/11, although some 9/11 families supported Park51.

FIGURE 7. Protests in New York City on August 22, 2010, to oppose plans to build the Park51 cultural center. Photograph by the author.

Abraham Foxman, national director of the Anti-Defamation League (ADL), defended the group's opposition to the plan by referring to 9/11 families: "their anguish entitles them to positions that others would categorize as irrational or bigoted."[3] While seeming to reject a notion of Muslims' collective responsibility for 9/11, ADL nevertheless defended such "irrational or bigoted" thinking, a stance that it is difficult to imagine the group taking in reference to the anti-Semitism of those who have been the victims of violence by Jewish people or the Israeli state.[4] A few months later, the ADL, without any recognition of the irony, announced its formation of the Interfaith Coalition on Mosques, in alliance with various Muslim leaders, to respond to "a disturbing rise in discrimination against Muslims trying to legally build or expand their houses of worship, or mosques, across the United States."[5] The distinction between defending a constitutionally protected right to build houses of worship and opposing the center as "offensive" obfuscated how the notion of offense depended on an assumption that all Muslims were associated with, and in a sense responsible for, the 9/11 attacks. Ultimately, such positions make Muslims responsible not only for their own presumed individual intolerance, or the intolerance of other Muslims, but also for the intolerance of those who oppose Muslims. The fact that the plan was presented as in the service of reconciliation and peace became ammunition for critics whose *own* opposition could serve as evidence that the proposal would not achieve its stated goal.

Another tactic used against the Park51 planners, and common in attacks against Muslim public figures, was the application of a political litmus test regardless of its actual relevance. Perhaps because Abdul Rauf passed so many of the tests of what is deemed a "moderate" Muslim, *Fox News* commentator Greg Gutfeld announced a plan to build a gay bar next door to the center, which he said would offer nonalcoholic beverages to cater to "Islamic gay men," even as he is neither gay nor Muslim. He framed this as an attempt "to break down barriers and reduce deadly homophobia in the Islamic world."[6] Park51 leaders eventually responded to Gutfeld, saying, "You are free to open whatever you like. If you won't consider the sensibilities of Muslims, you are not going to build dialogue." Gutfeld responded on his show, "It's weird being educated in tolerance by an incredibly intolerant ideology." A guest on his show suggested that a specialty drink at the bar could be named "Hang Me in the Middle of the Town Square."[7] Through this process, Abdul Rauf and the Park51 planners were transformed from people with apparently conservative views on homosexuality to people who represent an "incredibly intolerant ideology" to people complicit in public executions, even as the Park51 tweet expressed no opposition to Gutfeld's proposal to open a gay bar and hence evinced tolerance for that which one may not support.

While this example speaks to the ways in which Muslims are made collectively responsible for violence perpetrated by some Muslims, it also demonstrates how the variables of assessment deemed relevant to Muslims, such as views on gender and sexuality, can be used to defame a person who in other respects abides by the narrow definition of a moderate Muslim. Three years earlier, another New York City controversy foreshadowed many of these dynamics, including the malleability of discourses of tolerance and the tactical use of political litmus tests. Together these cases illustrate the narrow space that Muslim Americans must navigate to maintain their acceptability, a space that is reproduced by liberal discourses of tolerance. They also demonstrate that population racism is effectively exploited by liberal and conservative media outlets to garner audience attention and produce political effects.

TEACHING TOLERANCE AS TEACHING TERRORISM

The Khalil Gibran International Academy (KGIA), first announced in February 2007, was to integrate the teaching of Arabic language and culture into a standard college-preparatory curriculum for middle through high school grades and was modeled on the more than sixty dual-language schools and eleven culturally themed schools already existing in the New York public school system.[8] Similar to Park51, the school was conceived as focused on increasing tolerance and understanding among a diverse student body and hence was compatible with discourses of tolerance that articulate intercultural and interfaith dialogue as a solution to post-9/11 conflict. Its founding principal, Debbie Almontaser, a Muslim and Arab American educator of Yemeni descent, known for her interfaith activism bringing Muslim, Jewish, and Christian communities together in the wake of 9/11, was deemed by many an exemplary "moderate" and the perfect individual to lead the school. However, a media-generated controversy surrounding the founding of KGIA culminated in the resignation of Almontaser following the publication of a highly critical *New York Post* article in early August, less than a month before the opening of the school. As a result of Almontaser's resignation, and an abdication of support from the Department of Education, the school faced significant difficulties and failed to become a dual-language school.[9]

The *New York Post* article leading to the resignation of Almontaser served as a political litmus test and quickly produced a view, in the words of the teachers' union president Randi Weingarten, that Almontaser is "someone who doesn't instinctively denounce campaigns or ideas tied to violence."[10] In the *Post* article, headlined "City Principal is 'Revolting,'" Almontaser was represented as explaining the multiple meanings of *intifada* in response to the reporter's question about an unrelated organization's T-shirt bearing the words "Intifada NYC." What was reported over and over again as her "defense of the T-shirts" or her "failure to condemn" the use of the word *intifada* led many key allies to withdraw their support of

Almontaser. Irrelevant to these assessments of Almontaser's suitability for the job of principal was her widely available public record of service. How was it possible to so quickly cast as unacceptable a politically well-respected public figure who was seen by many as an exemplary "moderate" Muslim American? Indeed, Mayor Michael Bloomberg, in announcing Almontaser's resignation, said, "I know the woman. She's worked for the city in a variety of capacities. She's very smart. She's certainly not a terrorist." This tepid defense marked just how close this exemplary "moderate" had come to being transformed in the eyes of many into a "terrorist." In this chapter, I analyze the relationship of the center-left media's discourses of tolerance, as exemplified in assertions of Almontaser's status as a "moderate" Muslim, to the concerted right-wing campaign against Almontaser and the school to examine how these discourses together racialize Muslims.

Population racism, which produces a racial Other as a coherent yet internally diverse population, manifests differently in relation to high-profile Muslim Americans than in relation to Muslims in Muslim-majority societies. While population racism is undergirded by an absolutist conception of difference, which delineates one "population" from another, it also allows for diversity and variation *within* a racialized population. This diversity, however, exhibits as a distinctive distribution of characteristics, capacities, and risks and hence suggests the terms in which each individual of that population must be assessed. The coherence of the racialized population is articulated through the consistency of the particular measures or variables used to assess whether one is a more or less typical member of that population. While liberal discourses cast Muslims abroad as either "good" or "bad," they treat Muslim Americans through a much more ambivalent assessment-focused orientation. Hence the question of *who* is a "moderate" Muslim has been highly contested within both liberal and right-wing discourses, reinforcing population racism via the consistent evocation of distinct variables of assessment. These variables include relationships to U.S. patriotism, to Muslims abroad, to religion/secularism, to gender and sexuality, and to discourses of tolerance that have made tolerance–intolerance a main axis of the conflict between the "West" and "Islam." My analysis shows that the category of "moderate" is exceedingly narrow and that anyone not abiding by its parameters is easily shifted to the other side, as extremist, terrorist, or terrorist sympathizer.

Furthermore, for both center-left and right-wing media, the question of who is or is not a "moderate" Muslim has proved a useful controversy to capture audience attention. Population racism emerges not only in elaborated arguments and narratives but also in disaggregated evocations of distinct variables that circulate efficiently through sound bites, headlines, and images, allowing for rapid affective measurements of tolerability. Ultimately, the power of the attacks waged on Almontaser did not rest in the power of the better argument or the stronger evidence. The right's attacks were focused on what Tiziana Terranova describes as perception management.[11] Perception management does not treat the public as a body that seeks to be informed but rather as an element of the media ecology to be managed through "public relations work, knowledge of local conditions, information warfare and media manipulation."[12] While the right's opposition to the school was often articulated in terms similar to those of liberal critics, the aim of its attacks was to circulate discomfort, suspicion, and fear about Almontaser and KGIA. This was accomplished through highly suggestive, associational, and affective modes of attack, including through the use of images of Almontaser and of Arabic words. In effect, the language that the school was created to impart on its students became a highly manipulable weapon. Charged language and hyperbolic claims also had the ability to circulate broadly, as they were repeated in mainstream and liberal sources as framing questions or examples of critiques of the school.

Many liberals viewed the right's response as irrational and hysterical, but as Janice Irvine argues,

> overt emotion is not only increasingly acceptable but seemingly required in contemporary politics, where it conveys righteous solidarity and demands state intervention. Contemporary Western societies consider feelings the core of the self; they are constructed as a site of truth and ethics. Hence feelings, as Michel Foucault has argued, are 'the main field of morality.' . . . Because of its cultural authority, public emotion can pressure politicians, police, media, and other regulatory agents to respond to fierce community battles.[13]

The right claimed to express an authentic emotional response of horror and outrage to an existential threat, while liberals were represented as stymied by political correctness and unable to defend their own interests. These attacks were successful in building on and eventually transforming ambivalence, as expressed in many liberal critiques *and* defenses of the school, into a moral panic based on the accumulation of highly suggestive associations with the school. These associations resonated with variables of assessment particular to Muslims as a population, especially the question of connections to Muslims abroad. Early attacks created a general feeling of unease and suspicion that provided the context in which Almontaser could quickly be transformed into an unacceptable figure when she was represented as deviating from the script and role of a "moderate Muslim." The swiftness of this transformation points to the precarity of the position of all Muslim American public figures who seek to claim their roles within the liberal parameters of acceptability.

The remaining sections of this chapter address the media construction and framing of the KGIA controversy from a number of angles to examine population racism as a shared liberal-conservative terrain, as a media resource to gain audience attention, and as a political tool to close off Muslim American civic participation. The first section examines the arguments made by defenders and critics of the school plan to uncover their shared assumptions and highlight the most relevant variables of assessment. The second section explores the temporalities of New York press engagements with the story to demonstrate an interaction between the goal of garnering audience attention and political ends. The third section demonstrates how the right-wing media produced confusion, incredulity, and fear about Almontaser and KGIA, in part through the efficient circulation of Arabic-language words, which I argue functioned as what Terranova has termed "bioweapons" that infect everything with which they come into contact.[14] My final section further elucidates the role of the figure of the moderate Muslim in the center-left media, not so much as a figure to be defended from attack, but rather as a victim of shameful right-wing racism that allows liberals to establish their own tolerance. Rather than meaningfully countering the right-wing attack, the center-left media represented itself as an arena of civil and reasonable debate about the "substantive" issues of the controversy, while at the same time pointedly ignoring the central conflict that led to Almontaser's resignation. It also reinforced, rather than challenged, the population racism that informed attacks on Almontaser, even if it did challenge specific assessments of Almontaser. Therefore the moderate Muslim as an object of tolerance served to establish the center-left media as an essential component of a pluralist public sphere of civil discourse and debate, key to the functioning of democracy, even as this case demonstrates the effective closure of such an arena, particularly for Muslim Americans.

The analysis is based on a survey of a broad range of media, especially widely accessible press sources. In particular, I focused on the key local and city papers involved in attacking Almontaser and the school, the *Brooklyn Paper,* the *New York Post,* and the *New York Sun,* and the two center-left publications that provided the most extensive and significant coverage of the controversy, specifically, the *Brooklyn Daily Eagle* and the *New York Times.* I also reviewed a number of print and internet-based sources that catered to particular communities or niche audiences, along with television programs that brought the local controversy to a national audience.[15] My focus is on media discourses, rather than the debates occurring among various actors that were not represented in the media. As such, when I refer to the statements of defenders or supporters of the school, I am referring to the discourses in media outlets, rather than the actual views of activist and community-based supporters.[16] Certainly the latter were more diverse, nuanced, and complex than what was represented in the media.

POPULATION RACISM AND FRAMEWORKS
FOR ASSESSMENT

Many had long regarded Almontaser as an exemplary "moderate" Muslim, as the following description of her by Larry Cohler-Esses in *New York Jewish Week* makes clear:

> Since 9/11, the slight woman in a hijab had emerged as a prominent advocate in the Muslim community for reaching out and working with other faiths. After the attacks her son, an Army Reserve officer, served as a rescue worker at Ground Zero.
>
> Among other things, Almontaser had invited hundreds of Jews and Christians to her own home in the wake of the terrorist attack to help defang fear and anger towards Muslims. She had joined social action groups, such as We Are All Brooklyn, an inter-ethnic initiative supported by JCRC, to combat hate crimes in the dense, mixed neighborhoods of that borough. She had trained with ADL's anti-bias program, A World of Difference, to become a better facilitator for diversity and inter-group dynamics in the public schools.[17]

A *New York Times* article also notes that four of her cousins and nephews served in the U.S. military in Iraq and that Almontaser was twice profiled on Voice of America, a U.S. government–run international media organization.[18] While generally, *moderate* refers to a centrist position on a left–right political spectrum, for Muslims, the concept often comes down to a pro- versus anti-U.S. position. The concept of the moderate Muslim ostensibly distinguishes Muslims with "moderate" theological positions, but religion is seen as implicated in and by one's politics, making interdependent a set of religious and political positions to create a specific delineation of that which is acceptable from a hegemonic U.S. perspective. The narrowness of this category is demonstrated by how assessments take conservative or orthodox theological perspectives to be signs of anti-Americanism and place Muslims' political criticism of the United States on a continuum with violence against the United States. Therefore those who fail to be deemed moderate Muslims are likely to be seen as anti-American threats. As such, usage of the concept of the "moderate Muslim" reinforces an idea that Islam has a particular and unique problem with violent religious extremism and that the Muslim population requires distinct scrutiny.

In the case of Almontaser and KGIA, liberal defenses, liberal critiques, and right-wing attacks all focused on similar variables to assess Almontaser as moderate or not and the school project as consistent or inconsistent with American values. The main areas of contention included, on one hand, the issues of tolerance and patriotism and, on the other hand, the issues of secularism and gender equality. The argument that tolerance of cultural difference is a key solution to post-9/11 conflicts and that, as such, the school serves an important function in promoting peace was countered by arguments that multiculturalism produces dangerous separatism and that Muslims were seeking to enforce their incompatible culture on U.S. society. Similarly, arguments that the school would be secular were countered by claims that it was likely to proselytize Islam, a notion reinforced by reference to images of women and girls in hijab. Whatever position one took, there was agreement that culture and religion were primary objects of concern in relation to Muslims and the War on Terror, partaking in what Mahmood Mamdani has criticized as "culture talk," which reduces complex historical and political conflicts into a matter of civilizational difference.[19] Therefore defenses of the school, liberal ambivalence about the school, and right-wing attacks on the school were largely focused on the same variables, evidencing a common set of concerns about Muslims and Arabs.

As the entire framing of the school project by its defenders makes clear, KGIA was only acceptable if it fit a narrow set of parameters, claiming to be apolitical while also aligning itself with the U.S. position on the War on Terror. A Department of Education spokesperson described the school as "right for the times,"[20] which Almontaser clarified as promoting cross-cultural understanding and tolerance, thereby producing "ambassadors of peace and hope."[21] Building on Almontaser's reputation as "a moderate active in interfaith groups,"[22] the school's supporters, like Lena Alhusseini, executive director of the lead community sponsor of KGIA, argued, "It has nothing to do with politics. It's about tolerance, giving students a new language skill they can use in many international fields such as finance, and giving them a rigorous education."[23] Rather than presenting the school as an arena of critical engagement with multiple and competing political perspectives—a notion that Almontaser presents in an early interview but that is otherwise largely absent in defenses of the school—this representation of the school reinforces a notion that cultural differences and misunderstandings are a major cause of conflict in the post-9/11 era.

The school was also defended in relation to a particular set of War on Terror politics, implied in the claim of another defender of the school, Joel Levy of the ADL, who argued that the school would train students in conflict resolution and international diplomacy, thereby connecting it with a specific notion of politics.[24] Indeed, the school had to be aligned with the U.S. War on Terror, as made clear in a letter of support from a U.S. Army sergeant that Almontaser publicly read: "American society desperately needs this bridge to Arabic language and culture."[25] An article by New York University historian Jonathan Zimmerman further elaborates this line of argument:

> We should scrutinize any new Arabic program to make sure it's teaching in an evenhanded fashion. There is a war going on, and there are people who want to kill us. Enemies of America should not gain a voice in our public school curriculum.
>
> But there's no reason to think that the Gibran academy would turn patriotic Americans into Al Qaeda sympathizers. In fact, to win the War on

Terrorism, we're going to need many more people who know Arabic, get the difference between Sunnis and Shiites and understand the complex culture of the Middle East.[26]

In this case, a liberal ambivalence about the school was outweighed by a belief that the school was contributing to a U.S. victory in the War on Terror, clarifying the only acceptable ends of an education in Arabic language and culture.

Even as the school sought to abide by the narrow parameters of the War on Terror, it faced critique from liberals and conservatives opposing multicultural education and questioning its apolitical position. Some, such as the self-identified liberal Richard Kahlenberg, raised fears of Muslim separatism, a problem he argued was also produced by Afrocentric schools of the 1980s. Right-wing critics amplified such fears, refusing defenders' disaggregation of culture, religion, and politics and arguing that the school would necessarily promote a threatening anti-American ideology. While claiming to support Arabic-language instruction, they argued for strict scrutiny, then discredited the school by lodging various attacks on Almontaser to suggest guilt by association, as I discuss in greater detail later. Alicia Colon, referring to the school's naming after a Lebanese Christian, wrote, "As if we're stupid enough to believe that the school will only be teaching Arabic language and not Islamic culture." Colon exclaimed, "We're bending over backwards to appease those sympathetic to individuals who would destroy us again."[27] Hence defenders and opponents agreed on the need to assess the project through the framework of the War on Terror and an assumption of the presumed distinctive riskiness of Muslims as a population.

Similarly, assessment of the school's relationship to religion was a central task for defenders and critics. Supporters and the Department of Education felt the need to reiterate what should have been obvious—that as a public school, KGIA would abide by the same secular standards as all New York City public schools, teaching "college preparatory courses and history of the Arabic people, not Islam."[28] Defenders also emphasized that the school would not be exclusively serving the interests of the Muslim community, noting that many Arab Americans are Christian, that the school is open to everyone, and that it was intended to serve a half non-Arabic-speaking student body. However, both liberal and right-wing critics raised serious doubts about the secular status of the school, arguing that the Arabic language has a particular relationship to Islam that makes secular instruction of the language unlikely.

From a liberal perspective, law professor Noah Feldman, writing in the *New York Times Magazine*, dismissed the notion that the school would teach Arabic language and culture without also proselytizing Islam:

> Islam will presumably be taught—it would be educationally indefensible to teach Arab civilization without including it—and enrollment seems likely to include Muslim students in disproportionate numbers.... Khalil Gibran ... seems poised to teach religion as a set of beliefs to be embraced rather than as a set of ideas susceptible to secular, critical examination.[29]

While Feldman acknowledged that schools can teach about religion without proselytizing, he argued that this is unlikely simply because of his assertion that the student body will be "disproportionately" Muslim, without explaining why majority-Christian schools do not face a parallel problem. A key right-wing opponent to the school project, Daniel Pipes, made a strikingly similar argument, insisting, however, that not just Islam but a politicized religious ideology of Islamism would infiltrate the school. His main thesis, quoted and circulated broadly in the media, was that "Arabic-language instruction is inevitably laden with pan-Arabist and Islamist baggage," offering a motley of highly decontextualized, questionable, and irrelevant evidence.[30] While Feldman rejected the likelihood of secular instruction at KGIA, Pipes rejected the possibility of secular or apolitical instruction of the Arabic language at all, while defenders argued that learning Arabic is key to a U.S. victory in the War on Terror. KGIA founders' aspirations of staying out of politics were completely negated by this discursive terrain, which made clear that Arabic may only be viewed through the framework of the War on Terror.

The centrality of the debate surrounding the school's secular versus Islamic character was further demonstrated through divergent meanings ascribed to the school's name and supporters. The school's namesake, Khalil Gibran, the Christian Arab American author of the best-selling 1923 work *The Prophet*, highlighted the largely unrecognized role of Arab Americans in U.S. history but was framed almost exclusively in terms of what it said about the school's relationship to religion. On one side, supporters pointed to the name as evidence that the school was not "Islamic."[31] On the other side, critics like Feldman suggested that the name was an intentional obfuscation of the school's truly "Muslim" character. Similarly, defenders noted the school's support from the ADL, along with a wide range of interfaith organizations, such as the "Lutheran Medical Center, Tanenbaum Center for Interreligious Understanding, MSI Net, [and] American-Arab Anti-Discrimination Committee," to highlight its non-Islamic character.[32] By contrast, critics interpreted the school's primarily religiously identified, yet multifaith, sponsors as evidence of the school's *religious* character, which they argued would necessarily be Islamic.[33] As with many other elements of the debate surrounding the school, the same referent was interpreted in opposing ways, implying that every move made by the planners to demonstrate that the school fit within the narrow parameters of acceptability was open to manipulation to indicate its opposite.

The question of the school's relation to religion was often referenced through the image of the head scarf–wearing woman. References to the hijab were used to question the secular nature of the school, as in a Brooklyn parent's statement in the *New York Sun* raising concern that "the school population would end up becoming mostly 'girls in burkas.'"[34] The image of Debbie Almontaser, as a head scarf–wearing woman, also became an arena of contested meaning. On one hand, Almontaser's decision to wear the head scarf was presented as epitomizing her place in U.S. multiculturalism, where her "embrace of Muslim customs" is associated with being "part of the American melting pot."[35] On the other hand, there was much ambivalence and opposition expressed to the presence of head scarves in the public arena. Richard Bernstein, in his defense of the school, argued that while Almontaser has a right to wear the head scarf, her decision to do so "is probably a mistake" because it is also "a symbol of political Islam or . . . of the oppression of women."[36] Critics made similar associations by manipulating Almontaser's image to perpetuate a notion that the school was threatening. A much-commented-upon blog post compared pictures of Almontaser wearing different styles of head scarves to argue that she had undergone "An Extremist Hijab Makeover" to hide her true Islamist intentions.[37] While Almontaser's role as a visibly religious Muslim woman and community leader would challenge a notion that the head scarf is necessarily a symbol of women's oppression, the head scarf was represented by many as demonstrating the incursion of religion into public life and as a potent symbol of a potential "Islamic threat."

This terrain of debate demonstrated broad agreement that Arabs/ Muslims must be assessed in terms of specific characteristics articulated through the questions of tolerance, patriotism, secularism, and the status of women. Ultimately, all these measures were assessments of alignment, or nonalignment, with U.S. imperialism in the War on Terror. Even Almontaser's strong record as abiding by the standards of the moderate, patriotic Muslim Arab American was quickly recast as evidence that she was attempting to hide radical beliefs. Therefore, while establishing oneself as a moderate Muslim was necessary to garner a public platform, it did not offer inoculation to the potential of being recast as threatening within that same framework of tolerability.

THE TEMPORALITY OF MEDIA ATTACKS, DEFENSES, AND DEBATES

In the post-9/11 context, KGIA's Arabic language and culture theme contained the potentiality of controversy within its conception even before any significant critiques were lodged against it. Indeed, much early media coverage of the school, even when not describing the critiques of the school's theme, nevertheless referenced a likelihood of future controversy. However, media outlets dealt with this potentiality differently, and those that would prove most pivotal in attacking Almontaser, the *New York Sun* and the *New York Post,* did not choose to capitalize on this potentiality from the beginning of their coverage, suggesting rather a highly strategic timing of negative coverage. By contrast, the mainstream media outlet that lodged the most far-reaching defense of Almontaser, the *New York Times,* did not do so until more than eight months after she had resigned from her position, when such a defense could do little to alter the outcome of the controversy. In this section, I examine the temporality of engagement with the controversy, tracing a timeline of press coverage and demonstrating how this engagement was a reflection of both ideological interests and economic interests in garnering audience attention.

Different approaches to capturing audience interest and attention are evident in the patterns and inconsistencies in coverage within and across media outlets. Local Brooklyn papers provided regular coverage of the controversy over a longer period of time, reflecting the fact that any controversy over local schools was of interest to their audiences; in contrast, the coverage by city papers was much more episodic. Right-wing blogs engaged in a ceaseless attack on the school from very early in the controversy, yet right-wing papers often began with neutral or positive portrayals of the school, concentrating their negative coverage at particular moments, while the single center-left city paper, the *New York Times,* only published opinion pieces after the most severe attacks had taken place. These differences in coverage can be explained by the interaction of ideological positions with differing strategies of garnering audience attention. While the right-wing media saw the school as a potential source of controversy to be harnessed to greater effect—in terms of both audience attention and political consequences—through focused attacks, the center-left media did not function as a counterpoint to that attack. Rather, it approached the controversy largely retrospectively, long after the central battles had been lost, to generate sympathy for the victimized moderate Muslim. Hence the mode of engagement of different venues pointed to the unevenness of the media terrain in which controversies about Muslims are produced and debated, where baseless attacks face little timely counterattack and liberal ambivalences stymie substantive defenses of Muslim public figures.

Most initial press coverage, in the Brooklyn papers and the *New York Sun* from March through May 2007, focused on concerns regarding the location of KGIA, in terms of resource utilization and safety when colocating younger and older students. These more mundane debates offered the press the opportunity to introduce the concept of the school and pique audience interest in it, at times referencing a *potentiality* of further controversy.[38] At the same time, a group of bloggers began attacking the school's mission, becoming an arena for the collection, testing, and refinement of arguments against the school before their broader dissemination. These blogs included *Militant Islam Monitor; Pipeline News; Jihad Watch* by Robert Spencer, author of *New York Times* best sellers *The Truth about Muhammad, Founder of the World's Most Intolerant Religion,* and *The Politically Incorrect Guide to Islam (and the Crusades); Atlas Shrugs* penned by Pamela Geller; and *Daniel Pipes,* the blog of Daniel Pipes. Most prominent among them was Pipes, a neoconservative commentator and Harvard PhD who has marketed himself as an expert on Islamic extremism and founded the pro-Israel Middle East Forum and Campus Watch. As a columnist for the *New York Sun,* Pipes was a direct link between bloggers and the New York papers and would pen a number of highly critical and much-quoted columns on the school. Pamela Geller would rise to prominence through the KGIA controversy, laying the groundwork for her key role in the campaign against Park51, which brought her to the national stage.[39]

The local Brooklyn newspapers, the *Brooklyn Paper* and the *Brooklyn Daily Eagle,* also served an important early role, articulating the range of more mainstream negative and positive positions in relation to the school. On March 17, the *Brooklyn Paper,* a weekly publication, printed the first sensationalistic article on the school, under the front-page headline "Holy War!"[40] The article described some parents' objections to the school's theme and a PTA president's concerns regarding colocated schools losing "space . . . services, and . . . safety." After a series of critical letters from its readership, the paper's negative coverage became more subtle, with interspersed positive representations of the school.[41] The *Brooklyn Daily Eagle* more consistently gave voice to both the opposition and supporters of KGIA. One early article provided a lengthy explanation that the school would serve a diverse student body and teach tolerance, rather than promote any political or religious perspectives.[42] It also ran a sidebar profile of a prominent board member, described as a "patriotic" Republican, Christian, Lebanese American man.[43] The terms of debate regarding the school were already very clear. Attacks were in terms of sensationalistic associations with Islam ("Holy War!") or insinuations about the riskiness of the population being served, and defenses were in terms of tolerance, multiculturalism, and patriotism.

In contrast to Brooklyn papers, early coverage about KGIA in the *New York Sun* and the *New York Post* did not betray any strong opposition to the school, even though these papers would prove pivotal in attacks later. This moderation is striking given these papers' political stances. The *New York Sun,* a five-year-old neoconservative weekly paper, was known for campaigns against those it viewed as critics of Israel, such as the Ford Foundation for its funding of Palestinian NGOs and Muslim and Arab public figures, including a number of Columbia University faculty. Although its circulation was small, it was regarded as having an outsized political influence.[44] The *New York Post,* a right-wing tabloid owned by Rupert Murdoch, by contrast had the fifth largest circulation of all daily papers in the United States.[45] Each paper began covering the school controversy with neutral and positive portrayals of the school.[46] However, when coverage in each paper became critical, it did so in a manner that intensified reader attention, setting aside appearances of neutrality during their periods of concentrated attack—for the *Sun,* in late April and May, and for the *Post,* in August. Despite earlier reticence, the *Post* in August became the primary instigator in the event that would lead to Almontaser's resignation and, following her resignation, continued to publish a barrage of negative articles that focused audience attention on the issue for a short period of time (see Figure 8). Therefore, rather than simply responding to the school from a consistent ideological position, these media outlets allowed for a range of views to be represented, while concentrating negative coverage to produce moments of intense reader attention with specific political effects.

A close reading of coverage of the *Sun* and *Post* demonstrates notable shifts in their coverage of the story over a relatively short time. Although the first critical opinion piece the *Sun* published in March about KGIA was relatively reasoned in tone, a month later, the same author's tone changed dramatically, referencing "Islamists who see the potential of a mini-madrassa in Park Slope" (the term *madrassa,* which means "school"

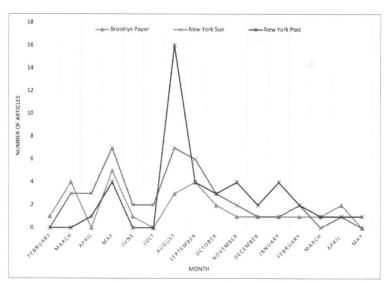

FIGURE 8. Right-wing press coverage of KGIA/Almontaser (number of articles per month).

in Arabic, is discussed in more detail later).[47] This shift foreshadowed two key attack pieces published in late April and early May: Daniel Pipes's "A Madrassa Grows in Brooklyn" and Alicia Colon's "Madrassa Plan Is Monstrosity," which would serve as the reference points for the main arguments of the opposition to the school.[48] The seven pieces published in May included an editorial repeating many of Pipes's and Colon's allegations.[49] Following this period of concentrated attack by the *Sun*, there was a spike in overall coverage about the school across outlets. Critiques shifted focus from the school's location to its theme, while a range of defenses also began to emerge. The ADL's Joel Levy wrote a strong statement of support for Almontaser and the school in the *Sun*.[50] The *Daily News* published expressions of ambivalent support and a "liberal" critique of the school, while editorializing that the school would foster Arab "Balkanization."[51] The *Brooklyn Daily Eagle* published an editor-authored opinion piece condemning attackers and presenting a confused defense, analogizing the school to various religious schools.[52] The *New York Times* ran in-depth news articles but no editorials or opinion pieces (see Figure 9). In contrast to this muddle of coverage and opinions, the *New York Post* was largely silent, only to emerge as a strident critic, an attack dog, at a moment when the stakes were highest.

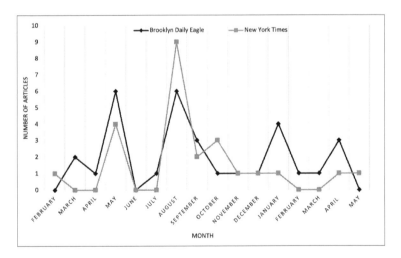

FIGURE 9. Center-left press coverage of KGIA/Almontaser (number of articles per month).

The *Post* participated little in the debate about the school in May but in August became the key venue for a renewed, focused, and highly effective attack on Almontaser, just weeks before the school's opening. Publishing a total of sixteen articles in August—more than any venue in any month—including the article that resulted in Almontaser's forced resignation and four highly critical editorials, the *Post* produced an atmosphere of incredulity, horror, and condemnation about the school. It also continued these attacks well past the time of Almontaser's resignation, maximizing the story's capacity to garner audience attention. In September, presumably having tapped out interest in the topic, the *Post* published just three articles. As such, the attack was swift, fierce, and relatively brief, maximizing the story's ability to capture attention and quickly move audiences to political effect.

The *New York Times*, by contrast, was slow to weigh in to the controversy, publishing its first opinion pieces related to Almontaser and the school in the weeks following her resignation. The paper initially positioned itself as a dispassionate outside observer and now presented a range of perspectives—two articles criticizing the school's theme and one defending Almontaser—in an "objective" tone that purported to reject fearmongering and racism. Eight months later, in April 2008, the *Times* published an in-depth and highly sympathetic article about the controversy, documenting how Almontaser became the object of a concerted right-wing attack with significant repercussions. However, at this point, the debate that determined the fate of Almontaser and the school was largely over, and the battle for Almontaser's vision of the school had already been lost. Nevertheless, despite its absence from the debate in the more formative periods, the *Times* was able to harness liberal displeasure at the type of attack Almontaser had suffered and emerge as the arena of civil discourse and debate.

Just as New York City newspapers mobilized the story to generate concentrated moments of attention, a similar dynamic is evident in national news coverage. On the day of the school's opening, CNN ran nine separate segments on the school, beginning in the morning and continuing into the evening, and giving significant airtime to opponents. One segment opened with "Well, you've never seen a school like the one that we're about to visit. It specializes in everything Arabic, the culture, Islam, that is scaring a lot of folks in New York." Another segment was introduced "Reading, writing, radical Islam?"[53] Following this daylong barrage, the topic was almost completely dropped, demonstrating a lack of interest in determining whether accusations lodged would be substantiated. Rather, racialized fear of Muslims was simply a means of garnering attention, with each media venue following a distinct temporality. I now turn to the particular affective power of the right's attacks and, following that, to the center left's dispassionate, objective framing of the controversy to examine the affective messages conveyed via each approach to the story and the precarious space for Muslim American public figures produced between them.

THE RIGHT'S AFFECTIVE ATTACKS

In the face of liberal discourses casting Almontaser as an exceptional moderate Muslim, the repetition of evidence suggesting that she had ties to and sympathies with ostensibly questionable Muslims cast doubt on that claim. The campaign against Almontaser and KGIA, similar to other media-generated campaigns against moderate Muslims, aimed to create doubt about Almontaser's true beliefs and loyalties, casting her moderate appearances as a calculated façade intended to hide her presumably Islamist views. Focusing on Almontaser rather than the school allowed critics to circulate fears based on her being a head scarf–wearing Muslim and Arab woman. Repeatedly using Almontaser's birth name "Dhabah," rather than "Debbie," which the *Post* did only during its period of concentrated attack in August, some sources suggested both foreignness and duplicitousness. Highly selective and decontextualized information about Almontaser was constantly repeated to reinforce a feeling that there was something untoward about her affiliations, statements, and behaviors. Her political views were misrepresented and scrutinized to portray her as unpatriotic, including through truncated quotes to suggest that she was a "9/11 denier."[54] Almontaser's arguments, shared by many others, that U.S. foreign policy had a role in producing the 9/11 attacks or that the New York Police Department was using questionable entrapment tactics in Muslim communities in Brooklyn were presented as proof that she was unpatriotic. Many efforts were made to connect her, in some way, with disreputable governments or organizations, for example, in portraying the New York chapter of the Council on American Islamic Relations, which had given Almontaser an award, as a "foreign-funded front organization."[55] Almontaser's refusal to respond to a reporter's question on whether Hezbollah or Hamas was a terrorist organization was presented as evidence of support for these groups.[56] Without a viable middle ground between moderate and extremist, Almontaser could be effectively moved from one side to the other.

In addition to these intense attacks on Almontaser, the right used Arabic words as a weapon against the school, words that could circulate efficiently in print media through headlines, sound bites, and quotations. The use of these words cast the school and Almontaser not only as connected to a foreign culture but as a shadowy and obscure threat, only knowable to a select group of experts. Much of Terranova's description of the functioning of images as powerful tools in perception management applies as much to the use of Arabic words in the right's campaign against KGIA. As she says,

> it is no longer a matter of illusion or deception, but of the tactical and strategic deployment of the *power of affection* of images as such. It is no longer a matter of truth or appearance, or even of the alienating power of the spectacle as "opium of the masses," but of images as *bioweapons,* let loose into the informational ecology with a mission to infect.[57]

Terranova argues that rather than acting as representations, or misrepresentations, of truth, images are "types of bioweapons that must be developed and deployed on the basis of a knowledge of the overall informational ecology." An image's power depends on the "kind of affect that it packs, the movement that it receives, inhibits and/or transmits."[58] In this case, words are as evocative, affective, and infectious as images and circulate more efficiently in print media. Words like *jihad, madrassa,* and *intifada* are not only often defined along lines that associate Muslims with violence, terrorism, irrationalism, and backwardness but also become a force that infects everything with which they are associated. They gain their power from stereotypes associated with Muslims but have become detached from specific definitions to function somewhat independently in garnering audience attention and producing a swift assessment. Arguments about the true meaning of a word, or the intentions of those associated with them, are ineffective in depleting the force of the word, in part because the arguments themselves were cast as suspect. As Jeffrey Wiesenfeld, CUNY Trustee, said, "let those who think jihad and intifada are nice terms—let them take those terms and shove it. Stop parsing the language."[59] These words are presented as both transparent, in that there can be no argument about their meaning, and impenetrable, as foreign, unfamiliar, and resistant to reinterpretation. Even when a word is described as being misinterpreted or misapplied, it can still do the work of infecting and repelling. Therefore, even when it is recognized by many that the school and Almontaser will likely never pose a threat to the United States, these words make associating with the school and Almontaser a risky endeavor.

Despite their vastly different meanings and usages in Arabic, such words were used very similarly to affiliate the school and Almontaser with Islam and violence. Though many words and phrases have come to function in this way, such as *Sharia, fatwa,* and *allahu akbar,* and others less commonly, such as *dhimmi* and *taqiyya,* in this case, three terms that became central to representations of the school and Almontaser were *jihad, madrassa,* and *intifada.*[60] *Jihad* is a multifaceted religious concept that refers to struggling in the path of God and can encompass a duty to take up arms under specified circumstances;[61] *madrassa* is the Arabic word for school and can refer to various types of educational institutions, both secular and religious; and *intifada* is a secular concept literally meaning "shaking off," used to refer to uprisings or rebellions, including two major periods of Palestinian resistance, via both nonviolent and violent means, to Israeli occupation of the West Bank and Gaza Strip (1987–93 and 2000–2005). Despite these different meanings, because of the particular history of usage of Arabic words in the United States, these words almost automatically connote violence and terrorism, becoming one-word distillations of the stereotype of the violent Muslim extremist.

While the usage of these words depends on particular meanings or interpretations of them, above and beyond questions of meaning, these words become bioweapons against Muslims. They travel quickly—repeated in sound bites, headlines, framing questions, and captions—capturing momentary attention. Rather than being processed simply as an interpretation, their usage packs a particular set of associations that trigger powerful emotions. On the first level, these words racialize as Muslim and Arab the institutions and people with whom they are associated, immediately raising the particular variables of assessment deemed relevant for this population. However, they also already make the assessment, through words that are almost inevitably associated with both Islam and violence—and particularly with what is called "Islamic terrorism." Tactics included alternating between more common and broadly accepted Arabic terms, like *jihad,* and newer, less familiar terms. Unfamiliar words that combine letters in unusual patterns for English speakers, while referencing seemingly unique and unusual concepts, create feelings of confusion and uneasiness. As new words are introduced, they fall into an assemblage of concepts all seeming to be elaborations on Islamic extremism and violence. These words attest to the expertise of those using them as knowledgeable about this shadowy threat. Furthermore, the use of Arabic distances the concepts from parallel ones in English, separating the Islamic tradition from other, more familiar ones with which it is connected, most notably Christianity and Judaism, and Arab societies from the United States. For example, use of the term *Allah* obscures the fact that it is the Arabic-language word for "God" used by both Muslim and Christian Arabs. Furthermore, the news media often emphasizes the usage of the phrase *allahu akbar,* meaning "God is great," in contexts of militancy and violence,[62] further connecting Islam to violence, despite the phrase's nonmilitant, quotidian usage among Muslims. Similarly, *jihad,* which is hardly ever understood in its nonviolent meaning, is rarely linked to the Christian concept of a "just war"; *intifada* is rarely connected to the revolutionary history of the United States; and *madrassa,* even when defined as the Arabic word for "school," continues to pack another set of unsettling associations.

Initially, the school was termed a "jihad school" by right-wing bloggers to indicate that it would both proselytize Islam and promote Islamic extremism.[63] Even more liberal papers used the term, as in a *Brooklyn Daily Eagle* article that led with the question "'Jihad School' or 'School for Everyone'?"[64] Jihad, here understood crudely as a Muslim holy war against non-Muslims, has become one of the central concepts of the War on Terror, and the term *jihadist* has become a broadly acceptable term for any Muslim who advocates or resorts to violence in the service of a cause identified with Islam.[65] However, before long, the concept of the "jihad school" was replaced by the term *madrassa.* Despite meaning "school" in Arabic, it had been used in the English-language media to reference conservative Islamic schools, as is clear in the following definition on PBS's website for its program *Frontline*: "A madrassa is an Islamic religious school. Many of the Taliban were educated in Saudi-financed madrassas in Pakistan that teach Wahhabism, a particularly austere and rigid form of Islam which is rooted in Saudi Arabia."[66] In January 2007, the word had been used in an attempt to defame presidential candidate Barack Obama by saying he had attended a madrassa while a child in Indonesia.[67] While *madrassa* was the technically correct word in that it refers to the school, critics clearly used it to evoke a conservative Islamic school, as they sometimes said explicitly.

The word *madrassa* was first put into circulation in a few key articles to make suspicion of the school seem common sense and obvious. Pipes's article "A Madrassa Grows in Brooklyn" produced a shock by placing the familiar "Brooklyn" with the unfamiliar, foreign, and seemingly dangerous. Colon's "Madrassa Plan Is Monstrosity," also frequently cited by other sources,[68] concluded,

> How delighted Osama bin Laden and Al Qaeda must have been to hear the news—that New York City, the site of the worst terrorist attack in our history, is bowing down in homage to accommodate and perhaps groom future radicals. . . . I say break out the torches and surround City Hall to stop this monstrosity.[69]

Although Colon risked alienating some readers in her strong language, it also guaranteed that her words would be circulated widely, bringing to the fore an apparently disturbing irony implied by the idea that a "madrassa" would be built in New York. In these circulating sound bites, even those who might not initially oppose the school might feel dissonance, expressed in a question like, Why should "they" have a school, or "madrassa," in New York, where so many were victimized by 9/11? Stop the Madrassa, an organization formed as the "grassroots" opposition to the school, further circulated this fear of Islam and especially Islamic education. Much like the later framing of Park51 as the "Ground Zero Mosque," the use of *madrassa* exploited a notion of Islam as a foreign and enemy religion, while functioning as an argument about the nature of the school that was powerful even without any evidence.

The power of an Arabic word to dislodge an entire narrative about a person became clear in the central event that led to Almontaser's resignation. Here the word functioned not simply as a label that associated Islamic violence with Almontaser and the school but actually served as an affective tool to assess the moderate status of Almontaser. This event revolved around a T-shirt, which bore the words "Intifada NYC," produced by Arab Women Active in Art and Media (AWAAM), an activist organization of young Arab women very tenuously connected to Almontaser, in that the organization sometimes rented space from an organization on whose board Almontaser sat. In the T-shirt's logo, we see a similar bringing together of elements from different contexts to capture attention: rather than a "madrassa" in Brooklyn, the T-shirt references "intifada" in New York City. These T-shirts were produced for a particular audience, presumably primarily Arab Americans, who were likely to understand intifada both as a general concept referring to resistance and as a reference to *legitimate* uprising by the Palestinian people in opposition to an illegal Israeli occupation. However, the logo was then unleashed by the *New York Post* in a media context where a wholly negative interpretation of intifada quickly congealed around the word, one that was based on an image of illegitimate Palestinian violence against Israeli civilians and that corresponds to the much circulating stereotype of Islamic terrorists. While the T-shirt exemplifies what Terranova describes as the power of images to circulate between local and global networks, jumping tracks from one segmented media environment to another, it is clear that it was also an image and set of words that were manipulated to produce particular effects in this local media milieu.

On August 6, 2007, the *Post* published an article based on an interview it had conducted with Almontaser in which it claimed that she had "downplayed the significance of the T-shirts," which "glorify Palestinian terror." Although Almontaser had conveyed that she had no knowledge of the T-shirts, the *New York Post* pressured the Department of Education to have Almontaser grant an interview. The resulting article, titled "City Principal Is 'Revolting': Tied to 'Intifada NYC' T-Shirts," combined reporting with editorializing, presenting an interpretation that soon shaped the consensus view about Almontaser. The article quoted Almontaser at length as saying

"The word [intifada] basically means 'shaking off.' That is the root of the word if you look it up in Arabic," she said.

"I understand it is developing a negative connotation due to the uprising in the Palestinian-Israeli areas. I don't believe the intention is to have any of that kind of [violence] in New York City.

"I think it's pretty much an opportunity for girls to express that they are part of New York City society . . . and shaking off oppression."[70]

While there has since been evidence to indicate that this was a misrepresentation of what Almontaser said in the interview,[71] my analysis is based on how the available information circulated at that time. While the article represents Almontaser as defending the T-shirts, the quote seems to be about the term *intifada* and the intentions of the girls in using it. Almontaser acknowledges the "negative connotation" of the term while also giving the youth organization the benefit of the doubt regarding its usage, suggesting that they understood the term differently. In the following weeks, responses to Almontaser either represented her statement as a gaffe, an error in judgment that does not truly represent her actual views, or as akin to a slur, demonstrating deep-seated prejudice. There was little debate over the meaning of the word *intifada* and almost no consideration of the possibility that the youth organization might not take the term to be synonymous with terrorism. Furthermore, whether the statement was deemed a gaffe or a slur, most agreed that Almontaser should step down from her position as principal of the school. When she did, the *Post* gleefully ran a front-page photograph of her with the headline "SHEIK UP: 'Intifada' Principal Quits City Arab HS."

Despite an apology in Almontaser's name released the evening of the August 6 article, taking responsibility for the statement and pointing to her record of work to demonstrate her opposition to violence, the outcry to the article was persistent and harsh. The apology failed to change responses because the question posed by the *Post* reporter was read as an affective litmus test of Almontaser, a way to assess whether she truly was the moderate Muslim she presented herself to be. In a context where some accused her of being a stealth "jihadist," no apology could transform the fact that she was deemed to have failed that test. There were calls for Almontaser's resignation and rallies planned outside the office of the schools chancellor. Everyone seemed to agree that the meaning of *intifada* is obvious and that the only proper response to the word was an immediate denunciation. The *Post*, presenting Almontaser's quotes as an indication of her true beliefs, ran a series of articles that also demonstrated the effective use of words to vilify. Andrea Peyser began an op-ed with highly suggestive language: "How many ways can you define 'suicidal'? The school hasn't even opened yet. But the hijab-wearing principal of a taxpayer-funded school founded especially for Arab students has issued a fatwa against the kids of New York."[72]

After evoking various versions of the figure of the Islamic fundamentalist, from the suicide bomber to the fatwa-issuing cleric, Peyser insists that the meaning of *intifada* "is as clear as the hole in the ground in lower Manhattan." The *Post* editorialized, "Now, if Dhabah Almontaser is going to be as disingenuous about something like this, why should New Yorkers believe her claim that 'you won't find religious or political indoctrination or anti-Americanism' at her Khalil Gibran school?"[73] A representative of Stop the Madrassa said that the T-shirts indicate that KGIA "will advocate terrorist violence,"[74] and politicians echoed this view, for example, Councilman Peter Vallone Jr. said, "This shirt should read, 'I promote terror and hate on a daily basis, and all I got for it is this lousy T-shirt.'"[75] Many explicitly called for Almontaser to resign and some urged that the school be closed. Indeed, one of the most damaging responses came in the form of a scathing letter to the *Post* from Randi Weingarten, president of the teacher's union and a former supporter, which expressed concern about a principal who "doesn't instinctively denounce campaigns or ideas tied to violence."[76] Ignoring Almontaser's apology, Weingarten made her failure to "instinctively denounce" intifada a litmus test of acceptability, suggesting it more appropriately captures Almontaser's authentic beliefs.

Others insisted that Almontaser's statement was a serious error in judgment but not necessarily one that indicated a support of terrorism. The *Sun* reported that Joel Levy of the ADL said Almontaser's comments were troubling: "The word intifada has a very specific meaning, and it's the violent uprising in the Palestinian territories. . . . We can't ignore that."[77] Others, such as the director of the American Jewish Committee and Rabbi Andy Bachman, separated their views on the school and Almontaser from their views on the T-shirt, which they resoundingly agreed deserved condemnation.[78] Bloomberg, in his radio announcement of Almontaser's resignation, most clearly articulated a notion that her statement was simply an error in judgment: "I know the woman. She's worked for the city in a variety of capacities. She's very smart. She's certainly not a terrorist. She really does care . . . she's not all that media-savvy maybe, and she tried to explain a word rather than just condemn."[79] Reiterating a view that the word required that one "just condemn," Bloomberg presents the resignation as a pragmatic matter for the sake of the school, rather than an act of giving in to anti-Muslim bias. His defense of her as "certainly not a terrorist," intended to indicate a lack of bias on the part of the city, only reiterated just how much the figure of the terrorist haunts Muslim Americans.

Errors in reporting and slippages between words point to the common associations of Muslims and Arabs with terrorism that shaped responses. Errors in reporting cast Almontaser and the school in worse terms than in the original *Post* article, for example, in referring to Almontaser as wearing the T-shirt.[80] A *Daily News* article described Almontaser as having resigned "after a published report tried to link her to a militant Islamic group,"[81] while Glenn Beck said that Almontaser was a "devout Islamist" who had "supported and sanctioned the sale of T-shirts to young girls that read 'Intifada New York.'"[82] Reporting also demonstrates an assumption that various Arabic terms are interchangeable and reference irrational Islamic violence. An article, in the *Brooklyn Paper,* by the reporter who had regularly covered the story describes Almontaser as having resigned "after she defined the word 'jihad' as 'struggle.'"[83] A reader comment by "anthony4" posted in response to a *Washington Post* article on August 4, 2007, read "Perhaps I am confusing the word [*intifada*] too much with jihad. As far as I can tell they boil down to the same thing, Muslim rage against any perceived slight (ie killing a nun because of a Mohammed cartoon)."[84] The quote succinctly demonstrates how divergent Arabic words all have been made to reference a stereotype of the fanatical, violent Muslim terrorist.

With their various meanings, associations, connotations, and usages, these words are available to manipulation, which was on clear display in a September 26 interview with an Almontaser supporter, then councilman John Liu, on Fox's *Hannity and Colmes.*[85] In response to Liu's objection to the use of the term *madrassa* in the network's introduction to the segment, Sean Hannity says, "Well, I did not say that word. But the fear of the community—see, we have a problem with extremists that believe in intifada in this battle, in this holy war, and jihad." Even as Hannity distances himself from the use of the term *madrassa,* he brings forward a range of other terms, demonstrating how much their differences are unimportant. When Liu seems to flummox Hannity by repeatedly asking whether he opposes all dual-language schools and pointing out that *madrassa* is written on the screen, Hannity bursts out with a nonsensical phrase: "Intifada. Intifada." Like a bomb meant to eliminate any critical thinking, he throws the word into the scuffle and ducks back. Alan Colmes, the liberal in the duo, comes to the rescue, clarifying that he at least has no problem with teaching Arabic, and explains, "I used the word madrassa because I understand madrassa means 'school.'" Defending the "accurate" usage of the word, Colmes demonstrates just how flexible these words are in bending to the needs of the moment, which maximizes their circulation. As such, they are very effective "bioweapons" circulating broadly in a range of discourses, while infecting those associated with them. Furthermore, these words often become tools for assessment of Muslims, as positions on the meanings and usages of terms are made sources of scrutiny. As a result, although a White media commentator like Colmes may be able to disassociate himself from racism by articulating the correct definition of *madrassa,* Muslim and Arab Americans' attempts to reclaim, or even simply define, Arabic words have become evidence of anti-Americanism and extremism.

LIBERALS' TOLERANCE, THE RIGHT'S SHAME

In contrast to the right's emotional, associational, and affective mode of attack, liberal commentators sought to present themselves as the voice of reason, dispassionately considering the merits of opposing perspectives to arrive at a rational position in relation to the school. With titles like "Arabic School's Critics Are the True Zealots"[86] and "'Madrasa' in New York? Hysteria Trumps Reason,"[87] many liberals accused the right of irrational zealotry and hysterical racism. As Anthony DiMaggio put it, "there has been no 'debate' going on here, only racist bullying. American media commentary has been hijacked by pundits who have zero commitment to intellectual debate of issues, and even less commitment to understanding the nuances that come along with learning about foreign cultures and languages."[88] However, defenses of Almontaser and the school also asserted the particular variables of assessing Muslims contributing to the swift defamation of Almontaser, by excluding more complex understandings of Muslim and Arab American experiences and perspectives. Indeed, though liberal voices in the media were willing to critique the bulk of attacks on Almontaser, they kept distance from central elements of these attacks, especially with regard to the "Intifada NYC" T-shirt incident. Although many community members and activists came forward to defend Almontaser in the months following her resignation,[89] these voices were largely excluded from the mainstream media. With time, as more evidence emerged to indicate that Almontaser's words had been misrepresented, more liberal voices articulated shame at the right-wing campaign against her. The *New York Times*'s April 28, 2008, front-page article and multimedia website was the culmination in this slow shift in perceptions, largely clearing Almontaser's name and laying blame for her defamation on the right-wing campaign against her. The *Times* emerged as a responsible media outlet providing objective analysis and competing viewpoints, while correcting misinformation. However, rather than addressing the context that allowed for the swift defamation of Almontaser in the eyes of people across the political spectrum, the paper put into circulation the image of the "moderate Muslim" victimized by a shameful right-wing attack to reproduce in its liberal readership a feeling of its own tolerance.

Excluded from discussion in the center-left media has been the fact that the defamation of Almontaser depended on the delegitimization of the political perspectives of many Muslim and Arab Americans, especially with regard to the Palestinian–Israeli conflict. While neoconservative right-wing campaigns seek to frame all kinds of Palestinian resistance to occupation as terrorism and delegitimize any critiques of Israel, including those lodged by those who are neither Arab nor Muslim, the racialization of Muslims and Arabs casts their criticism of Israel as indicative of their purported anti-Semitism and intolerance and their solidarity with Palestinians as indicative of their sympathies for "Islamic terrorism." As such, their views become of concern not only to Israel's defenders but to anyone concerned about the "threat of Islam" in the United States. Therefore, while the strength of the pro-Israel lobby and of supporters of Israel, especially in New York City politics, was a significant factor in responses to Almontaser's quoted statement, her speedy defamation was also a result of how the figure of the "Palestinian terrorist" resonates with the broader racialization of Muslims as susceptible to religious fanaticism, intolerance, and violence. Anti-Muslim racism and prevalent, normalized pro-Israel bias explain why the center-left media depicted the "Intifada NYC" T-shirt controversy in terms that implicitly legitimized outcry against Almontaser and never considered the controversy through the perspectives of other New York Arabs.

Indeed, even ostensibly neutral news coverage in center-left media betrayed a reading of the concept of intifada that implied Almontaser had clearly erred in not simply condemning it. For example, the *Brooklyn Daily Eagle* reported,

> *Rather than immediately denounce the shirts,* Almontaser initially *tried* to explain that "intifada" literally means "shaking off" and the shirts represented women "shaking off" oppression. As the political implications became clear, however, she condemned the T-shirt's apparent connection to Palestinian terrorism.[90]

The *New York Times* similarly referred to Almontaser's "attempt to explain away the term intifada on the shirts."[91] It also reported in multiple news articles that Almontaser had "defended the word 'intifada' as a T-shirt slogan" and described *intifada* as having "come to be associated with Palestinian attacks on Israel."[92] Even after Almontaser made a public statement on October 16, which the *Times* published on its website, explaining that her statement was largely a response to a question about the origins of the term *intifada,* the *Times* continued reporting the controversy in the same terms.[93] Furthermore, even the opinion pieces that were critical of attacks on Almontaser did not come to her defense in relation to the *Post* interview. The single *Times* article defending Almontaser published in the weeks following her resignation largely sidestepped the controversy surrounding the T-shirts,[94] while a piece in the *New York Jewish Week,* lauded by many as documenting the unfair attacks on Almontaser, referred to a "disastrous interview in which Almontaser failed to denounce [the] T-shirts."[95] Similarly, an editorial in the *Brooklyn Daily Eagle* referred parenthetically to Almontaser's "unfortunate, misinterpreted 'intifada' statement" without any further explanation.[96] While more sympathetic in tone, these statements never question that Almontaser's statement deserved condemnation.

Strikingly, no New York City newspapers actually presented the central issue in this controversy, which by contrast was briefly described in a *Washington Post* article:

> At core in the debate is a linguistic disconnect. The word "intifada" crystallized in its current Arabic meaning during the first Palestinian uprising in the late 1980s and early '90s. It is seen by many Arabs as a valid term for popular resistance to oppression, while for many English speakers it has come to conjure images of violent attacks on civilians.[97]

While hardly a defense of the perspective of many Arab Americans, this piece articulated that a fundamental difference in interpretation of an international conflict was central to the controversy. A more detailed and sympathetic rendition of the Palestinian Intifada was evident in a *World Socialist* piece on the controversy:

> The Intifada, which began at the end of 1987, was a popular uprising by the Palestinian people in the West Bank and Gaza, involving mass demonstrations, strikes, civil disobedience. It was provoked by conditions of grinding oppression and the brutal destruction of the basic rights of the Palestinians under Israeli military occupation. To transform any positive reference to these events as tantamount to advocacy of terrorism . . . represents a sinister attempt to suppress any political challenge to the policies pursued by Israel and Washington in the Middle East.[98]

By contrast, center-left New York City sources maintained an equation of intifada with unjustified violence, foreclosing any possibility of discussion about the word, its literal meaning in Arabic, or its political meanings for different communities. By repeating horrified condemnations from various commentators, these sources also contributed to making the actual political perspectives of many Muslim and Arab Americans on intifada not only taboo but a sign of terroristic sympathies. When Almontaser's reputation was eventually restored, through an April 28, 2008, *New York Times* piece, it rested on the argument that the *Post* had misquoted her, rather than a consideration of whether the responses to the article as published were appropriate.

The *Times* piece, which presents itself as a definitive piece correcting the historical record and resuscitating Almontaser's tarnished reputation, came following many months of protests from supporters seeking Almontaser's reinstatement, an unsuccessful lawsuit against the city, and the hiring of a new permanent principal for the school. The article by Andrea Elliott, titled "Her Dream, Branded a Threat," appeared on the front page of the paper, above the fold, with an image of Almontaser surrounded by her supporters.[99] It continued on a two-page spread, which included additional photographs, a timeline of major events, and a reference to additional materials on the website. The website includes videos of opposing viewpoints on various issues and a more detailed timeline, with additional photographs and links to primary source documents.[100] The website also has a reader comments section in which 482 comments were posted within thirty-six hours of the article's release and could be ranked by other readers. Offering this space for reader comments, the website appears to be an active civil forum for discussion, and in producing a reader-ranked hierarchy of comments, it creates an appearance of reflecting "public opinion." The article gives significant space to perspectives on various sides, giving voice to Almontaser and her opponents, especially Pipes, thereby appearing balanced. Nevertheless, in describing Almontaser's personal life, work, and involvement with the school project, the article provides substantial evidence against most of the accusations made against her and the school. Therefore the article appears to be not only thoroughly documented and reliable but also a correction of the record on Almontaser, who is presented as a victim of a right-wing smear campaign. However, there are significant gaps in the article, which defends Almontaser in large part by making her exceptional to her community, rather than examining how her connections

FIGURE 10. Almontaser shown center surrounded by her supporters in a church in Brooklyn. This image was printed on the front page of the *New York Times,* above the fold, on April 28, 2008. Photograph by James Estrin/The New York Times/Redux.

to her community made her vulnerable to these attacks. It also roots her defamation solely in the attacks by Pipes and his allies and leaves unexplored the intifada controversy itself and how it was possible for Almontaser to so quickly lose the support of many key allies.

The article resuscitates Almontaser in part by making her exceptional to broader Muslim and Arab communities via images and the description of her relationship to local Arabs. The front-page photograph of Almontaser shows her smiling with hands clasped in front of her, in the aisle of a beautiful church, the pews filled with predominantly White supporters giving her a standing ovation. The juxtaposition of this image of interfaith support for Almontaser with the one created by the right is emphasized by the caption "Debbie Almontaser, labeled a 'jihadist' by some opponents, amid supporters at a church in Brooklyn in January." This notion is repeated in another image of Almontaser standing solemnly on the steps of City Hall flanked by multiracial and interfaith supporters, one holding a sign that reads "The Torah and the Koran Both Teach Peace." While the school was partly intended to serve Arab communities, the article emphasizes conflicts that produced discord and distance between Almontaser and these communities. Describing criticism of Almontaser's work with the ADL by a local Arab American paper, *Aramica,* the article presents it as evidence of Arab discomfort with "Almontaser's ties with Jewish groups," despite the fact that the article's complaints were in regard to ADL's well-documented anti-Arab political positions and activism.[101] It also disregards the fact that some Arab Americans criticized the *Aramica* piece,[102] in effect presenting Almontaser as an exceptional moderate caught between two extremes: anti-Muslim right-wing and apparently anti-Semitic Arab Americans.

Furthermore, the *Times*'s establishment of Almontaser as a moderate Muslim is in the service of demonstrating its own tolerance, in contrast to right-wing intolerance, which is experienced as "shameful." Elliott's piece gives a great deal of space to the views of Daniel Pipes and his allies, thereby placing blame for Almontaser's demise squarely on their campaign. Visually, the paper represents these opponents as a small media-hungry fringe through an image of a White man and a White woman standing on the steps of City Hall, with a reporter's microphone awkwardly held out before them. In the video section of the website, each interview clip of Almontaser, or members of Communities in Support of Khalil Gibran Academy, is counterposed by a clip of either Daniel Pipes or Jeffrey Wiesenfeld, an adviser to the Stop the Madrassa Coalition and a trustee of the Board of the City University of New York. The article emphasizes that Pipes and other anti-Muslim activists were increasingly focusing their attacks on "law-abiding Muslim-Americans," whom they depict as "lawful Islamists" seeking to institute Sharia by "working through the system," including the schools.

Reader comments on the *Times* website indicate horror at this type of thinking, which incriminates virtually all Muslim Americans in a nefarious project to take over the United States. Of the 182 comments I reviewed, selected based on being recommended by ten or more readers, I found that two-thirds expressed support of Almontaser and/or the school. The most common sympathetic response deemed Almontaser a victim of a shameful witch hunt, dissociating from Daniel Pipes and his allies by comparing their tactics alternately to the Japanese internment, historical anti-Semitism, the Ku Klux Klan, and, most frequently, McCarthyism. Commenters, often referencing their own identities as Jewish, Christian, or Muslim, also argue that learning Arabic is important in the current global context and should not be equated with Islam, and even occasionally note double standards applied to Muslims. However, the strongest reaction in these comments and in supportive blog posts was to criticize the shameful attackers, particularly Daniel Pipes as the chief villain.[103] Indeed, not a single supportive reader comment I analyzed directly addressed the intifada controversy, which mirrored the article's framing.

While the *Times* piece describes how the *Post* article precipitated the Department of Education's pulling of support from Almontaser, it offers no analysis of why the *Post* article was so effective in hurting Almontaser's reputation. Elliott addresses the intifada controversy as a product of the *Post*'s misrepresentation of Almontaser's responses, offering a detailed account of Almontaser's perspective on the interview and noting that in March 2008, a federal judge found that her words were "inaccurately reported by The Post and then misconstrued by the press." Given that the *Times* had up to then ignored Almontaser's October 2007 account of being misrepresented, it appears that the judge's assessment finally created the space for representing her side of the controversy. The *Times* website also includes a clip from Mona Eldahry, of AWAAM, the girls' media organization that produced the T-shirts, in which she explains the word *intifada* as "awakening or to shake off" and the shirts as applauding activism in New York. She also notes that Almontaser had only defined the word and never defended the Palestinian Intifada, but these comments, which begin to touch on the political heart of the controversy, do not appear in print, nor does any discussion of the actual perspectives of Arab or Muslim New Yorkers on the Palestinian Intifada. The right-wing and Zionist interpretations of *intifada*, which cast all pro-Palestinian politics as taboo, are never challenged or even explained. Hence the article never actually elucidates why this defamation was so effective, resulting in the loss of support of key allies—the ADL, the mayor, the Department of Education, and the head of the teacher's union—who had previously defended the school.

Almontaser's defamation admittedly was temporary. Indeed, Randi Weingarten, head of the teacher's union, later said, "I deeply regret that my comments were used as a basis of continuing that treatment because Debbie is an incredible educator and a gift to the city,"[104] while reiterating her concern about the word *intifada*.[105] Nevertheless, attacks on Almontaser were also important in determining the fate of the school, in signaling to Arab and Muslim New Yorkers how their civic participation would be treated, and in emboldening right-wing anti-Muslim activists in New York and nationally. Almontaser's redemption was largely in the service of creating a feeling that the *New York Times* and its liberal readers were tolerant Americans, engaged in civil discourse and debate and disassociating themselves from the shameful, racist, right-wing attacks. While the controversy was treated by the *Times* as an opportunity for the defense of the values and presumed practices of pluralism, it and other New York City venues in fact failed to protect Almontaser from attacks they would later deem unconscionable. As such, the controversy also demonstrates the failure of the center-left media in meaningfully defending the liberal values for which it stands.

The absence in discourses of tolerance of substantive discussion of experiences and political views of Muslims and Arabs that challenge U.S. imperialism, including the United States' alliance with Israel, makes it impossible to imagine an alternative understanding of concepts like *intifada*. Indeed, when the *Times* defined the field of reasonable debate, it excluded not only the types of conspicuous lies and affective attacks present in right-wing sources but also many of the actual linguistic and political perspectives of Arab and Muslim Americans, especially views on the Palestinian–Israeli conflict. Rather than creating an arena for critical engagement with the central accusations against Almontaser, regarding her explanation of the word *intifada* and, by extension, the views of many Arab and Muslim Americans about what *intifada* means, the center-left media focused on reasserting an image of Almontaser as an exceptional "moderate" Muslim, distinguishing her from these communities and itself from the right-wing media attack on her. At the same time, the idea that Almontaser was at fault for "failure to condemn" the word *intifada* implied that she as a Muslim held some personal culpability for violence by Muslims in other parts of the world. As such, even though Almontaser was widely regarded as a "moderate" Muslim, she was judged in relation to a Muslim population assumed to have greater association with violence. In turn, Almontaser's redemption was dependent on distancing her from Muslim and Arab American communities.

Both critics and defenders of KGIA and Almontaser in the mainstream media shared the assumptions of population racism that sees individual Muslims as needing to be assessed in relation to the particular distribution of threat associated with the Muslim population. As a result, the figure of the "moderate" Muslim is part and parcel of this population racism, sometimes described as the "norm" but increasingly represented as the "outlier." The moderate Muslim is a highly contested figure that encapsulates a tension in U.S. War on Terror discourses between articulating the United States as exceptionally tolerant and defining an enemy in terms of a religion and/or ethnicity. As a result, it has also become a useful figure to be manipulated by both right-wing and liberal media to garner audience interest and produce moments of intense attention. While the specific assessment of a Muslim as moderate or not changes from context to context, the variables by which she is assessed are relatively consistent, including religiosity/secularity, patriotism, relation to gender equality and sexual freedom, and relation to discourses of tolerance.

Furthermore, highly affective words that encapsulate a particular threat most strongly associated with Muslims—irrational, intolerant, Islamically motivated violence—function as bioweapons and tools for assessing particular Muslims. As bioweapons, words like *jihad, madrassa,* and *intifada* circulated quickly and broadly in the media, disseminating incredulity and horror at the idea of the school. Words are also compatible with an assessment-oriented and variables-based population racism, because they offer a fast and flexible means of assessing the affective responses of individuals in relation to particular variables. In this case, Almontaser's quoted response to the "Intifada NYC" T-shirts functioned as such an affective assessment. Although many of the right's claims initially seemed so outlandish as to not even warrant a counterpoint, they accumulated around Almontaser, and when there was an accusation that seemed to carry some credence, they provided an affective background into which that accusation could fall and stick. Because words are flexible and can change meaning and connotation from context to context, battles over literal meanings, intended meanings, and connotations offer a space for the insertion of suspicion and doubt—or also for distancing oneself from overt racism.

Therefore, when it becomes useful to discredit a Muslim American, as in both the cases of KGIA and Park51, right-wing commentators represent deviations from the parameters of the "moderate" Muslim—parameters laid out most clearly in defenses of Muslims in liberal media source—as evidence that an individual is intentionally obfuscating his true values and intentions and is therefore a potential threat. They also produce moments of attention and fear by unleashing Arabic words that they make to reference a uniquely Islamic threat. Although liberal defenders may reassert that an individual is *truly* a moderate, these defenses rarely address the legitimacy of the framework for assessing Muslims in relation to a racialized population. As a result, they simply become a means of representing themselves as an arena of civil debate, in contrast to the right-wing media. In effect, rather than a debate, both liberal and right-wing media sources use the figure of the moderate Muslim American as part of a broader strategy to momentarily garner attention in an affectively and informationally saturated media milieu. As a result, both forms of engagement contribute to producing Muslims as a racial population with a distinct set of characteristics and capacities that requires constant surveillance and assessment.

5. Making Muslims Worth Saving

Humanitarianism and the Syrian Refugee Crisis

The photograph shows a boy lying on his stomach almost seeming to be sound asleep, waves lapping at his face and fully clothed body on a beach. Documenting a cruel, untimely death through the familiar scene of a sleeping child, the image is very disturbing, bringing together the quotidian and the unthinkable. The image, at least momentarily, shook publics into recognizing something of the desperation and cruelty that shaped what was being discussed in 2015 as the migrant or refugee crisis in Europe. Focusing on the singular and undeniable tragedy of this death, the image demanded a response. Migrants described as faceless waves, as subhuman creatures, could now be personified through the innocent child. This and other images of "Aylan Kurdi"[1] went viral, viewed by twenty million in twelve hours,[2] with the information that the three-year-old boy had washed ashore on a Turkish beach on the morning of September 2, 2015, after he and his family attempted to cross the Aegean Sea from Turkey to Greece. Of his family of four, only his father survived. The photographs, also printed on the front pages of more than a dozen newspapers across the world, powerfully brought viewers into the already-circulating narrative of a "crisis" in Europe. The suffering and deaths of migrants and refugees arriving from Syria, Afghanistan, Iraq, Sudan, and Somalia were already apparent, including in an April report of eight hundred perishing in a single incident in the Mediterranean.[3] While Kurdi's death certainly deserved to be mourned and questioned, responses to it speak to a distinction between grievable and ungrievable life, making his unexceptional death one requiring mourning and action.

The photographs were both emotionally and politically powerful, creating connection and empathy, while offering evidence for specific truths that created a sense of urgent responsibility. While aestheticized images of horror can distance and desensitize the viewer, in their initial dissemination, these images were more likely to create a feeling of presence and familiarity. Many spoke of relating to the images of Kurdi as a parent, making his death comparable to the loss of one's own child.[4] Kurdi's neat clothes and particularly his shoes, placed on him by an adult, were noted as evidence of parental love.[5] When viewed as a transparent documentation of reality, they also offered proof of the extreme hardship of refugees who would be forced to take such a risk. Their surreal quality produced a surface onto which reactions could be overlaid, with new user-modified versions of the photograph placing Kurdi into a bed or giving him angel wings, which are "designed to mitigate the brutality of the original images in order to sustain the visual narrative of the story and its diffusion."[6]

These dynamics produced a powerful platform for engagement with the "refugee crisis" through grief and outrage, resulting in documentable shifts. The crisis in question became increasingly viewed as an issue of "refugees" fleeing persecution, rather than "migrants" seeking opportunities.[7] Public opinion became more supportive, with a jump in French polls from 44 percent to 53 percent supporting refugees over the course of a week.[8] Charitable giving rose for the next month, with donations to the Swiss Red Cross increasing a hundredfold.[9] A Facebook group, "Refugees Welcome to Norway," grew from about two hundred to more than ninety thousand in September, and the right-wing Norwegian Progressive Party lost at the ballot box.[10] Justin Trudeau was elected as prime minister of Canada while promising to admit twenty-five thousand more Syrian and Iraqi refugees by the end of the year.[11] European leaders agreed to resettle 120,000 refugees in Greek and Italian camps to other European countries, a plan that ultimately fell far short of its goals.[12] Germany, an outlier among European nations, vowed to accept up to eight hundred thousand refugees per year.[13]

Perhaps best exemplifying the power and the limits of this image was the response of British prime minister David Cameron. Months before, he had complained of "a swarm of people coming across the Mediterranean,

FIGURE 11. Mikel Agirregabiria Agirre, *Homenaje a Aylan.* One of the many images produced in response to the photographs of Aylan Kurdi, in this case showing Aylan standing and interacting with others who had died, hence further removed from the original image than most.

seeking a better life, wanting to come to Britain because Britain has got jobs, it's got a growing economy, it's an incredible place to live," casting refugees as a subhuman "swarm" and an undeserving drain on resources.[14] Following Kurdi's death, however, he spoke of how he "as a father . . . felt deeply moved" and that Britain "will fulfil our moral responsibilities,"[15] promising that the United Kingdom would resettle twenty thousand Syrian refugees over five years. The United Kingdom would accept ten thousand in the following two and a half years, but they were disproportionately sent to the poorest regions of the nation.[16] More broadly, the number represented a tiny portion of the refugees entering Europe that year, and the policy gave priority to those experiencing additional hardship, such as disability, rape, or torture, distinguishing a narrow category of the deserving refugee.[17]

Furthermore, the discourse of sympathy that the Kurdi images elicited was quickly superseded by a discourse of threat when Muslim refugees became associated with violence and perverse sexuality. The November

Paris attacks committed by a small number of assailants, likely all European nationals,[18] and claimed by the Islamic State, along with New Year's Eve reports of sexual assaults on women in Cologne and other parts of Germany by men of apparent Arab and North African descent, created a media frenzy. These incidents reanimated border security discourses about the deportability of refugees. As Nicholas De Genova has analyzed, "the figure of the refugee—so recently fashioned as an object of European compassion, pity, and protection—was refashioned with astounding speed, first as the potential terrorist who surreptitiously infiltrates the space of Europe, and then as the potential criminal/rapist who corrodes the social and moral fabric of Europe from within."[19] Making the link between these moments explicit, the anti-Muslim French satirical paper *Charlie Hebdo* ran a cartoon with an image of Kurdi that read, "What would little Aylan have grown up to be? / Ass groper in Germany."[20] Islam, a mutable signifier of religion, culture, or political ideology, was the explanatory glue that connected refugees with terrorists and the sexual assailants, facilitating the affective shift from widespread sympathy to suspicion.

Similarly, in the U.S. context, during the period of the 2015–16 presidential campaigns, the terrorist and the refugee emerged as closely entwined figures, both racialized through their presumed shared Muslim identity. While Donald Trump's vehemently anti-Muslim and anti-immigrant presidential candidacy explicitly cast refugees as terrorists, a presumed link was also present in humanitarian discourses that sought to garner sympathy for the refugee. This chapter analyzes the relationship of U.S. discourses of sympathy for Muslim refugees and the racialization of Muslims, finding that an assessment-oriented stance pervades these representations. I first consider the affinity between the figures of the Muslim, the refugee, and the terrorist, each an outsider to the liberal-democratic nation-state, especially during the long War on Terror. Next, I examine how humanitarianism can feed into population racism by presenting refugees through a framework of exceptionalism, which accepts the need to vet and separate deserving and undeserving victims. I then analyze the work of Brandon Stanton, amateur photojournalist and creator of the immensely popular Humans of New York (HONY), and his 2014 and 2015 series on Syrian and Iraqi refugees in Europe. Even as HONY humanizes refugees, it reproduces a narrow standard of acceptability thereby reinforcing distinct standards of assessment for refugees as Muslims, demonstrating that Muslim refugees must contend with the figure of the terrorist to establish their claims for dignity. While these refugees elicit a sense of obligation, I also raise questions about the form and expression of that obligation.

RACIALIZED MUSLIMS: THE REFUGEE AND THE TERRORIST

The overlapping figures of the Muslim, the terrorist, and the refugee inform each other, while also establishing the full circle of the long War on Terror, when those whom the war was said to be saving arrive on the shores of Europe, seeming to demand that savior. However, precisely in this moment when the war's ever-widening destabilization of the Middle East and North Africa demanded response, those Muslims worth saving were made continuous with a Muslim threat to produce an alibi for evading the responsibility implied in a liberal defense of war. What Mimi Nguyen describes as liberalism's "gift of freedom" was incomplete given violence, poverty, environmental disaster, and political disorder, and yet freedom cannot be gifted to those who "hate" freedom, which is how terrorists were defined.[21] Within this logic, the refugee can only be saved if her desire for freedom is confirmed, a confirmation that is not sufficiently produced by a dead child but must be established through interrogation of the body and the soul of the refugee.

As in the rest of the book, I am primarily focused on how the racialization of *Muslims* occurs through the construction of the refugee crisis in liberal and humanitarian discourses. Much as the state demands the vetting of individual refugees, U.S. humanitarian discourses functioned to vet refugees, to separate refugees from the terrorist, and to assess them against the characteristics deemed problematic for Muslims as a population. As in earlier chapters, I use *population racism* to refer to the separation of one category of people from another based on a presumed distinct distribution of characteristics within each population. These variables of assessment emerge from long-standing stereotypes and representations but are understood as propensities of a population rather than characteristics of all individuals in that group, recognizing diversity within any population. Muslim refugees who are deemed worthy of saving must at minimum demonstrate themselves as acceptable in relation to the variables of assessment of Muslims as a population, including tolerance–intolerance, feminism–misogyny, secularism–true religion–politicized religion, and pro-Americanism–anti-Americanism. As such, these representations reinforce population racism, even while articulating sympathy for the plight of the refugee.

White Americans encountered the refugee crisis through not only anti-Muslim racism but also alignment with Europeans as geopolitical allies and presumed racial-cultural kin. The "refugee crisis" was so dubbed in 2015 to refer to a European crisis, not the actual crisis that Syrians, Iraqis, and others had been facing for several years. The Syrian Civil War, which began in 2012 and led to the displacement of millions of people, was now producing an increase in refugees entering Europe seeking more sustainable life circumstances. The civil war emerged out of the 2011 Arab Spring, a striking period of people-led uprisings and revolutions in numerous Arab countries, which in Syria was met with an iron-fisted response by the authoritarian president Bashar al-Assad. Countering peaceful protesters with mass arrests, torture, and executions, a splintered resistance movement emerged, including defectors from the Syrian army, leading to the long-waged and devastating Syrian Civil War. The war was further exacerbated by outside influencers—notably Russia, Turkey, Iran, Saudi Arabia, the United States, the United Kingdom, and France—who offered military and/or intelligence support to Assad or various resistance forces. In addition, decades of U.S.-led military and political incursions in the region, particularly Iraq, were having ripple effects, most notably in the rise of the militant group Islamic State of Iraq and Syria, ISIS, also known as ISIL or Daesh, which was vying for power in Syria. By 2015, the war had led to the displacement of fully half of Syria's population of twenty-two million and to a refugee population of five million seeking resettlement outside the country. In June 2015, the United Nations High Commissioner for Refugees reported that at sixty million, the number of refugees and internally displaced people worldwide had reached the highest level since World War II.[22] One in six of these displaced people was Syrian.[23]

In 2015, about a million refugees and migrants, half of whom were Syrian, entered Europe.[24] Traveling by foot, boat, bus, or train, and being stopped and held at borders by the thousands, refugees were a very material presence in parts of Europe and at its borders. By contrast, distance and restrictive policies meant that only highly controlled numbers of refugees, and very few Syrians, were being resettled in the United States. Fewer than two thousand refugees from Syria were resettled to the United States in 2015, a number that increased to thirteen thousand in 2016 and decreased under President Trump.[25] Nevertheless, in the United States, Syrian refugees were evoked via campaign discourses raising the specter of invasion and terrorism to produce a moral panic. As of 2017, however, the majority of the millions of displaced Syrians were in Syria (6.3 million), and of those who had left the country, the vast majority were in Turkey (3.4 million), Lebanon (1 million), and Jordan (660,000), in part as a result of the 2016 European Union–Turkey deal.[26] About one million were in Europe, with more than half this number in Germany, followed by Switzerland (110,000) and Austria (50,000). Hence Turkey, a country roughly a quarter of the population of the United States, hosted one hundred times the number of Syrian refugees as the United States.

Trump's position on Syrian refugees was initially deemed extreme, given a tradition of bipartisan support for the refugee program, rooted in a Cold War ideology of the United States as global defender of democracy. Dovetailing with his stance against Mexican and Central American immigration, Trump complained of a "mass migration" of Syrian refugees to the United States and vowed to deport them.[27] In contrast to Europe, the photographs of Kurdi had little effect in shaping U.S. political discourses. Rather, Republican candidates used the November Paris attacks to call for closing the borders or stopping admission of people from countries with ISIS or al-Qaeda presence, that is, Iraq and Syria, hence following Trump's lead. Ted Cruz, a son of refugees himself, called it "lunacy" to allow the entry of "tens of thousands of Syrian Muslim refugees."[28] Governors of thirty-one states opposed the resettlement of Syrian refugees, though no U.S. city had accepted more than a hundred Syrian refugees that year.[29] Riskiness was attached to refugees' presumed Muslim identity, and some candidates proposed that the United States only accept Christian Syrians.[30] Trump became more explicitly anti-Muslim, calling for shutting down mosques and a "total and complete shutdown of Muslims entering the United States."[31] In August 2016, Trump described a plan for "extreme vetting" of Muslims, where "applicants will be asked their views about honor killings, about respect for women and gays and minorities. Attitudes on radical Islam . . . and many other topics as part of this vetting procedure."[32] The Syrian refugee-terrorist became a bogeyman justifying what would become Trump's ban on visitors, immigrants, and asylum seekers from Muslim-majority countries.

While the leading Democratic candidate, Hillary Clinton, called for the admittance of sixty-five thousand Syrian refugees, she also emphasized border security, framing a refugee program as a voluntary, humanitarian act limited by national security priorities.[33] Rather than challenge the association of refugees with terrorism, Clinton emphasized that admitted refugees undergo a highly stringent multiyear vetting process, one described by a *Washington Post* columnist:

> Screening includes health checks, repeated biometric verification of identity, several layers of biographical and background screening, and in-person interviews. Multiple agencies are involved in the process, including the FBI's Terrorist Screening Center, the State Department, the Department of Homeland Security, the National Counterterrorism Center and the Department of Defense. And all of this happens before a refugee's application for resettlement is ever approved or rejected and long before a refugee enters the United States.[34]

Indeed, vetting was the common ground across these discourses, as there was agreement that it was absolutely essential to keep the United States safe from the terrorist threat Muslim refugees implied.

While the racialization of Muslims ties Syrian and other refugees to the figure of the terrorist, in fact the refugee and the terrorist are already conjoined in liberal theory. The figures of the refugee and terrorist bring forth a fundamental contradiction within the liberal-democratic nation-state, as they are both excluded from presumably universal rights in the name of state sovereignty. The refugee, as Yen Le Espiritu notes, is a by-product of the nation-state system: "in a world imagined to be composed of mutually exclusive, territorially bound spaces, refugees, lacking the qualities of the citizen, do not properly belong anywhere."[35] Mimi Nguyen describes the refugee and terrorists as "limit figures" within the liberal nation-state:

> On the one hand, the terrorist ranges out of the reach of any single state, and thus often demands (or justifies) strategies of radical disenfranchisement and extraterritorial murder in order to meet, and extinguish, this

enemy. On the other, the refugee cannot appeal to the state from which she is fleeing, or expelled, to recognize her as legitimate life, a human being worthy of rights.[36]

The consequence for both these figures is that statelessness results in a lack of access to human rights that are supposed to be inalienable. Falguni Sheth, drawing from Hannah Arendt, notes that "recognition of one's human rights is *predicated not on one's status as human, but on one's recognition as a member of a polity.*"[37] Statelessness produces dehumanization and reduction to a status of a life that need not be respected or saved.

Indeed, Muslim U.S. citizens who are deemed to be terrorists have been legally treated as noncitizens who are rightless and expendable. Abdulrahman al-Awlaki, a sixteen-year-old U.S. citizen, was killed in a 2011 drone attack in Yemen approved by President Obama because of his father's political advocacy; his father, Anwar al-Awlaki, also a U.S. citizen, had been killed by the same method two weeks earlier.[38] Hoda Muthana, an American citizen born in New Jersey who joined ISIS, had her citizenship rescinded on a technicality by the Obama administration in 2016, resulting in her becoming a refugee in Syria.[39] For Muslims, affiliation with terrorism, an ambiguous construct that is determined by the state, has become grounds for wholesale exclusion from the political community and the reciprocal obligations that it implies; an accusation of terrorism results in being excommunicated and treated as life not worthy of respect. These examples demonstrate a dynamic that Sherene Razack argues is central to the racialization of Muslims: the "casting out" from political community, or a denial of rights that is systemic and constitutive. As Razack explains, "communities without the right to have rights . . . are constituted as a different order of humanity altogether by virtue of having no political community willing to guarantee their rights, and whatever is meted out to the 'rightless' becomes of no concern to others."[40]

Even as Muslims are systematically cast out through law, statecraft, and geopolitics, humanitarians partake in a discourse that aims at inclusion or reentry; however, they *also* participate in the racialization of Muslims, as the terms of inclusion are entwined with the processes of exclusion. Jodi Melamed has argued that geopolitical conditions of war, violence, and migration contribute to a differential valuing of populations, while "appearing to be (and being) a rationally inevitable normative system that merely sorts human beings into categories of difference."[41] This dynamic allows for some refugees to be put forward as worthy of saving, even as millions are violently neglected and excluded, the former process justifying the latter. These refugees must establish not only their worthiness for receipt of the "gift of freedom" but also their credit and ability to repay the debt that the gift produces.[42] In the humanitarian discourse I analyze here, this worthiness is often established by representing refugees as already "American" in disposition and values and good for "America" through their human capital and potential economic and moral contributions to the nation. This process is necessary to separate the refugee, as abject victim *and* future contributor, from the terrorist, to be worthy of U.S. "generosity."

HUMANIZATION AND RACIALIZATION OF SYMPATHETIC REFUGEES

Humanitarian discourses that challenge the treatment of refugees as negligible or threatening seem to operate through universalistic registers that undermine the particularism of race. This universalism is expressed through the idea of "our common humanity," which avoids analysis of power relations and the causes of violence and exploitation. A pronounced commitment to remaining neutral and "above" politics produces other forms of differentiation to focus humanitarian attention.[43] As anthropologist Miriam Ticktin has argued, the object of humanitarianism is not actually everyone who suffers but rather one who establishes his innocent victimhood and hence is deemed deserving of compassion and pity.[44] The paradox of humanitarianism lies in this tension between universalism and exceptionalism. The impulse to identify worthy victims produces the need to speak to the stereotypical perceptions of identities that otherwise these discourses claim to be irrelevant. As a result, apolitical humanitarianism must partake in assessment processes, such as the vetting of refugees to determine their worthiness for sympathy and care, as evident in representations of refugees by HONY, analyzed later.

Ticktin places this dynamic in historical context as a feature of what she terms the "new humanitarianism," which is avowedly apolitical.[45] Analyzing the history of Médecins Sans Frontières (MSF, or Doctors without

Borders), Ticktin argues that the new humanitarianism emerged as a shift away from the 1960s Third Worldism that sought to transform the causes of suffering and inequality through anti-imperial and anticapitalist politics of collective self-determination. As she explains,

> MSF's new universalism marks a shift from the universalism imagined in May 1968—a form of leftist solidarity—to a universalism based on the individualism of human rights, grounded in a moral, *not* a political, imperative and enacted in the temporal present. In other words, this universalism also produced a different vision of humanity and a new strategy to protect it.[46]

As revolutionary movements gave rise to authoritarian governments, the French MSF leadership decided to refocus the organization on alleviating individual suffering. The result was an "antipolitics" that refused to stake out positions in relation to political conflicts. Recipients of aid became victims in need of saving, not political agents in history. MSF removed itself from commenting on the power relations and politics that contributed to this suffering. MSF still saw its mission to be to bear witness to and publicize human atrocities, even as this created tension with its principle of neutrality. Furthermore, humanitarianism operated through the logic of exception, a response to "crisis." The suffering had to be exceptional rather than woven into the daily life of any specific group. Representations of horrifying experiences of sympathetic victims, what Ticktin calls the "morally legitimate suffering body," contrasted with those who did not receive care. In turn, lack of care could cast someone as having "failed in some important moral way," legitimating condemnation and criminalization.[47]

These dynamics of differentiation are also evident in media representations of suffering, which often do not produce humanization of those who are suffering. Lilie Chouliaraki argues, "in the analytics of mediation, *humanization* is a process of identity construction that endows the sufferers with the power to say or do something about their condition, even if this power is simply the power to evoke and receive the beneficiary action of others. The humane sufferer is the sufferer who acts."[48] Contrasting European representations of New York victims of the September 11 attacks and of Bangladeshi homeless people, she notes, "The September 11th sufferers speak; the Bangladeshi sufferers do not."[49] In her analysis, with Tijana Stolic, of 2015 European news representations of refugees, she argues that these representations only ascribe agency to refugees when they are seen as threats to the nation or potential terrorists and otherwise portray them as victims, unable to speak for themselves. Nevertheless, they identify diverse modes of representing refugees, which they categorize as regimes of visibility: (1) "visibility as biological life," (2) "visibility as empathy," (3) "visibility as threat," (4) "visibility as hospitality," and (5) "visibility as self-reflexivity." Even within the most sympathetic activist discourses, for example, in "Refugees Welcome" marches, categorized as "visibility as hospitality," refugees are not presented as actors with their own voices, suggesting the limitations of prevailing liberal discourses in Europe.[50] I utilize this framework to demonstrate how HONY representations of refugees seek to humanize refugees, attributing to them their own perspectives, motives, and agency, in a context where such representations were largely absent. As such, HONY provides a compelling case for considering the potential and limitations of self-avowed apolitical humanitarianism.

Although claims of humanity are in theory universal, they are validated in HONY through representations of individuals. This mode of representation aligns with a liberal valuing of individuality and individual autonomy and also regimes of asylum that assess claims on an individual basis. When the refugee is recognized, she is in some mode separated from that population, either as representative, the one who exemplifies the experiences of others, or as exceptional, the one who is different and more worthy of saving than others. The refugee is not brought forward as a political representative of a *community*, one who speaks for and makes demands on behalf of others, corresponding with both the depoliticization of refugee discourses and a liberal humanitarian valuing of the autonomous individual over a community imagined as traditional and repressive. As such, the individual refugee is separated from the politics and cultures of his communities, both at home and ones formed in displacement, and is forced to fit his story into a "universalistic" frame that in fact evinces liberal preferences. While it became urgent to counter demonization and exclusion of Muslim refugees, this liberal humanitarian discourse is greatly limited by its mode of representation.

RECLAIMING LIBERALISM AND HUMANIZING REFUGEES

On March 14, 2016, Brandon Stanton released an open letter to Donald Trump:

> I've watched you advocate the use of torture and the murder of terrorists' families. I've watched you gleefully tell stories of executing Muslims with bullets dipped in pig blood. I've watched you compare refugees to "snakes," and claim that "Islam hates us."
>
> I am a journalist, Mr. Trump. And over the last two years I have conducted extensive interviews with hundreds of Muslims, chosen at random, on the streets of Iran, Iraq, and Pakistan. I've also interviewed hundreds of Syrian and Iraqi refugees across seven different countries. And I can confirm—the hateful one is you.[51]

While Stanton explicitly defends Muslims, he implicitly defends a liberal positionality that was threatened by the rise of Trump, articulating a vision of what it means to be a good, tolerant American. He posits himself, a White, heterosexual, Christian man, as one who can produce an unbiased representation of Muslims, evoking objectivity as a "journalist" speaking to people "at random." Notably, this is a rare instance in which Stanton speaks of the Muslim identity of the refugees he profiles. Even as HONY representations of refugees rarely explicitly reference religious identities or beliefs, this statement highlights that refugees are to be understood in reference to Muslims as a population. In the face of a right-wing discourse that suggested that *Muslim* refugees posed an existential threat to the United States, Stanton's work presented religion as private, politics as irrelevant, and the refugee crisis as only properly engaged through a universal humanistic lens. As Stanton said elsewhere of his international work, "those are the places most skewed in people's heads. The work has a very humanizing effect in places that are misunderstood or feared." He also claims an apolitical stance: "I purposely and pointedly try to avoid infusing any meaning in the work."[52] However, as my analysis makes clear, while Stanton's work does compellingly humanize refugees, giving them the voice to tell their own stories, it also produces meanings consistent with U.S. global hegemony and the racialization of Muslims as a population of risk.

Despite its avowed apolitical stance, HONY's individualized and humanizing narratives align with a demand to surveil, police, and assess refugees as Muslims. It distinguishes among refugees, highlighting some as more worthy of sympathy and bringing them into distinctly U.S. discourse as fitting the image of the good immigrant and the good, patriotic Muslim. Although there initially is an attempt to represent refugees as a population or a multiplicity, over time the project is distilled to a few stand-out representatives, who ultimately appear exceptional to all the rest. Stanton's work also dismisses the possibility of legitimate and rational critique of U.S. imperialism emerging from Muslim-majority societies, while naturalizing the American Dream as a global phenomenon, exported through popular culture and U.S. militarism and internalized by "our friends" across the world. Individuals profiled needed to be separated from characteristics deemed problematic among Muslims, such as strongly felt religious, ethnic, or political identities, including explicit religiosity or political affiliations; conservative views on gender, family, or sexuality; and critical views of U.S. culture and foreign policy. The story of the individual, particularly in the truncated and highly circulatable form that predominates in social media and is exemplified by HONY, emerges as a technology of assessment, consistent with discourses of vetting. These representations thereby reinforce population racism by engaging and circulating the distinct variables of assessment associated with Muslims as a population.

HONY emerged as a very popular and powerful social media site with a Facebook following of nine million in 2014, a number that increased dramatically over the next year and a half to seventeen million in 2016.[53] Stanton, a former bond trader, created HONY in 2010, posting daily photographs of people he met on the streets of New York City. Within three years, Stanton's popularity had grown so much that he published a book, *Humans of New York*. With thirty thousand preorders, the book debuted at number one on the *New York Times* hardcover best-seller list, staying in the list's top fifteen for twenty-one weeks.[54] In 2014 and 2015, Stanton published two other successful books, *Little Humans of New York* and *Humans of New York: Stories*. In 2017, the HONY enterprise added video, with a television series that ran exclusively on Facebook, the first episode of which had more than two million views in twenty-four hours.[55] In addition to commercial success, Stanton's international work has given him respect as a humanitarian voice. Of the three series that include a focus on refugees, the first was part of a fifty-day tour sponsored by the United Nations as part of its efforts to promote the Millennial Development Goals.[56]

Soon after HONY's inception in 2010, and despite the title of his project, Stanton's geographic focus broadened beyond the perimeter of New
York City. As an Iranian American, I remember the excitement and relief
among my circles when Stanton went to Iran in 2012 and released, in a very
digestible and circulatable format, images and stories of Iranians as regular
people. I was moved by these stories, by the fact that a simple act filled such
a gaping vacuum in the portrayals of Iranians. These seemed like accounts
that a curious and perceptive tourist—one who actually speaks with the
people he encounters—would bring back. Even as I thought about and
analyzed the limitations of discourses of tolerance and sympathy, I "liked"
Stanton's Facebook page, as did many of my Iranian family members and
Iranian American friends. Stanton's success in Iran led him to many more
locales, including Iraq, Pakistan, Jordan, and Turkey. Stanton's work on
refugees similarly offered broad audiences a view of a population that had
been largely maligned or ignored, increasing awareness and shifting perceptions in important, but I argue also very limited, ways.

From its inception, HONY has framed itself at the nexus of the individual and the population, a dynamic that operates differently in representations of New Yorkers, as opposed to refugees. Conceptualized as a
mapping of the ten thousand "humans" of New York, the HONY project
began by documenting a city full of visually striking, unique figures. With
the addition of pithy quotes, interesting vignettes, and longer "life" narratives, quirky style was supplemented with reflections on hopes, regrets,
traumas, and accomplishments. As a body of work, these "photo-stories,"
as dubbed by Jennifer Nish,[57] seemed to attest to the diversity of New York,
where people rubbing shoulders on the subway can see each other more
fully through the HONY project. In contrast to the individuality and diversity that define New Yorkers, the HONY series on refugees focuses on
the relationship of individual experiences to a population-level phenomenon. Stanton said, "Together, these migrants are part of one of the largest
population movements in modern history. . . . But their stories are composed of unique and singular tragedies."[58] While the individual is the focus
of each representation, the goal is to bring attention to a population-level
problem of the "refugee crisis," although without any analysis of the historical and geopolitical dynamics that have given rise to these movements
of population.

HONY's photo-stories have a number of qualities that produce "humanization" of their subjects, offering a more agentive vision of the refugee than is evident in news media representations that Chouliaraki and Stolic analyze. In stark contrast to Chouliaraki and Stolic's "visibility as biological life," where refugees are presented as masses of people in need of assistance for survival, HONY shows the agency of refugees, including collective agency. In his 2014 images from Jordan, including the Zaatari camp housing eighty thousand refugees, HONY images and text emphasize the ingenuity of refugees in a context of extremely limited resources.[59] In addition to the stories of individuals, a number of images demonstrate the infrastructure, such as wires rigged to maximize access to electricity, and spaces, including neat homes and functional stores that were maintained by the refugees. The refugee population is represented as upright and entrepreneurial, building a city with its own economy.

More commonly, HONY presents highly humanizing representations of individuals, fitting in Chouliaraki's frame, giving refugees voice to tell their stories, and granting them "interiority" or "'depth' of consciousness."[60] HONY, operating in the mode of documentary realism, offers close-up images of its subjects, often looking into the camera or contemplatively to the side, paired with a direct quotation that appears unfiltered, creating a sense of transparency and authenticity. Sometimes a close-up image of the body, such as clasped hands, creates intimacy, while allowing for anonymity, the reason for which is often apparent. First-person accounts convey beliefs and experiences, often telling of how one became a refugee. These photostories fit most closely with "visibility as empathy," which Chouliaraki and Stolic describe as "intimate snapshots of individuals or couples, such as a crying child, a mother with her baby or a rescue worker in action."[61] However while HONY's work does evoke the audience's guilt and benevolence, it does not fall into the most problematic elements of the "visibility as empathy" schema, which they argue infantilizes refugees as lacking voice and agency and focuses disproportionately on children. In contrast, Stanton centers refugees as their own storytellers, presenting men and women, young and old, but these stories do give inordinate focus to hardship and traumas that cause and confound the refugee experience.

Extreme trauma, interspersed with enduring hope, is the most commonly repeated theme in these stories. In describing how humanization of distant others "widen[s] my awareness of the spectrum of human experience," Stanton notes "the depth and the extent of the tragedy that people go through and still keep going and living and laughing has really been shocking."[62] The refugee series consistently provides stories of extreme physical violence and emotional trauma, articulating a humanization wedded to suffering and producing sympathy as a predominant mode of viewer connection. For example, the September 2015 Refugee Stories series, collected from people in Greece, Hungary, and Austria, tells of the horrors in home countries leading to a need to flee and of the process of escaping, traveling by rickety boats, dealing with dishonest smugglers, and benefiting from the generosity of individuals.[63] Even as the specifics of each story differ—in this one, a father was blown up by a suicide attacker, whereas in another, a child was kidnapped and held for ransom, and in a third, a brother was shot in his backyard, resulting in disabling injuries requiring continuing medical care—there is a uniformity through the ever presence of extreme bodily violence. While these narratives also document perseverance and strategies for survival, refugees are consistently asked to bring forth the worst experiences of their lives. As a whole, the stories attest to the legitimacy of the refugee claim of persecution, while also capturing the attention and sympathy of audiences far away through the shock of horrors.

HONY often pushes against the prevailing stereotypes of Muslims, challenging a notion of refugees as primarily threats to state security. Chouliaraki and Stolic note the prevalence of the media representations of refugees as only agentive when threatening, portrayed as young men, whose skin color, facial hair, and dress suggest racial difference ("visibility as threat"). In contrast, HONY offers many representations of highly sympathetic men, including ones that directly counter the association of the young, bearded Muslim man with terrorism. For example, the image featured on the Syrian Americans page is of a solitary, relatively young bearded man, sitting, Middle Eastern style, cross-legged and barefoot on some cushions, with a cigarette dangling from his hand.[64] The image, dated December 2015, is taken in Amman, Jordan, and the man tells of how war interrupted his studies and that fear of being drafted into the army led him to flee Syria. Emphasizing that he "had no interest in religion or politics," the man is an innocent bystander to civil war. In Jordan he was hopeless, saying, "I felt so alone that I wanted to kill myself," a hardship that attests to his being worthy of sympathy.[65] Fortuitously, he made a phone call that led to a friendship with a woman he did not know, another refugee from Syria. Now the two are married with two children and pleased to be awaiting their resettlement in Michigan. In a story told over three images, the single bearded man is placed next to his wife, and later two children, his solemn expression replaced by a smile. Ending with the quote "I'm done with religion and politics forever. I only want to worry about milk and diapers," the man who visually fits the image of a terrorist becomes a family man, and audiences are left to feel pleased with the happy ending.[66]

This example, however, highlights a dynamic common in HONY, where characteristics deemed problematic for Muslims as a population are disavowed, rather than interrogated. The Syrian man's repeated denial of affiliation with "religion or politics" mirrors the absence of both of these as meaningful elements of the experiences of the refugees profiled, suggesting one of the key dynamics through which refugees are made sympathetic. Stanton's own apolitical stance is reflected in the narrative accounts, which consistently represent political actors as perpetrators—usually ISIS, Syrian and Iraqi armies, and, less frequently, smugglers and European police—while the refugees are almost always innocent bystanders, never playing an active role in the political conflicts. More confounding is the complete absence of references to religion or God in these accounts. Indeed, religion appears to be as taboo as politics, even as the subjects often appear to be Muslim based on dress. Everyday references to God, references that are present in HONY's broader body of work, are absent. These refugees do not "thank God" for having survived or put their faith in God in thinking about the future. The absence of religious references of any sort suggests a tendency to see Islam as a political religion, which leads to a need to represent refugees as separated from their religion to make them universal sympathetic victims.

While HONY adds an additional layer of nuance that is lacking in typical news coverage, there are still specific gaps, suggesting that the problem is not a refusal to "humanize" refugees, in the sense of demonstrating their voice and agency, but rather the refusal to politically contextualize them. Even as Stanton offers these first-person accounts, he clearly solicits and edits them to certain effect, presenting these stories within an acceptable frame that garners sympathy by emphasizing extreme suffering but otherwise does not challenge the audience. There is a distinct pattern of omission and emphasis that suggests a set of parameters of assessment relative to Muslims as a population, which places refugees on a spectrum of more or less worthy of care. This set of assessments becomes especially apparent when analyzing the few profiled individuals whom Stanton chose to highlight, granting them a larger platform and garnering much broader interest in their narratives. The subjects who become most prominent in the HONY series are presented as exceptional to the broader population of refugees, more fully disavowing characteristics that are deemed problematic for Muslims as a population and more deserving of sympathy and care.

EXCEPTIONAL REFUGEES AS "SYRIAN AMERICANS"

In Stanton's work on refugees, two stories stand out among the rest: a man referred to as "the scientist" and Stanton's interpreter, "Aya." Stanton highlighted these two figures over others, granting them much more space to tell their stories—in the case of the scientist, through seven images posted over the course of one day, and in Aya's case, through eleven images posted over the course of three days. In turn, the scientist and Aya both received much broader attention, including press coverage, targeted advocacy, and a response from President Obama. Both of these stories are within the Syrian Americans series, which Stanton gathered in Turkey with individuals and families with approved U.S. asylum applications.[67] These two photostories are consistent with the HONY representation of the refugee experience but distinct in the particular highlighted characteristics of their subjects. As in other narratives portrayed, the subjects tell of the intense violence and severe loss they witnessed and experienced, hardships that attest to their legitimacy as refugees. However, in contrast to other refugees portrayed, the scientist and Aya stand out in how much they fit a U.S. framework of acceptability, through their alignment with an image of the United States as a nation of immigrants where hard work and ingenuity will lead to the achievement of the American Dream, and of themselves as "good" Muslims, that is, apolitical, private or secular in their religious belief and practice, nonsexist, tolerant, and supportive of U.S. global hegemony.

The story of "the scientist," who later was identified as Dr. Refaai Hamo, is a heart-wrenching narrative of a hardworking entrepreneurial and successful man who, through the course of the narrative, comes to embody the violated and devastated refugee, the ingenious and industrious immigrant, and the tolerable, good Muslim. The scientist follows the general formula of the series: telling of the trauma of becoming a refugee through the Syrian Civil War and ending with the good fortune of receiving news of resettlement in the United States, hence becoming, in Stanton's framing, "Syrian American." The first image, posted on Facebook on December 8, 2015, shows a striking white-haired man with sharp features and wearing a shiny blue suit sitting on a futon in a green room. Two suits hang behind him on the wall, and a door opens into a dark hallway; things seem out of place and yet orderly. He sits in a thoughtful pose, head tilted, a hand holding his chin, the other hand on his leg. The seven images appear to have all been taken in one sitting, all but one showing Hamo alone, in one case holding up a drawing of his complex of buildings. In the fourth image, he sits between his two children, a sixteen-year-old boy and a young woman. The final image is a close-up with Hamo's tilted face fully lit, solemn and thoughtful, chin resting in his hand, and looking directly at the camera.[68]

As in other portrayals of refugees, Hamo meets the demand to relive his worst traumas to establish his status as a legitimate refugee. He describes losing his wife, a daughter, and fourteen other family members when, during the war, President Assad's military bombed a compound of buildings Hamo had built for his family. He tells of how his son had to carry out pieces of his mother after the bombing and has since never been the same. His surviving daughter has shrapnel in her neck. Hamo concludes, "We survived but we're dead psychologically. Everything ended for us that day."[69] This bodily devastation has found another form today as Hamo explains that he has stomach cancer but cannot receive care in Turkey.

Despite these adversities, Hamo also distinguishes himself in ways that align with an image of the good Muslim and the good immigrant. As a Muslim, his acceptability is established through his status as a "modern" man who entered a love marriage, supported his daughter studying medicine, and comes from a family with no party affiliation. This apolitical positioning omits Hamo's Kurdish identity and support of the Kurdish people, which he describes in later interviews once settled in Michigan.[70] Hamo also fits the image of the good immigrant who will contribute to the U.S. economy, describing himself as hardworking, entrepreneurial, and innovative. He says he became a scientist to make "a lasting contribution to humanity."[71] A self-made man, he funded his education by working in construction, eventually earning a PhD. Referencing inventions he has made, books he has written, and work he continues to do in Turkey despite not being able to get credit for it, Hamo documents both his achievements and his current situation. Despite the challenges, he insists that he still has hope and can be productive:

> I still think I have a chance to make a difference in the world. I have several inventions that I'm hoping to patent once I get to America. One of my inventions is being used right now on the Istanbul metro to generate electricity from the movement of the train. I have sketches for a plane that can fly for 48 hours without fuel. I've been thinking about a device that can predict earthquakes weeks before they happen.[72]

The jarring shift in Hamo's narrative from being "dead psychologically" to having hope for his future and the possibility of "mak[ing] a difference in the world" speaks to the dual demands of claiming one's worthiness as a refugee. One must be devastated yet not broken, traumatized yet still optimistic and future oriented. Within the U.S. culture of positive thinking and self-confidence, it is this inexplicable optimism, along with his claims of exceptionalism, that make Hamo an appealing figure to support.

On December 9, President Obama commented on this final post, saying in part, "Yes, you can still make a difference in the world, and we're proud that you'll pursue your dreams here. Welcome to your new home. You're part of what makes America great."[73] In contrast to Hamo's experience of exclusion in Turkey, the United States can present itself as "a land of opportunity" where human capital does not go to waste and Hamo will be able to pursue his dreams, ignoring the vastly unequal conditions in these two countries. This parallels a dynamic Espiritu notes where poor treatment of Vietnamese refugees in first-asylum countries leads to the racialization of these countries, while the United States can claim itself as a place of democracy and opportunity, even as it severely limits the number of entering refugees.[74] Even though Hamo has never set foot in the United States, he is actively incorporated into "America" first by Stanton, in his naming of this series as Syrian Americans, and second by President Obama. Reframing Trump's "Make America Great Again" campaign slogan, Obama staked out a humanitarian patriotism that welcomes refugees, although, in this case, a single highly educated, entrepreneurial one. Hamo was invited to and attended Obama's 2016 State of the Union address and Trump's 2017 inauguration.[75] Hamo seems to have fully internalized the discourse of identity, saying in an interview following his arrival that because of his experience with Obama, he does not consider himself an immigrant but rather an American citizen, suggesting the two are mutually exclusive.[76]

Aya, unlike the others profiled in the Syrian Americans series, is originally from Iraq and ultimately has her asylum case rejected by the United States, in some respects standing in for the vast majority of asylum seekers who will have their cases denied. Aya is Stanton's interpreter, presumably assisting him on the other interviews with refugees. The images show a young woman wearing a black scarf, leopard print top, black pants, purple socks, and tan slippers, sitting on a couch. Most of the eleven images show her alone, either from the side or front, from a distance of several feet or in close-up; one shows her with her mother, another with her dog, and another with her female family members. She tells of her multiple displacements: from Iraq to Jordan and back to Iraq, then to Syria after the start of the U.S.–Iraq war, and finally to Turkey after the Syrian Civil War. Aya's life story of displacement, violence, and perseverance is told punctuated by vivid and horrifying details. In contrast to the photographs of a serene young woman, Aya's words create images of stark brutality.[77]

Her story begins with Aya almost being euthanized as a baby in Iraq due to a disease the doctors considered incurable. Was Aya's poor care in the mid-1990s due to the devastating effects on Iraq's medical infrastructure as a result of the U.S.-backed economic sanctions?[78] This possible contributing factor, however, is not mentioned. Rather, the United States appears as savior in the form of a U.S. doctor who treats Aya in Jordan. After returning to Baghdad, she tells of the start of the war, presumably the 2003 U.S. invasion of Iraq, but the U.S. role is not mentioned. Rather, she tells of finding her friend following a bombing: "She didn't have any legs and she was screaming and I can still hear that sound now."[79] Two years later, Aya witnesses a car bombing, offering more images of dismemberment.[80] Threats from the Iraqi military led the family to escape to Syria, but after two years there, the civil war began, presumably in 2012, again marked by images of violence: "I was studying one afternoon, and I looked out the window, and a man smashed another man's head with a stone. Right in front of me."[81] In Turkey, Aya describes experiencing physical attacks, apparently due to antirefugee sentiment. Aya's telling of her narrative abides by the demand that the refugee demonstrate her own exceptional suffering while seeming to stay above the fray of politics, not being a political actor herself.

However, there is a clear politics articulated in the narrative, as Aya consistently emphasizes a strong pro–United States stance and her compatibility with U.S. culture and values, abiding by a narrow construct of the patriotic Muslim American, even as Aya is not an American. Aya, like Hamo, is hardworking and academically successful, but she also defends the U.S. military in Iraq and emphasizes her family's strong appreciation of and alignment with U.S. culture. The U.S. role in Iraq is either omitted or described as liberatory. Aya is a bright, ambitious child and teaches herself English from music, movies, and speaking with U.S. soldiers. In Syria, Aya is able to study and prosper, so much so that her teacher declared she would become "the voice of refugees."[82] In Turkey, Aya is providing for her family through her work as an interpreter, emerging as a self-made, hardworking, independent young woman.

Aya's pro-Americanism comes through even more strongly as her narrative continues. Aya mistakenly believed that her family's application for resettlement had been approved, and the family is ecstatic as they begin planning a Christmastime trip to New York. When they realize they have been rejected, Aya is incredulous, exclaiming,

> Our family loved America. My father always told me about America. He made us go talk to American soldiers during the war. Other people were afraid of Americans, but he told us they were here to help us and not to be afraid of them. He told us that America was a place where so many different people lived in peace. So many religions. So many communities. We loved America! Every day we watched Oprah. My father promised me that one day we would go on her show and meet her. We even wrote about Oprah for our assignments in school. Why would we ever hurt America?[83]

Aya's overstated love for "America," articulated through love of U.S. culture and celebrities, and appreciation of the U.S. military and its political role in Iraq, establishes the family's worthiness. She distinguishes herself from other Iraqis in her attitude toward U.S. soldiers and later by emphasizing how she has veered from stereotypical cultural expectations. In the final post, we discover that Aya's father disappeared some six months ago and the family's situation is increasingly tenuous, even as Aya is economically supporting them through her work. Aya concludes, "I never wanted to be the traditional Arabic girl who marries her cousin and spends all day in the house. I've worked so hard to escape it all. . . . But if things don't change for me, I think I'll have to go back to Iraq."[84] Aya, the modern, independent, America-loving young woman, presents another vision of herself as an Arab (Muslim) girl forced by circumstances to marry a cousin. Aya emerges like Hamo as an exceptional refugee, one who not only experienced exceptional suffering but is exceptional in aligning with U.S. values.

While HONY representations do humanize refugees through close-up images and first-person accounts that create feelings of direct connection, they also reinforce the logics of racialization. The scientist and Aya, compared to other "Syrian Americans" in the series, fit exceedingly well within a U.S. framework of acceptability for Muslims. Both have shed sexist traditions and ways of thought; are hardworking, educated, and independent thinkers; and retain a positive attitude and hopeful worldview despite the devastation that they have experienced and continue to experience. Even as their loss and suffering are shared with other refugees, their alignment with the specific "American" values distinguishes them from the crowd and helps to explain why Stanton chose to provide much more extensive narratives for them. Their stories seem to highlight elements that rub against the stereotype of Muslims, for example, in the emphasis on Hamo's love marriage, apparently secular attachment to science, and entrepreneurial spirit, while details of political agency evident in other press coverage, such as Hamo's support for Kurdish nationalism, are excluded. As such, these representations reinforce the variables of assessment deemed necessary for holding up sympathetic Muslims and separating them from what is deemed risky in Muslims as a population.

RACIALIZED ASSESSMENTS AND COMMUNITIES OF CARE

HONY consists not only of Stanton's images and quotations but also of HONY's millions of Facebook followers, and especially the tens of thousands of Facebook followers who react to and comment on these images. Chouliaraki argues that humanization is manifest in how the sufferer interacts with the spectators to create feelings of responsibility through a dynamic of "request-response." The "HONY community" emerges through these accumulated individual responses and sees itself as having a shared moral vision and the power to transform an individual's life. This moral community, however, rejects political conceptions of responsibility and solidarity, emphasizing a person-to-person ethic of care. Even when organized, through a fund-raising plea or a petition drive, responses take the form of providing assistance to individuals. Rather than advocate political changes that might have broader impact for refugees as a whole—for example, by raising the annual refugee quotas or opposing U.S. militarism—the HONY community stays focused on the individuals they have deemed worthy of sympathy and care. Furthermore, through this process, Muslim refugees are individually assessed via Stanton's posts and commenters' responses to distinguish them from a potential threat. As such, the HONY community produces itself as not only a moral community but also a community of vetters who can assess the worthiness of Muslim refugees for their attention and care.

Analyzing *top comments* (with more than one thousand reactions and showing at the top of the comment feed) on Aya's and Hamo's photostories, I found that even as occasional comments name the United States as contributing to conditions that have produced displacements, there is never a suggestion that this community could organize to advocate a shift in U.S. policies. For example, Kristina Collins writes a lengthy critique of the Bush-led invasion of Iraq, saying, "Saddam was a terrible dictator but what we created was 100 times worse than what he did there. . . . A war created under false pretenses and it took 10 more years to get to the one who actually attacked our towers. From the shambles ISIS was created and allowed to rise to power and so many want to turn their backs on what we helped create."[85] However, the few top comments like this do not build to a call for broad political change. This is despite the fact that the power of the HONY community is widely recognized among his followers. In February 2015, Stanton was able to raise more than a million dollars to fund students at a predominantly African American Brooklyn school to visit Harvard University.[86] A few months later, Stanton raised another million

dollars to support the work of a Pakistani activist seeking the emancipation of bonded laborers.[87] As such, followers of HONY are aware of this
potential for action when engaging HONY, a platform they see as connecting millions of people who could be activated through the right image and
story.

As Nish notes, transformation of self is centered over transformation
of "the relevant structures of power . . . through which refugees' precarity is
reproduced."[88] Top comments suggest that Aya's and Hamo's photo-stories
are broadly experienced as a means to reestablish one's own values by recognizing the humanity of others. This dynamic is articulated in mundane
terms—"these refugees are really making me motivated to work harder in
my life and career"[89]—or national terms, such as "you are our salvation
to being human again. . . . Have faith in our fellow Americans, they will
rise up and be the amazing people that I believe they can be."[90] HONY's
project becomes the redemption of America, one person at a time, as expressed in the twenty-five thousand reactions garnered by the comment "a
month ago, I was against refugees coming to America. HONY has single-
handedly broken down that so-very-wrong viewpoint."[91] By centering the
transformation of themselves, they also resonate with the message that "it
is because 'we' feel this way that refugees are worthy of 'our' attention," in
Chouliaraki and Stolic's framework of "visibility as self-reflexivity."[92]

Individual and collectively organized offers of assistance further mark
Hamo and Aya as exceptional refugees worthy of care. Commenters offer
direct assistance, for example, offering Hamo medical help and inviting
Aya to apply for a scholarship to study in the United States. One commenter provides Aya detailed instructions on how to take a dog across
national borders. Stanton also organizes collective responses, such as a December 13, 2015, Change.org petition titled "Let's Bring Aya to America,"
described as an "invitation" to Obama to learn about Aya's case as she seeks
an appeal of her rejection.[93] On Christmas Eve, Stanton initiated a fund-
raiser for the eleven families portrayed in the Syrian Americans series, raising more than $700,000 in three days.[94] Hamo was also the recipient of at
least two other fund-raising efforts, one led by the actor Edward Norton,
raising $400,000, and another by an individual in Troy, Michigan, raising
$12,000.[95] These activities further separated Hamo and Aya from the other
nine profiles in the Syrian Americans series, making them exceptional
among this already exceptional group of refugees who had been admitted

to the United States. While there is occasional recognition of the inadequacy of these responses—for example, one commenter exclaims, "What about the others? And what about their homes?"[96]—such statements do not produce in the forum suggestions for broader action.

While Stanton holds up individuals as worthy of sympathy, he struggles with and yet still reinforces the framework of assessment used to determine the acceptability of Muslims as refugees. On a December 12 appearance on CNN's *On GPS*, Stanton makes an impassioned plea for Aya, saying the United States is being too selective in who it allows to enter, his voice cracking with emotion.[97] Four days later, on a PBS *NewsHour* segment, Stanton addresses some of the challenges of telling these stories: that although they are stories of individuals, millions more are suffering who do not have the opportunity to tell their stories. He argues that the United States is being too selective, noting that the few Syrian refugees accepted to the United States were exceedingly exceptional, with PhDs, a major disability, or a serious health condition needing immediate attention. While Stanton's profile of Aya represents her as highly exceptional as well, her application rejection forces him to contend with the limitations of the logic of exceptionality. His plea for Aya shifts to a plea for other refugees:

> Yes, she's just one person. But she's also representative of so many people that are in a similar situation that don't have the benefit of speaking English, that don't have the benefit of speaking for themselves and telling their own stories. These are smart, educated people who through no fault of their own are just languishing in near homelessness.[98]

Even here, however, Stanton must offer an assessment of these other refugees as "smart, educated people" lacking any "fault" in their circumstances. While Stanton is attempting to broaden the parameters of acceptability for refugees, he and the entire HONY project nevertheless reinforce the logic of assessment, whether it takes the official form of refugee vetting or the unofficial form of profiling individuals against the standards by which Muslims can be deemed acceptable. Unsurprisingly, despite the immense trust Stanton's followers seem to have in him, skeptics suggest that perhaps Stanton himself has failed to adequately vet Aya. Anna L'Abbate, for example, emphasizes the vetting undertaken by the U.S. government: "I have a feeling the father's situation has a lot do why the family is being denied entry into the US. Remember, a lot of background work goes into assessing their application."[99] Whether commenters align with Stanton's assessment or not, however, they share an assumption that refugees who "do everything right" or who are "motivated and hardworking" are worthy of sympathy and support, while others are not.

If the HONY community chooses to do so, they have the power to transform a person's life; therefore assessment of a person's worthiness for sympathy and support becomes a powerful task of the HONY community. While these HONY series do humanize refugees, they also reinforce population racism that demands that Muslims be assessed in terms of their worthiness and risk of threat, bringing forward exceptional individuals who can garner sympathy within the U.S. context. While these representations may raise the profile of refugees, they also reinforce the set of measures through which Muslim refugees' acceptability must be established. In fact, to the extent that Hamo and Aya are distinguished from other refugees, they do more to promote their own cases than to produce feelings of responsibility for refugees as a whole. HONY's emphasis on person-to-person connections results in further separation of these more prominent subjects, who become recipients of much more intense care and advocacy than any other refugees profiled. Rather than establish ties of complicity and responsibility between different contexts and populations, given U.S. militarism and imperialism, HONY garners responses of individualized pity or compassion based on compelling personal narratives by refugees who can attest to their own individual worthiness. Ultimately, an avowedly apolitical and humanizing discourse reveals itself to be complicit in the racialization of Muslims as a population of risk, one that must be vetted to establish their acceptability in the United States and imbricated with U.S. patriotism and militarism.

ALTERNATIVES TO LIBERAL INDIVIDUALISM: POSSIBILITIES FOR HUMANIZING POPULATIONS

While HONY offers a highly individualistic, voluntarist model of human connection and responsibility built on the portrayal of the refugee as innocent, worthy victim, Ai Weiwei's documentary film, *Human Flow*, builds a feeling of human mutuality through a portrayal of refugees as a population.[100] While the liberal focus on the individual narrative and identifying the worthy victim operates as a mode of assessing and policing Muslims and other refugee populations, Ai's film suggests a nonindividualized, non-narrativized model of building feelings of connection and responsibility for the conditions of life of human populations. I end the chapter with an analysis of Ai's film not to suggest that it is an exemplary representation of refugees but rather because I see it as abiding by some of the same humanitarian conventions of apolitical engagement and witnessing, and yet breaking with one key convention of documentary realism predominant in HONY: telling the stories of "unique" individuals. Ai's work also has broad reach and seeks to represent refugees from the "outside," as an observer, notwithstanding his own claims to identification with a refugee experience. In contrast, the work of Abounaddara, a Syrian filmmaking collective that released films approximately weekly from 2011 to 2017, offers a rich body of work that documents human hardship and resilience through everyday experiences, caused by the Syrian Civil War, while also representing community life and a contested political terrain. Even as Abounaddara's work is far more complex and informative, it requires a level of audience knowledge and engagement that neither HONY nor *Human Flow* assumes. The latter two, made for U.S. and European audiences, offer for my purposes a useful contrast point in illustrating the limitations of individualized representations in countering racist stereotypes, given the logics of population racism that I have analyzed throughout this book. *Human Flow,* I argue, offers an example of how the material and ideological construction of human populations could be represented, challenging racializing frameworks of assessment prevalent in liberal discourses. Refusing to separate those worthy of sympathy from other sufferers, *Human Flow* asks viewers to see moving populations as fundamentally human and thematizes the production of the population of refugees. Although *Human Flow,* like HONY, maintains distance from questions of the specific causes of such displacements, including the roles of U.S. and European powers in promoting neoliberal economics and decades-long wars, its approach allows for the greater possibility of recognizing connectivity, difference, and responsibility between people.

Ai, a globally known Chinese artist with a large body of work spanning three decades and often engaging social and political issues, has an immense following. He has also been the recipient of scathing critique, including that his recent body of work profits from or sensationalizes the suffering of refugees.[101] His restaging of the Aylan Kurdi image, taking the form of showing Ai lying face-down in the same position as the child, was condemned as reducing the horror of the child's death to an aestheticized and self-centered portrayal of the artist.[102] I observed his 2017–18 *Good Fences Make Good Neighbors* installations throughout New York City, appreciating the integration of refugee experiences into the urban landscape, while feeling dissatisfied with the message that fences or cages with doors and passageways could form the basis of a more "humane" border security system. Ai's body of work on migrants and refugees is vast and varied, and a thorough engagement with the politics of representation of this work is beyond the scope of my analysis. Hence I present my reading of *Human Flow* not to make a statement about Ai's aesthetic or political choices more broadly, nor even to argue that the film radically challenges existing discourses on refugees; rather, it serves as a wide-reaching example of nonindividualized and nonnarrativized representation that brings forth the experiences and humanity of populations without reinforcing an assessment-oriented disposition that contributes to population racism.

In some regards, *Human Flow* seems to shirk many of the humanizing conventions that Chouliaraki describes, particularly the focus on the individual as agent who tells her own story. The film's at times highly aestheticized representation of refugees as masses and flows of human bodies aligns with seeing refugees as biological life in need of assistance. People are filmed as moving lines or large sedentary collectives; the camps are filmed from above, as rows and rows of identical tents in a sterile landscape. On one occasion, people appear as dots on a landscape that slowly take human form as the drone camera moves closer to the ground. These images of flows and masses, however, are interspersed with the close-up, including a series of awkwardly shot silent images of one person after another standing, as if posing for a picture that is never taken. These particular individuals, however, are never given voices. The narratives that are conveyed in brief interviews are fragmented and decontextualized, never presenting the viewer with a complete story of a single individual. However, in refusing to take up the coherent individual and the story as the heart of the humanization, *Human Flow* suggests possibilities for seeing humanity as population and the refugee experience as a central ethical question of our time.

FIGURE 12. Still from *Human Flow* by Ai Weiwei. Participant Media and Amazon Studios, 2017.

FIGURE 13. Still from *Human Flow* by Ai Weiwei. Participant Media and Amazon Studios, 2017.

Whether represented through the individual or the collective, in movement or stationary, the refugees are still agents, managing under dire conditions, and mostly surviving. In one scene, a line of moving migrants arrives at a rough, cold river they must wade cross. Early attempts are unsuccessful as bags are lost and float downstream. As we keep watching, the line becomes better populated and more organized as people work together to traverse the river. In a similar spirit, in the camps, the film shows people fortifying their tents with extra plastic, doing their laundry in buckets, and staying connected via cell phones charging on generators. One repeated image is of groups of refugees forced to sit on the ground, usually due to the demands of police and immigration agents. However, in the face of the threat of being pushed back into Turkey, groups of men sit on the ground and hold up signs that read "EU don't send us back," "Am I human," and "Respect." The repeated images of seated passive refugees now become a seated protest, a refusal to move, and a demand for recognition. Some of the more disturbing scenes show the treatment of refugees from Africa, distinguished from the Arab, Afghani, and Iranian refugees by their skin color, who are made to line up, wearing matching white overalls; ordered around; and subject to medical inspection before being placed on busses. These images are intercut with commentary from Hanan Ashrawi, the Palestinian leader and activist, who defines being a refugee as

> the most pervasive kind of cruelty that can be exercised against a human being, by depriving the person of all forms of security, the most basic requirements of a normal life, by cruelly placing that person at the mercy sometimes of very inhospitable host countries that do not want to receive this refugee, you are forcibly robbing this human being of all aspects that would make human life not just tolerable but meaningful in many ways.[103]

This juxtaposition suggests that dehumanization for the refugee does not take place only, or primarily, through spectacular acts of violence but rather through the persistent disregard of one's personhood and the treatment of a person as a thing to be inspected and managed, at times in the guise of humanitarian procedures.

The film's refusal to represent any single individual "fully" acts in part as acknowledgment of the impossibility of representing trauma. It also speaks to the fact that such representations sensationalize the pain of others for the benefit of the spectator's growth. While traumatic experiences are mentioned in passing, their full impact is left unexplored. There are, however, inklings of the bodily impact of these traumas, for example, in a scene showing a woman from behind and at several feet distance, who has just been telling of her difficult travels with her son. Only a few sentences in, she breaks off and vomits into a bucket. With the camera running, Ai sits with her, offers her some paper towels, then gives her some space, but we never return to complete her story. The scene speaks to Clough's claim that "the traumatic event is an unsymbolizable event and, being severed from language, becomes a bodily memory."[104] No part of what she has conveyed is distinctly horrifying, and we will never know what caused her bodily response, and yet there is no denying that the refugee experience produces trauma.

The absence of any complete narrative also refuses to grant the audience the power to judge the individuals portrayed as worthy or unworthy of sympathy. As such, the film does not traffic in variables of assessment, which place Muslim refugees against some distinct set of standards by which they can be deemed sympathetic or tolerable. There is no effort made to show that these refugees are educated or hardworking. Their cultural values are not erased, and some do make references to God and their faith. Their cultural values are also not emphasized as either aligning with or contradicting Western values. Rather, the interspersing of poetry and quotations from writers from a range of cultures speaks to that possibility that all cultures create beauty and insight. The women are neither distinctly submissive and oppressed, even as there is mention of sexual assault, nor Westernized feminists railing against their culture. This is in part simply because Ai is not seeking answers to these questions and is not operating within these frameworks of assessment. There are no exceptional victims here; all are worthy of sympathy simply due to their humanity and circumstances. Furthermore, Ai's focus is almost entirely on the experience of being displaced, rather than on the initial violence that caused the displacement. Rather than attest to the legitimacy of anyone's claim that he deserves refuge because of a fear of persecution, Ai focuses on what responsibility societies have to those at their doorsteps seeking more viable life conditions.

In place of sensational scenes of horrifying brutality that are repeated in the HONY stories, ones that most viewers cannot fathom except as spectacle, Ai offers an image of a persistent grinding down of humanity through active negligence and exclusion. Many of the hardships Ai shows are more intense versions of experiences many people are likely to have had: people endlessly walking, carrying children and bags, tolerating constant cold and wet, sleeping in tents, and standing in hours-long lines for bowls of soup. While the viewer may not fully understand how the accumulation of these experiences affects a person, the existence of a point of connection allows viewers to stay with the film. Yet the film is unrelenting, lasting two hours and twenty minutes and showing innumerable people experiencing constant challenges. Even within this broader context of ever-present hardship, Ai attunes the viewer to the minutiae of everyday life. In one moment, we are watching a woman care for her child, whom she has stand on an inflated tube to keep his socked feet dry as he puts on winter boots. In another, a woman shows photographs on her cell phone: one of her cat, who has come with her on the journey, and another of her brother, who is still in Syria. These experiences, whether challenging or mundane, add up to a view of the lives of refugees as dramatically shaped by hostile social and political structures, and yet continuing on.

Where the film reaches the limit of providing a full account of the ties of responsibility between the viewer, particularly a European or American one, and refugees is in its somewhat ambivalent acceptance of an apolitical stance that treats human mobility through the frame of crisis. Europe's relationship to the "refugee crisis" is entirely in the present as recipients, rather than as already intertwined and implicated through historical and present-day ties of colonialism, imperialism, and asymmetrical political, economic, and military relations. The film maintains the divide Chouliaraki describes between spectator and sufferer, separating Europeans from people of the Global South, particularly South Asia, the Middle East, and Africa, and does not provide information about how that divide is produced and maintained. It therefore naturalizes the refugee crisis as tragedy, rather than a series of events with political grounding that implies possibilities for prevention or mitigation. However, Ai's inclusion of the long-term displacement of Palestinians, generations of whom have been born and raised in refugee camps, and a repeated point that the average length of being a refugee is twenty-six years, acknowledges that for most refugees, the status is not temporary; the "crisis" is persistent. As such, the film also disrupts a notion that this is a temporary state of emergency, which suggests that a deeper analysis of the causes and perpetuators of the displacement, movement, and confinement of populations is necessary.

Furthermore, the film does offer a scathing image of the effects of the EU–Turkey deal of March 2016, which enforced the return of asylum seekers arriving from Turkey, in return for which Turkey was given six billion euros in aid money. Ai shows the immediate tangible effects of the policy on refugees, including the violent closure of camps and coerced movement of people, who consistently opposed the forced transfer. The film also offers another kind of implicit analysis, beginning in Europe but moving back and forth between Europe and the Global South, showing that the scope of human displacement is much broader than what the West has been interested to see, with countries of the Global South taking up a much greater burden. A few horrifying scenes from Iraq of enormous fires, desolate landscapes, a charred body—perhaps the most sensational in the film—also give a hint of the scope of the devastation wars have wreaked, a devastation rarely shown to U.S. viewers. Europe emerges as an insular fortress seeking to protect itself, while effectively losing any claims to a cosmopolitan or humanistic ethic. As a result, the film does not allow its European or U.S. audiences to imagine themselves as the benevolent saviors, in stark contrast to the feeling produced through HONY for its "community."

This reading of *Human Flow* is not intended to be a counterpoint to HONY in the sense of offering the right way to represent Muslim refugees. No single representation can be burdened with the responsibility of portraying any experience or group of people fully or with complete nuance. However, I present *Human Flow* to disrupt the predominant liberal assumptions that shape the conventions of humanization and to raise the possibility of other approaches. Through my analysis of HONY, I argue that stories of Muslim refugees that fit within a paradigm of liberal humanitarianism can function as a technology of assessment. In presenting stories of acceptable or exceptional refugees, as a means of producing sympathy for the refugee experience, HONY reinforces a notion that one must know and assess Muslim refugees. As such, it reinforces a population racism that portrays Muslims as a population that contains within it a distinct threat. This humanization may counter stereotypes on an individual level, but it does not challenge a notion that vetting is necessary. Downplaying the ties of responsibility between the United States and the countries it has invaded or destabilized, Muslims are expected to support U.S. militarism. It also reinforces a perception that critique of U.S. imperialism from Muslims is always suspect as an indicator of potential support for terrorism. While

Human Flow does not offer a direct political analysis, it also does not pre-judge or preclude analysis of the relations of power. If humanization is the production of ties of mutuality and reciprocity, ties that are necessary for solidarity, then *Human Flow* offers a possibility for humanizing refugees as populations as an alternative to the liberal focus on the unique story of the individual.

Conclusion

On the last evening of the July 2016 Democratic National Convention, about an hour before Hillary Clinton would accept the party's nomination for president, Khizr Khan, a Pakistani immigrant and Muslim American man, delivered one of the most memorable speeches of the convention. Viewed by an estimated thirty million people across the United States, the speech quickly went viral, remaining in the headlines over the next week. The speech was an exquisitely delivered rebuke of much that Trump stood for among liberals. In the face of Trump's bigotry and fearmongering, Khan embodied and articulated an alternative vision of U.S. society, one that returned to the "founding" values of liberty, equality before law, religious freedom, and service to country, updated through a multicultural version of militarism and patriotism. In one of the most commented-upon moments, Khan, speaking directly to Trump, said, "Let me ask you: have you even read the United States Constitution?"[1] Removing from his breast pocket a miniature Constitution, he added, "I will gladly lend you my copy," as the audience whooped and whistled. It was an undeniably powerful moment. Carrying a Constitution where some might expect the Qur'an, an unknown Muslim immigrant educated the bigoted Republican presidential candidate about the "true" values of this country. As the refugee crisis was manipulated by Republicans to foment fear and animosity toward Muslims, the Democratic Party responded by putting forward a Muslim American to attack Trump.

Underneath this moment, plainly for everyone to see, was an affective and ideological infrastructure that granted Khizr Khan the podium from which to speak. The speech was preceded by a video recounting the life of Khan's son, U.S. Army captain Humayun Khan, who had died in Iraq in June 2004, when defending his unit from a suicide attack. Khan's speech also deftly positioned his family within the narrow parameters of acceptable Muslims, introducing himself and his wife, Ghazala Khan, who stood beside him, "as patriotic American Muslims . . . with undivided loyalty to our country." He told of arriving to the United States "empty handed" but believing that they could succeed "with hard work and goodness of this country." The ultimate proof of their patriotism, however, was in their son's willingness to "sacrifice . . . his life to save the lives of his fellow soldiers," earning Clinton's praise as "the best of America." Khan's claim to the podium rested on his identification as a patriotic American Muslim and also on the tangible evidence of that claim, a dead child, a Muslim sacrificed in the line of duty. The speech then pivoted to an attack on Trump's Muslim ban that would keep families like the Khans out and his derision of people of different faiths and ethnicities, despite the diversity of those buried in Arlington National Cemetery. Impassioned, with a finger pointing for emphasis, and garnering large applause, Khan admonished Trump, "You have sacrificed nothing and no one." Khan powerfully maneuvered his family's Muslimness—cast out by the likes of Trump—to bring attention to the Trump family's lack of appropriate patriotism, including lack of military service and rejection of multiculturalism.

More fundamentally, however, violence was the groundwork upon which Khan's performance of the good Muslim was possible, particularly the violence of U.S. imperial wars. The innocence of U.S. militarism was assumed, even though the attack that took the life of Khan's son, an occupying soldier, occurred a month after the U.S. military's pervasive sexualized torture of Iraqis in Abu Ghraib prison became widely known. Nevertheless, ethical ambiguities about the U.S. role in Iraq are swept away, and Khan's speech effectively legitimates the U.S. role in Iraq, its bombing campaign, prisoner torture, countless civilian deaths, and destruction of society. The speech was followed by numerous military speakers representing war as defending liberalism from threat and Clinton as fit to be commander in chief, while over the course of the convention, there was little mention of the millions of refugees produced through these wars.[2]

Khan's enactment of the patriotic Muslim American also rested on the violence of the American Dream narrative and the notion of the United States as a multicultural land of immigrants. These narratives erase the history of the formation of the United States via settler colonialism, including Indigenous genocide and the enslavement of Africans, a violence that formed the basis of White private property and generational wealth. The narrative of the United States as a nation of immigrants and land of opportunity erases not only the violent foundations of the nation but also the continuation of these systems of domination through normalized violation of Native sovereignty and the persistence of state-sanctioned anti-Black violence and exploitation. Economic success attained by some immigrant communities, often dubbed "model minorities," requires an aspiration toward and an alliance with Whiteness. At the same time, the War on Terror, which has been mobilized toward a broader war on immigrants, parallels the War on Drugs in producing domestic and global populations subject to militarized policing, detentions, incarcerations, deportations, and displacements. The role of the "good Muslim" requires an unquestioned acceptance of this legacy and the willingness to uphold white supremacy and its institutions, structures, and logics.

Nevertheless, Khan was not entirely immune to a counterattack, and unsurprisingly, Trump mobilized two variables of assessment particular to Muslims, sexism and violence, to undermine Khan's status and claims. In an interview with George Stephanopoulos, Trump insinuated that Khan was oppressing his wife, saying, "She had nothing to say. She probably—maybe she wasn't allowed to have anything to say."[3] Despite the irony of Trump suggesting that another man is sexist, it is clear that the problem of sexism sticks to Muslim men differently than to White, Christian men. Whereas Trump's domination over women is regarded as a presumed, if contested, benefit of White male power, a Muslim immigrant man's quiet wife casts that man as barbaric. The accusation was powerful enough that it required a response, in the form of a *Washington Post* article by Ghazala Khan explaining why she had chosen not to speak.[4] Trump also defended his Muslim ban against Khan's critiques by evoking a stereotype of Muslims as inherently violent: "we have had a lot of problems with radical Islamic terrorism," referencing attacks in San Bernardino, Orlando, and Paris, concluding, "something is going on and it's not good."[5] Despite the ambiguity of the connection of these attacks to the millions of people restricted by the proposed Muslim ban, Stephanopoulos did not seek further clarification. Nevertheless, Trump was widely criticized for his response to Khan, but not on the grounds I have noted here. Rather, he was perceived as failing to give due respect to a military family who had made the ultimate sacrifice, reinforcing the narrow terms upon which Muslims were deemed tolerable or sympathetic.

This book traverses two decades beginning with the initiation of the War on Terror as a war "for civilization" and ending with the rise of Trump through the white nationalist motto of "Make America Great Again." Trump's rejection of state-sponsored multiculturalism, which was threaded through both George W. Bush's and Obama's framings of the War on Terror, marked an abandonment of discourses of tolerance or sympathy. While some initially saw the election of Obama as evidence of the triumph of U.S. multiculturalism and the emergence of a post-racial society, the ensuing right-wing backlash became the groundwork for Trump's anti-immigrant, anti-Black, and U.S. nationalist campaign. Trump also tapped into and amplified a circulating distrust and animosity of Muslims, building on the work of an organized and well-funded Islamophobia Industry that promoted fear of all Muslim Americans, such as through the Park51 controversy.[6] Moreover, the election of Donald Trump, as part of the global rise of right-wing populism, nativism, and explicit racism, was an outgrowth of decades of neoliberal policies and warfare supported by liberals and conservatives. Such policies have produced greater economic inequality, unfolding environmental crises, and large population displacements, and racialized migrants have become one of the key scapegoats of rising right-wing movements. Even as some look back with nostalgia at the "compassionate conservatism" of George W. Bush or the multiracial romance of the Obama era, their policies at home and abroad failed to achieve the freedom and prosperity they promised, laying the groundwork for the confrontational politics of resentment that followed.

In the face of the right's increasingly racist rhetoric, liberal responses—like the image of the Muslim woman in the American flag hijab that I described in the first pages of this book, the platform given to Khizr Khan, or the stories and images of refugees circulated by Humans of New York—emphasized Muslims as "upstanding" individuals, culturally and politically loyal to the United States. Such multicultural visions offer support for the existence of Muslims within the United States but fall far short of opposing anti-Muslim racism. As I have argued, such liberal defenses reinforce an assessment orientation toward Muslims that justifies their surveillance and policing in the United States and at the borders, while acquiescing to warfare and neglect in relation to Muslim populations abroad. In these final pages, I connect the central threads of my different cases to consider how liberal discourse about Muslims in the United States and in Muslim-majority societies interact to racialize Muslims in the War on Terror. I conclude by considering various methods of challenging such dynamics of racialization, including by refusing the application of variables of assessment to broaden the public space for fuller engagement with diverse Muslims and Muslim Americans. With an understanding of anti-Muslim racism as a deeply rooted element of U.S. imperialism linking global and domestic realms, and irreducible to religious intolerance, U.S. progressives can construct a more effective counternarrative to the constructed threat of "Islamic terrorism" that casts Muslims as a population of risk and justifies ongoing wars at home and abroad.

"HERE" AND "THERE"

The racialization of Muslims is produced through dynamic interactions of representations in various contexts of "here" in the United States and "there" in Muslim-majority societies. Whereas a strongly delineated us–them conception is produced through discourses of sympathy in relation to Muslims abroad, more ambivalent and assessment-focused discourses of tolerance are predominant in relation to Muslim Americans. This contrast is in part a reflection of the fact that the War on Terror has been a global war with overlapping, yet variable, tactics addressing the international and domestic fronts. Discourses of sympathy toward Muslim-majority societies tend to produce a stark line delineating "us" from "them," in part by redrawing this line to bring some sympathetic Muslims over to "our" side. While these discourses produce identification with some Muslims, generally victims of violence within their own societies, this sympathy produces an enemy that is all the more malevolent and barbaric, justifying a by-any-means-necessary response. On the domestic front, closeness creates anxiety and the need to control and police, manifested in an impulse to inculcate the ability to see and measure the threat. While this threat is largely perceived as originating over "there" through Islamist ideologies, it is also perceived to be active and hiding over "here" through the formation of "homegrown" terrorists. Just as Americans are reminded to be the eyes of the state and to monitor their surroundings for "suspicious activities or packages," as announcements on public transportation repeat, discourses of tolerance toward Muslims in the United States offer a range of interacting variables by which their trustworthiness or threat can be measured.

What have representations of "here" done for the global War on Terror "there"? Articulations of U.S. tolerance for Muslims in the United States were initially important in justifying U.S. military incursions and its broader War on Terror, as a war for freedom and not against Islam. As this imperative of the War on Terror decreased, in part through the entrenchment and normalization of the war, the claims for U.S. tolerance diminished. The extension of the warfront to the domestic sphere was justified through exaggerated fears of self-radicalized terrorists and no longer required the counterbalance of tolerance discourses. Rather, the intolerance and untrustworthiness of Muslims in the United States became a justification for the expansion of the domestic front of the War on Terror. When patriotic Muslim Americans were put forward, it was no longer toward justifying the War on Terror but rather toward a performative multiculturalism circulating liberal values to garner attention in the United States, while obfuscating global geopolitical realities.

Conversely, what have representations of "there" done for the surveillance and policing of Muslims "here"? Variables of assessment are more starkly articulated in representations of "there." Gender inequality, homophobia, religious intolerance, and anti-U.S. politics have been most effectively produced as Muslim risk factors through highly selective and insufficiently contextualized representations of Muslim-majority societies. Instances of violence against girls, women, LGBTQ people, or non-Muslims in Muslim-majority societies have been represented as a reflection of a fundamental cultural/religious/political difference. These narratives of Muslim-majority societies delineate the riskiness of Muslim populations, producing powerful variables of assessment that are used to measure the threat of individual Muslims in the U.S. context. Despite all the evidence that Almontaser and Abdul Rauf abided by the narrow parameters of acceptability for Muslims demonstrated not only through their words but also through their years of work, their continued association with a Muslim population, conceived in global terms, left them vulnerable to attack. Sexist, homophobic, or anti-Semitic remarks—or those construed as such—may be deemed an objectionable part of a Christian Right worldview but, in the mouth of a Muslim, come to indicate complicity with irrational, barbaric violence and a potential for terrorism. These representations produce a view that Muslims are incapable of tolerating that with which they disagree, despite much evidence to the contrary.

While my cases are treated separately in the book, these connections between them suggest the importance of understanding the racialization of Muslims produced in a global arena. The intimate interrelation between representations of Muslims here and Muslims abroad suggests that any politically calculated attempt to divorce the former from the latter is likely to fail. Therefore it becomes essential to bring to light the political points of view, perspectives, and rationalities that shape the actions and beliefs of Muslims both "here" and "there," especially those whose perspectives one does not understand or opposes. In the following section, I draw out additional insights my project offers for countering the racializing dynamics of liberal discourses of tolerance and sympathy.

RESISTING LIBERAL RACISM

My analysis unsettles the assumptions of many well-intentioned journalists, activists, and social scientists that the best way to counter stereotype-fueled bigotry is to show misunderstood identities in a truer light that captures their diversity. While certainly there is value to endeavors to give voice to more people and diversify representations, such work can reinforce problematic assumptions about Muslims as a population. To resist complicity in this process of racialization, liberals and leftists need to interrogate the terms on which Muslims are made acceptable. Even as these discourses counter representations of Muslim Americans as a monolithic and threatening population, they can participate in disseminating a technology of assessment that casts Muslims as a population of risk. The questions repeatedly asked of Muslims—on women's rights, LGBTQ rights, religion, U.S. foreign policy, and so on—make evident and further circulate the variables deemed necessary to assess that risk. We need to think creatively about how to interrupt the fast circulation of variables of assessment to dislodge their distinct associations with Muslims, while also creating more representations of Muslims that do not traffic in these variables. More fundamentally, it is necessary to examine prevalent Orientalist, colonialist assumptions that undergird anti-Muslim racism, an endeavor that requires a deeper and more nuanced engagement with the histories and struggles within Muslim-majority societies and in Muslim communities in the United States and Europe. Finally, with greater understanding of the harms caused by the narrow parameters of acceptability for Muslims, there also needs to be greater commitment to protecting Muslim public figures, rejecting the application of narrow litmus tests, and creating space to engage and understand positions we find challenging.

Liberals have taken a podium to defend the public sphere from the "cancel culture" of social media, where the failure to abide by specific norms can lead to rapid assessments and loss of privileges, but liberals have generally failed to examine the material and discursive power relations enacted in those encounters. Outcry against a high-profile individual perpetuating malice toward a less powerful community must be distinguished from the kinds of attacks Muslim public figures have experienced, often due to their association with political views cast as taboo. The fall of Debbie Almontaser had serious implications not only for her but also for the school and the community she represented. Even liberal defenders of Almontaser conveyed a message that the linguistic knowledge and political beliefs of many Arab and Muslim New Yorkers were irrelevant to the public debate. Therefore, while articulations of tolerance disavow explicit racism, they do not create space for a diverse range of Muslims to participate in public life. This is most obvious in the inability, or resistance, of purveyors of tolerance to making the anti-imperialist politics of many Muslims in the United States and abroad legible. As such, discourses of tolerance function more to establish the commitment to liberal values of those who "tolerate" or "sympathize" than to substantively engage the lives and beliefs of those they seek to represent.

Variables of assessment function in highly fragmented ways, manipulated in a media milieu where the goal is audience activation. While such speedy assessments must be interrupted, we also should not romanticize an imagined public sphere of rational debate between equals, which has never existed. Rather, it may be more effective to recognize the potential role of social media in experimental, but conscientious, forms of activism that aim to produce new associations and open up pathways for the acquisition of new forms of knowledge. Taking inspiration from the impact of media-savvy activist movements that have successfully shifted the terms of debate on intersecting social movements, including Occupy Wall Street, Black Lives Matter, and the #MeToo movement, activism to disrupt anti-Muslim racism could adopt methods that are emotionally and aesthetically attuned and capable of garnering attention to move publics. Such activists would also need to be conscious of and creatively undercut the role of liberal sensibilities in perpetuating anti-Muslim racism. Since representations of Muslims are most likely to circulate when they engage the stereotypes beneath variables of assessment—either by abiding by or negating the stereotypes—one method may be to turn the variables of assessment onto others. Moving the variables, like misogyny or the propensity toward irrational ideological violence, in ways that associate them with new objects might undercut their power and demonstrate the speciousness of their apparently uniquely problematic association with Muslims. Such interruptions of the circulation of variables of assessment would be important, even as the temporality of the media and activism is not always conducive to deeper shifts in understanding.

Such deeper shifts depend on interrogating the assumptions beneath representations of Muslims. Even when the information circulating about Muslims is accurate, it is often interpreted through preexisting frameworks that produce systemic and interested misunderstandings. Therefore it is also necessary to challenge the more fundamental ideological infrastructure that undergirds anti-Muslim racism, including the exceptionalism that presumes religion and culture to be determinant in Muslim-majority contexts and the Orientalist construct that produces what Edward Said termed the "flexible positional superiority" of the West.[7] This oppositional construct takes different forms yet consistently positions the "West" as modern, secular, and rational, relative to Muslim-majority societies, which are cast as irrationally controlled by backward cultures and anti-modern Islamic/Islamist ideologies. As Said and others have articulated, it is essential to reiterate that there are no civilizations, no discrete self-contained cultural entities. It is necessary to question the primary causal role given to a monolithic understanding of culture that does not account for political and economic struggles. Furthermore, as Mamdani argues, terrorism cannot be explained as an expression of culture or, even more specifically, religious extremism; rather, "terrorism is born of a *political* encounter."[8] Similarly, as Haj has said,

> today's Islamists and their actions have to be simply explained in the context of modern politics and institutions rather than as having originated in Islam or the Wahhabiya dynasty. . . . The point is not to deny either the zealotry or the violence of any of these movements but to try and understand their violent actions not as something fixed and inevitable but as the product of historical events and social and political forces.[9]

It is important to focus attention on those political encounters that produce state and nonstate violence, while disrupting a binary opposition between Islam/Islamism and secularism, in order to recognize the linkages and continuities between ostensibly religious and secular violence.

Responses to anti-Muslim racism can highlight the connections across different forms of state violence and repression, not to equate them, but to disrupt the oppositional construct of "Islam" and "the West." When U.S. hikers Shane Bauer and Josh Fattal spoke, following two years in an Iranian prison after their arrest for crossing the Iraq–Iran border, both emphasized that solitary confinement was the most cruel part of their experience—as Bauer said, it was a form of "psychological torture."[10] They in turn drew on their experiences to articulate their solidarity with thousands of California prisoners who were on hunger strike, in part opposing the extensive use of solitary confinement. Bauer also noted that every day, approximately twenty thousand people are in solitary confinement in the United States. These statements undercut anti-Muslim racism by noting the similarities in forms of state repression in Iran and the United States, while lodging critiques of both Iranian and U.S. carceral systems. A media-focused activism can find ways of maximizing such moments, when an unpredictable confluence of events creates an opening, to disrupt circulating associations and dominant narratives that reinforce anti-Muslim racism.

It is also essential to refuse the constant assessments of Muslims in relation to the particular set of variables that are articulated in my case studies. The most pernicious of these, because it tends to be the most deci-sive in marking someone as trustworthy or threatening, is the question of loyalty to the United States. Participating in these forms of assessment only reinforces their legitimacy and perpetuates the circulation of these vari-ables of interest. Furthermore, on a practical level, as the Park51 contro-versy demonstrated, even being a pro-capitalist, patriotic "man of peace" who promoted U.S. interests abroad was not enough to mark Abdul Rauf as worthy of trust. Therefore it is necessary to ask other questions and high-light characteristics that are outside the binaries of religiosity–secularism, gender equality–gender oppression, sexual liberation–sexual repression, patriotism–disloyalty, and so on. That is not to say that such topics are off-limits when they are of actual direct relevance; rather, it is to say that Muslims should not be judged by distinct standards simply because they are Muslim. Ultimately, rather than focusing on representing particular Muslims as worthy of tolerance or sympathy, it is more important to chal-lenge cultural assumptions that make such assessments of Muslims seem necessary.

A shifting political and cultural landscape, including the emergence of antiracist, antisexist, anticapitalist social movements, and the growing strength of the progressive wing of the Democratic Party are producing a new context for Muslim American public figures and politics more broadly. The year 2018 saw the election of the most diverse U.S. Congress, includ-ing an unprecedented number of women and people of color and the first two Muslim women. Rashida Tlaib of Michigan is a child of Palestinian immigrants, and Ilhan Omar of Minnesota is a Somali American who came to the United States as a refugee. Both Tlaib and Omar have rejected the narrow role for Muslim American public figures, staking out political posi-tions that have been treacherous for high-profile Muslims, particularly by critiquing U.S. foreign policy and the U.S. alliance with Israel. Omar has been particularly vilified as a Black, hijab-wearing, Muslim woman who, as a member of the House Foreign Affairs Committee, has been vocal on foreign policy issues. While Trump has cast these and other congress-women of color as perpetual foreigners who should "go back" to the "crime infested places from which they came,"[11] Omar and Tlaib have refused to articulate their belonging through a narrow script of upholding U.S. impe-rialism, which has been demanded of Muslim Americans.

Even as accusations of disloyalty continue to be lodged against Muslim

American public figures, the mobilization of social movements on the left has raised the voices of Muslim public figures who have been actively contesting narrow parameters of acceptability applied to Muslim Americans. One notable example is Linda Sarsour, a Brooklyn Muslim American activist of Palestinian descent. While she has been an active community organizer in New York since the 2001 attacks, Sarsour gained national prominence as a key organizer of the 2017 Women's March on Washington and as a Bernie Sanders surrogate in his 2015–16 and 2019–20 presidential bids. She has also deftly taken on weapons used against Muslims, proclaiming herself a patriot not by donning a figurative American flag hijab but rather by aligning herself with a tradition of dissent. Rejecting the narrow script of the moderate Muslim, Sarsour has challenged the founding myths of this nation, while arguing that it is her love of the United States that has made her want to push the country to do better.[12] Centering a critique of U.S. settler colonialism, anti-Black racism, and imperialism, she has allied herself with movements grounded in U.S. history. This rhetoric is borne out by Sarsour's decades of political organizing, including her work in countering the surveillance and policing of Muslim communities in Brooklyn, her efforts to win the addition of Muslim holidays to the New York City public schools, and her organizing of Muslim communities in solidarity with Black communities and against anti-Black violence and police brutality. While Sarsour has long been a lightning rod, viciously targeted by right-wing and pro-Israel activists who focus on her Muslim Palestinian identity and her uncensored political views, she has also articulated an intersectional, anti-imperialist, and feminist politics to a large body of multifaith, multiracial progressive activists. Sarsour has done this work at great risk to herself, but a revitalized, reimagined antiracist left must create space for her and others to step outside narrow frames and open new possibilities of engagement across communities, societies, and borders.

The power of tolerance discourses has waned over the last two decades as, on one hand, more vociferously exclusionary and violent racist discourses and practices are proliferating and, on the other hand, there is greater recognition of anti-Muslim racism and the need to directly defend Muslims from such frontal attacks. Discourses of tolerance and sympathy still circulate, but their failure to protect Muslims, to create space for them in their full complexity, humanity, and diversity, is also becoming more apparent. I see some reason for hope in the changing political landscape, even as there is also great need for vigilance in the face of intensifying and violent anti-Muslim mobilization and an emboldening, explicitly white supremacist politics. Indeed, it remains to be seen whether the ongoing confrontations of interests and identities will produce new possibilities for Muslim American political life or for life itself in Muslim-majority societies and across the globe. The question may be, can we, in the midst of persistent crises, imagine and build new forms of economic and political organization locally and globally to meet the needs of the many, rather than the benefits of the few, so we all can thrive?

Acknowledgments

Countless people over the years have intellectually, emotionally, or materially supported me; engaged or challenged my thinking; and left a mark on this project. This book originated in my dissertation research conducted in the Department of Sociology at the Graduate Center, City University of New York. I am deeply indebted to the support I received there from faculty and fellow graduate students. Hester Eisenstein was the first person to offer enthusiastic support for my ideas and to push me to write for publication. Samira Haj provided essential intellectual guidance. Patricia Clough, my ever-inspiring and tireless advisor, in the spirit of true mentorship, gave me the freedom to pursue my interests and then pushed me to think beyond my horizons. I also benefited from formative courses with Ervand Abrahamian, Talal Asad, and Shiva Balaghi. I found a vibrant intellectual community and critical feedback for my work through a fellowship from the Center for Place, Culture, and Politics under the direction of the late Neil Smith, whose absence is deeply felt. Also absolutely essential was the intellectual engagement, support, and critical feedback of fellow graduate students in sociology and beyond, including Elizabeth Bullock, Jeffrey Culang, Kim Cunningham, Andrew Greenberg, Karen Gregory, Christopher Gunderson, Aleksandra Majstorac Kobiljski, Doug Meyer, Nada Moumtaz, Soniya Munshi, Sara Pursley, Catherine Sameh, Rachel Schiff, Andrea Siegel, Kara Van Cleaf, and Craig Willse.

More broadly, Raha Iranian Feminist Collective—a truly formidable group of thinkers and doers whom I will not name individually here but who continue to shape me—has been an intellectual and activist home for many years. I have also benefited from intellectual interlocutors at numerous conferences and panels, including Evelyn Alsultany, Carol Fadda-Conrey, Aisha Ghani, Zareena Grewal, Persis Karim, Maryam Kashani, Arun Kundnani, Neda Maghbouleh, Amy Malek, Maya Mikdashi, Rupal Oza, Dina Siddiqi, and Saadia Toor, among others. The "Engaging Islam" conference organized by Elora Chowdhury and Leila Farsakh at University of Massachusetts Boston was one earlier formative experience.

In developing this manuscript, I am truly indebted to the generous support of many thinking and writing partners, including Ujju Aggarwal, Emmaia Gelman, Caroline Hong, Laura Y. Liu, Manijeh Moradian, Soniya Munshi, Sahar Sadjadi, and Linta Varghese. In Liberal Studies at New York University, I have been blessed with a vibrant community: interdisciplinary and global scholars; thoughtful and committed staff; bright and inspiring students, including those with whom I have had the honor to partner through the LS Diversity, Equity, and Inclusion Committee; and the faculty of LS Islamicate Culture and Society. I have appreciated the support of Dean Julie Mostov and a 2018 Summer Stipend for Research from NYU Liberal Studies.

This project is especially indebted to the very generous and constructive feedback offered by reviewers of the manuscript, particularly Evelyn Alsultany and Falguni Sheth. Two chapters grew out of formerly published articles, which also received productive feedback from mostly anonymous reviewers, including David Butz. I received a very generative review of one chapter from Craig Willse. At the University of Minnesota Press, Danielle Kasprzak offered pivotal guidance in revising and completing the manuscript, while Jason Weidemann, Zenyse Miller, Anne Wrenn, Mike Stoffel, Eric Lundgren, and Ana Bichanich stewarded the project through the final stages. I am humbled by the generous endorsement of this project by the editors of the Muslim International series, Sohail Daulatzai and Junaid Rana. A Book Subvention Grant from the Center for the Humanities at New York University provided support for indexing, and Denise Carlson expertly compiled the index.

In addition to the friendships at the basis of many of the relationships already named, the camaraderie of Nancy Agabian, Chad DeChant, Laura Meyers, and Lesley Oram has held me up through the years. Small Idea

Preschool and Manhattan Country School, second homes for my children, have connected me with others who seek to live their values, especially through their relationships with children. The guidance and love given to my children by caregivers, teachers, and especially family members have also been essential in providing me space to do my work. None of this would have been possible without the love, support, and impossibly high standards of my immediate and extended family, including my parents, Faye and Asghar Rastegar, and my brothers Darius and Kamran Rastegar. Kamran treaded the academic path before me and has been more than generous with advice at every step of the way. I have been lucky to have a large and loving family, who, spanning continents and cultures, has been central to leading me to the questions I raise here. They, more than anyone, have taught me the value of a tolerance of deep-seated differences that comes from a space of love and respect.

Finally, Shadi Nahvi, I cannot ever fully express my gratitude to have had you by my side through it all, supporting my life and this project, as an intellectual partner, through your humbling love—and through your passion for justice and delicious food. I dedicate this book to S and O: may they blossom in the light you cast upon them and experience something of the immense joy they bring to me every day.

Notes

INTRODUCTION

1. Janice Monti Belkaoui, "Images of Arabs and Israelis in the Prestige Press, 1966–74," *Journalism Quarterly* 55 (1978): 732–38; Edmund Ghareeb and American-Arab Affairs Council, *Split Vision: The Portrayal of Arabs in the American Media,* Rev. and Exp. ed. (Washington, D.C.: American-Arab Affairs Council, 1983); Jack G. Shaheen, *Reel Bad Arabs: How Hollywood Vilifies a People* (New York: Olive Branch Press, 2001); Shaheen, *The TV Arab* (Bowling Green, Ohio: Bowling Green State University Popular Press, 1984); Yahya R. Kamalipour, ed., *The U.S. Media and the Middle East: Image and Perception,* Contributions to the Study of Mass Media and Communications (Westport, Conn.: Greenwood Press, 1995); Edward W. Said, *Covering Islam: How the Media and the Experts Determine How We See the Rest of the World,* Rev. ed. (New York: Vintage Books, 1997); Lawrence Michelak, *Cruel and Unusual: Negative Images of Arabs in American Popular Culture* (Washington, D.C.: ADC Research Institute, 1988).

2. Melani McAlister, *Epic Encounters: Culture, Media, and U.S. Interests in the Middle East, 1945–2000,* American Crossroads (Berkeley: University of California Press, 2005).

3. Su'ad Abdul Khabeer, *Muslim Cool: Race, Religion, and Hip Hop in the United States* (New York: New York University Press, 2016), 13.

4. Sohail Daulatzai, *Black Star, Crescent Moon: The Muslim International and Black Freedom beyond America* (Minneapolis: University of Minnesota Press, 2012).

5. Arun Kundnani, *The Muslims Are Coming! Islamophobia, Extremism, and the Domestic War on Terror* (London: Verso Books, 2014).

6. Sylvia Chan-Malik, "'A Space for the Spiritual': A Roundtable on Race, Gender, and Islam in the United States," *Amerasia Journal* 40, no. 1 (2014): 17–33.

7. Burnham et al. estimated in 2006 more than 650,00 excess deaths in Iraq as a consequence of the war, the largest portion of them due to violence, most

commonly gunfire. Gilbert Burnham, Riyadh Lafta, Shannon Doocy, and Les Roberts, "Mortality after the 2003 Invasion of Iraq: A Cross-Sectional Cluster Sample Survey," *The Lancet* 368, no. 9545 (2006): 1421–28. Iraq Body Count maintains a database of publicly recorded violent deaths, reporting approximately two hundred thousand civilian deaths from 2003 to 2019. Iraq Body Count, "Documented Civilian Deaths from Violence," https://www.iraqbodycount.org/database/. The Brown University Watson Institute estimates that more than 480,000, including 244,000 civilians, have died as a result of direct combat in Afghanistan, Iraq, and Pakistan, and many more as a result of indirect effects of the war. Neta C. Crawford, "Human Cost of the Post-9/11 Wars: Lethality and the Need for Transparency," Watson Institute for International and Public Affairs, Brown University, https://watson.brown.edu/costsofwar/figures.

8. Stephanie Savell, "Map: Current United States Counterterror War Locations," Watson Institute for International and Public Affairs, Brown University, https://watson.brown.edu/costsofwar/papers/2018/map-current-united-states-counterterror-war-locations.

9. Zareena Grewal, *Islam Is a Foreign Country: American Muslims and the Global Crisis of Authority,* Nation of Newcomers: Immigrant History as American History (New York: New York University Press, 2013), 342.

10. Jodi Melamed, *Represent and Destroy: Rationalizing Violence in the New Racial Capitalism,* Difference Incorporated (Minneapolis: University of Minnesota Press, 2011).

11. Melamed.

12. Richard Rorty, "On Ethnocentrism: A Reply to Clifford Geertz," in *Objectivity, Relativism and Truth: Philosophical Papers* (Cambridge: Cambridge University Press, 1991), 204.

13. Susan Mendus, *The Politics of Toleration in Modern Life* (Durham, N.C.: Duke University Press, 1999).

14. Marjorie Garber, "Compassion," in *Compassion: The Culture and Politics of an Emotion,* ed. Lauren Gail Berlant (New York: Routledge, 2004), 23.

15. Amit Rai, *Rule of Sympathy: Sentiment, Race, and Power, 1750–1850* (New York: Palgrave, 2002), 57.

16. Garber, 24.

17. Wendy Brown, *Regulating Aversion: Tolerance in the Age of Identity and Empire* (Princeton, N.J.: Princeton University Press, 2006).

18. Joseph Andoni Massad, *Islam in Liberalism* (Chicago: University of Chicago Press, 2015).

19. Talal Asad, *Formations of the Secular: Christianity, Islam, Modernity* (Stanford, Calif.: Stanford University Press, 2003).

20. Hester Eisenstein, *Feminism Seduced: How Global Elites Use Women's Labor and Ideas to Exploit the World* (Boulder, Colo.: Paradigm, 2009).

21. Rai, *Rule of Sympathy.*

22. In the U.S. Census, the "White" category includes "Middle Eastern entries, such as Arab, Lebanese, and Palestinian; and North African entries, such as Algerian, Moroccan, and Egyptian." Lindsay Hixson, Bradford B. Hepler, and Myoung Ouk Kim, *The White Population: 2010* (Washington, D.C.: U.S. Census Bureau, 2011).

23. Helen Hatab Samhan, "Not Quite White: Race Classification and the Arab-American Experience," in *Arabs in America: Building a New Future,* ed. Michael W. Suleiman, 209–26 (Philadelphia: Temple University Press, 1999).

24. Nadine Naber, "Ambiguous Insiders, an Investigation of Arab American Invisibility," *Journal of Ethnic and Racial Studies* 23, no. 1 (2000): 37–61; Neda Maghbouleh, *The Limits of Whiteness: Iranian Americans and the Everyday Politics of Race* (Stanford, Calif.: Stanford University Press, 2017); Sarah M. A. Gualtieri, "Strange Fruit? Syrian Immigrants, Extralegal Violence, and Racial Formation in the United States," in *Race and Arab Americans before and after 9/11: From Invisible Citizens to Visible Subjects,* ed. Amaney A. Jamal and Nadine Christine Naber, 147–69 (Syracuse, N.Y.: Syracuse University Press, 2008); Nabeel Abraham, "Anti-Arab Racism and Violence in the United States," in *The Development of Arab-American Identity,* ed. Ernest N. McCarus, 155–214 (Ann Arbor: University of Michigan Press, 1994).

25. Erik Love, "Confronting Islamophobia in the United States: Framing Civil Rights Activism among Middle Eastern Americans," *Patterns of Prejudice* 43, no. 3–4 (2009): 401–25; Suleiman, *Arabs in America.*

26. Saher Selod and David G. Embrick, "Racialization of Muslims: Situating the Muslim Experience in Race Scholarship," *Sociology Compass* 7/8 (2013): 649.

27. For discussion of the use of *Muslim American* in relation to Muslim communities, see the conversation between Khabeer and Alsultany in Chan-Malik, "A Space for the Spiritual."

28. Nikhil Pal Singh, *Race and America's Long War* (Oakland: University of California Press, 2017), xvi.

29. Michael Omi and Howard Winant, *Racial Formation in the United States,* 3rd ed. (New York: Routledge/Taylor and Francis, 2014), 111.

30. Omi and Winant, 110.

31. Omi and Winant, 110.

32. Eduardo Bonilla-Silva, *Racism without Racists: Color-Blind Racism and the Persistence of Racial Inequality in America,* 4th ed. (Lanham, Md.: Rowman and Littlefield, 2014).

33. Erik Love, *Islamophobia and Racism in America* (New York: New York University Press, 2017), 65.

34. Sarah Beth Kaufman and Hanna Niner, "Muslim Victimization in the Contemporary US: Clarifying the Racialization Thesis," *Critical Criminology* 27 (2019): 485–502.

35. Etienne Balibar, "Is There a 'Neo-Racism'?," in *Race, Nation, Class: Ambiguous Identities,* ed. Etienne Balibar and Immanuel Maurice Wallerstein, 17–28 (London: Verso, 1991); Tariq Modood, *Multicultural Politics: Racism, Ethnicity, and Muslims in Britain,* Contradictions (Minneapolis: University of Minnesota Press, 2005); Amaney Jamal, "Civil Liberties and the Otherization of Arab and Muslim Americans," in Jamal and Naber, *Race and Arab Americans,* 114–30; Louise Cainkar, "Thinking Outside the Box: Arabs and Race in the United States," in Jamal and Naber, 46–80; Nadine Naber, "Look, Mohammed the Terrorist Is Coming!," in Jamal and Naber, 276–304; Sherene Razack, *Casting Out: The Eviction of Muslims from Western Law and Politics* (Toronto: University of Toronto Press, 2008); Selod and Embrick, "Racialization of Muslims."

36. Balibar, "Is There a 'Neo-Racism'?," 22.

37. Jamal, "Civil Liberties and the Otherization of Arab and Muslim Americans," 119.

38. Naber, "Look, Mohammed the Terrorist Is Coming!," 280.

39. Naber.

40. Razack, *Casting Out,* 7–9.

41. Junaid Akram Rana, *Terrifying Muslims: Race and Labor in the South Asian Diaspora* (Durham, N.C.: Duke University Press, 2011), 5.

42. Falguni A. Sheth, *Toward a Political Philosophy of Race* (Albany: SUNY Press, 2009).

43. Patricia Ticineto Clough, *The User Unconscious: On Affect, Media, and Measure* (Minneapolis: University of Minnesota Press, 2018).

44. Ruth Wilson Gilmore, *Golden Gulag: Prisons, Surplus, Crisis, and Opposition in Globalizing California,* American Crossroads (Berkeley: University of California Press, 2007), 28.

45. Melamed, *Represent and Destroy,* 2.

46. Michel Foucault, *Security, Territory, Population: Lectures at the Collège de France, 1977–78,* ed. Michel Senellart, François Ewald, and Alessandro Fontana (New York: Palgrave Macmillan, 2007), 104.

47. Tiziana Terranova, "Futurepublic: On Information Warfare, Bio-Racism and Hegemony as Noopolitics," *Theory, Culture, and Society* 24 (2007): 136.

48. Sheth, *Toward a Political Philosophy of Race,* 8.

49. Sheth, 5.

50. Melamed, *Represent and Destroy*, 147.

51. Lisa Gannett, "Racism and Human Genome Diversity Research: The Ethical Limits of 'Population Thinking,'" *Philosophy of Science* 68 (Proceedings) (2001): S489.

52. Gannett, S487.

53. This dynamic, which Clough terms a "sociologic," "is meant to evaluate the individual in terms of a statistical profile in order to assess his or her risk factors, or what his or her future might or might not be." Clough, *User Unconscious*, 28.

54. George M. Fredrickson, *Racism: A Short History* (Princeton, N.J.: Princeton University Press, 2002).

55. Balibar, "Is There a 'Neo-Racism'?"; see, e.g., Omi and Winant, *Racial Formation in the United States*.

56. Nikhil Singh notes that while "race . . . is a modality of group domination and oppression . . . it requires a story (whether biological, sociological, anthropological, or historical) explaining how and why such practices persist and can be justified." Singh, *Race and America's Long War*, xviii.

57. Clough, *User Unconscious*, 29.

58. Evelyn Alsultany, *Arabs and Muslims in the Media: Race and Representation after 9/11*, Critical Cultural Communication (New York: New York University Press, 2012), 21.

59. While reality television shows allow for other modes of representing Muslims, Alsultany finds that these shows more subtly speak to the problem of Muslims as threatening by emphasizing either their patriotism or their secularism. Evelyn Alsultany, "The Cultural Politics of Islam in U.S. Reality Television," *Communication, Culture, and Critique* 9, no. 4 (2015): 595–613.

60. Wendy Brown, "Tolerance as/in Civilizational Discourse," in *Toleration and Its Limits,* ed. Melissa S. Williams and Jeremy Waldron, 406–41 (New York: New York University Press, 2008); Brown, *Regulating Aversion*.

61. Tiziana Terranova, *Network Culture: Politics for the Information Age* (Ann Arbor, Mich.: Pluto Press, 2004); Patricia Ticineto Clough, "The Affective Turn: Political Economy, Biomedia, and Bodies," in *The Affect Theory Reader,* ed. Melissa Gregg and Gregory J. Seigworth, 206–28 (Durham, N.C.: Duke University Press, 2010).

62. William E. Connolly, *Why I Am Not a Secularist* (Minneapolis: University of Minnesota Press, 1999), 27.

63. Sianne Ngai, *Ugly Feelings* (Cambridge, Mass.: Harvard University Press, 2005).

64. Mark Poster, *Information Please: Culture and Politics in the Age of Digital Machines* (Durham, N.C.: Duke University Press, 2006), 36.

65. Connolly, *Why I Am Not a Secularist.*

66. McAlister, *Epic Encounters*; Said, *Covering Islam.*

1. NEWS STORIES, POLICE PROFILES, AND OPINION POLLS

1. The Council on American Islamic Relations documented 1,717 "bias incidents and hate crimes" against those perceived to be Muslim, Arab, or South Asian reported in the six months following the attacks. Louise Cainkar, "The Impact of September 11 Attacks on Arab and Muslim Communities in the United States," in *The Maze of Fear: Security and Migration after 9/11,* ed. John Tirman (New York: New Press, 2004).

2. Office of the Press Secretary, "'Islam Is Peace' Says President: Remarks by the President at Islamic Center of Washington, D.C.," September 17, 2001, http://www.whitehouse.gov/news/releases/2001/09/20010917-11.html (no longer online).

3. Mark Silk, "Islam and the American News Media Post September 11," in *Mediating Religion: Conversations in Media, Religion and Culture,* ed. Jolyon P. Mitchell and Sophia Marriage (London: T & T Clark, 2003), 73–79.

4. "Reactions People Are Having to Suddenly Being Suspicious of Anyone Who Is Muslim or Arab," *NPR Morning Edition,* September 20, 2001.

5. Mitra Rastegar, "Managing 'American Islam': Secularism, Patriotism, and the Gender Litmus Test," *International Feminist Journal of Politics* 10, no. 4 (2008): 455–74.

6. Brigitte Lebens Nacos and Oscar Torres-Reyna, *Fueling Our Fears: Stereotyping, Media Coverage, and Public Opinion of Muslim Americans* (Lanham, Md.: Rowman and Littlefield, 2007).

7. Jodi Wilgoren, "After the Attacks: The Hijackers; a Terrorist Profile Emerges That Confounds the Experts," *New York Times,* September 15, 2001, http://www.nytimes.com/2001/09/15/us/after-attacks-hijackers-terrorist-profile-emerges-that-confounds-experts.html.

8. Rex A. Hudson, *The Sociology and Psychology of Terrorism: Who Becomes a Terrorist and Why?* (Washington, D.C.: Federal Research Division, Library of Congress, 1999).

9. Emily Badger, "The Long, Halting, Unfinished Fight to End Racial Profiling in America," *Washington Post,* December 4, 2014, https://www.washingtonpost.com/news/wonk/wp/2014/12/04/the-long-halting-unfinished-fight-to-end-racial-profiling-in-america/; Nicole Davis, "The Slippery Slope of Racial Profiling," *ColorLines,* December 15, 2001, http://colorlines.com/archives/2001/12/the_slippery_slope_of_racial_profiling.html; Public Agenda, "Half of Amer-

icans Say There Is No Excuse for the Racial Profiling of African Americans, but Two-Thirds Say Greater Scrutiny of Middle Eastern People Is 'Understandable,'" 2002, http://www.publicagenda.org/charts/half-americans-say-there-no-excuse-racial-profiling-blacks-two-thirds-say-greater-scrutiny-middle; Stuart Taylor Jr., "The Case for Using Racial Profiling at Airports," *Atlantic,* September 25, 2001, https://www.theatlantic.com/politics/archive/2001/09/the-case-for-using-racial-profiling-at-airports/378030/.

10. "Terrorism 2002/2005," Federal Bureau of Investigation, U.S. Department of Justice, 2005, https://www.fbi.gov/stats-services/publications/terrorism-2002-2005#terror_05sum.

11. Nancy Murray, "Profiling in the Age of Total Information Awareness," *Race and Class* 52, no. 2 (2010): 3–24; "Guidance for Federal Law Enforcement Agencies Regarding the Use of Race, Ethnicity, Gender, National Origin, Religion, Sexual Orientation, or Gender Identity," U.S. Department of Justice, December 2014, https://www.dhs.gov/publication/guidance-federal-law-enforcement-agencies-regarding-use-race-ethnicity-gender-national; David Cole, "Obama's Civil-Rights Legacy—and Ours," *Nation,* January 2, 2017, https://www.thenation.com/article/obamas-civil-rights-legacy-and-ours/.

12. Edward W. Said, *Orientalism,* 1st Vintage Books ed. (New York: Vintage Books, 1979).

13. Jack G. Shaheen, *Reel Bad Arabs: How Hollywood Vilifies a People* (New York: Olive Branch Press, 2001).

14. Edward W. Said, *Covering Islam: How the Media and the Experts Determine How We See the Rest of the World,* Rev. ed. (New York: Vintage Books, 1997), 83.

15. Edward Tabor Linenthal, *The Unfinished Bombing: Oklahoma City in American Memory* (Oxford: Oxford University Press, 2001).

16. David Cole, "Secrecy, Guilt by Association, and the Terrorist Profile," *Journal of Law and Religion* 15, no. 1/2 (2000–2001): 267–88.

17. American Civil Liberties Union, *Analysis of Immigration Detention Policies* (New York: ACLU, 1999).

18. Cole, "Secrecy."

19. Shirin Sinnar, "Patriotic or Unconstitutional? The Mandatory Detention of Aliens under the USA Patriot Act," *Stanford Law Review* 55, no. 4 (2003): 1419–56.

20. Leti Volpp, "The Citizen and the Terrorist," *UCLA Law Review* 49, no. 5 (2002): 1575–99.

21. Nadine Naber, "'Look, Mohammed the Terrorist Is Coming!,'" in Jamal and Naber, *Race and Arab Americans before and after 9/11, 287.*

22. Deborah A. Ramirez, Jennifer Hoopes, and Tara Lai Quinlan, "Defining

Racial Profiling in a Post–September 11 World," *American Journal of Criminal Law* 40 (2003): 1202.

23. Wendy D. Fitzgibbon, "Institutional Racism, Pre-emptive Criminalisation and Risk Analysis," *Howard Journal of Criminal Justice* 46, no. 2 (2007): 128–44.

24. Center for Human Rights and Global Justice, *Targeted and Entrapped: Manufacturing the "Homegrown Threat" in the United States* (New York: NYU School of Law, 2011).

25. Cainkar, "Impact of September 11 Attacks," 219.

26. Mark Tessler and Michael D. H. Robbins, "What Leads Some Ordinary Arab Men and Women to Approve of Terrorist Acts against the United States?," *Journal of Conflict Resolution* 51, no. 2 (2007): 305–28; Yener Altunbas and John Thornton, "Are Homegrown Islamic Terrorists Different? Some UK Evidence," *Southern Economic Journal* 78, no. 2 (2011): 262–72.

27. Diego Gambetta and Steffen Hertog, "Why Are There So Many Engineers among Islamic Radicals?," *European Journal of Sociology* 50, no. 2 (2009): 201–30.

28. Marc Sageman, *Understanding Terror Networks* (Philadelphia: University of Pennsylvania Press, 2004); John Horgan, "From Profiles to Pathways and Roots to Routes: Perspectives from Psychology on Radicalization into Terrorism," *Annals of the American Academy of Political and Social Science* 618, no. 1 (2008): 80–94.

29. Kundnani, *The Muslims Are Coming!*, 133.

30. Amber Michel, "Countering Violent Extremism: Islamophobia, the Department of Justice and American Islamic Organizations," *Islamophobia Studies Journal* 3, no. 1 (2015): 127–37.

31. Mitchell D. Silber and Arvin Bhatt, *Radicalization in the West: The Homegrown Threat* (New York: New York City Police Department, 2007).

32. In 2012, the Associated Press released a series of articles documenting the extent of NYPD surveillance of Muslim communities. See also CUNY Law School Creating Law Enforcement Accountability and Responsibility, Asian American Legal Defense and Education Fund, and Muslim American Civil Liberties Coalition, *Mapping Muslims: NYPD Spying and Its Impact on American Muslims* (New York: Creating Law Enforcement Accountability and Responsibility [CLEAR] Project, CUNY School of Law, 2013).

33. Murray, "Profiling in the Age of Total Information Awareness."

34. Chris Hayes, "Before Prism There Was Total Information Awareness," September 12, 2013, http://www.msnbc.com/all-in/prism-there-was-total-infor mation-awar; Murray, "Profiling in the Age of Total Information Awareness."

35. Edward Tverdek, "The Limits to Terrorist Profiling," *Public Affairs Quarterly* 20, no. 2 (2006): 175–203.

36. Tina G. Patel and David Tyrer, *Race, Crime and Resistance* (London: Sage, 2011); Jeremy Kearney and Catherine Donovan, *Constructing Risky Identities in Policy and Practice* (Basingstoke, U.K.: Palgrave Macmillan, 2013).

37. Manar Waheed, "Countering Violent Extremism: Harming Civil Rights and Hurting Communities," in *Countering the Islamophobia Industry: Toward More Effective Strategies* (Atlanta, Ga.: Carter Center, 2018).

38. Murtaza Hussain, Cora Currier, and Jana Winter, "Families at Risk for Extremism: Social Workers, Educators to Rate 'Expressions of Hopelessness,'" *Intercept,* February 9, 2015, https://theintercept.com/2015/02/09/government -develops-questionnaire-see-might-become-terrorist/.

39. Sam Howe Verhovek, "Americans Give In to Race Profiling," *New York Times,* September 23, 2001.

40. Barbie Zelizer and Stuart Allan, *Journalism after September 11,* Communication and Society (London: Routledge, 2003); Richard Perez-Pena, "Times Wins 5 Pulitzers, for Coverage of War, Scandal, Art and the Campaign," *New York Times,* April 21, 2009; James W. Carey, "American Journalism on, before, and after September 11," in *Journalism after September 11,* ed. Barbie Zelizer and Stuart Allan (London: Routledge, 2003).

41. Matthew Gentzkow and Jesse M. Shapiro, *Ideological Segregation Online and Offline* (Chicago: University of Chicago, Booth School of Business, Initiative on Global Markets, 2010).

42. See, e.g., Somini Sengupta, "Arabs and Muslims Steer through an Unsettling Scrutiny," *New York Times,* September 13, 2001.

43. Robert Worth, "For Arab-Americans, a Time of Disquiet," *New York Times,* September 30, 2001.

44. E.g., Margo Nash, "'A Big Knife through My Heart': Middle Eastern Performers Face Slowing Business and Fears after the Terrorist Attacks," *New York Times,* October 7, 2001; Worth, "For Arab-Americans, a Time of Disquiet"; Timothy Egan, "Tough but Hopeful Weeks for the Muslims of Laramie," *New York Times,* October 18, 2001; Laurie Goodstein, "Muslims See Acceptance and Scrutiny as Holy Month Nears," *New York Times,* November 16, 2001; Jodi Wilgoren, "Struggling to Be Both Arab and American," *New York Times,* November 4, 2001.

45. John Fountain, "Sadness and Fear as a Group Feels Doubly at Risk," *New York Times,* October 5, 2001; Daniel J. Wakin, "Ranks of Latinos Turning to Islam Are Increasing," *New York Times,* January 2, 2002; Evelyn Nieves, "A New Minority Makes Itself Known: Hispanic Muslims," *New York Times,* December 17, 2001.

46. Laurie Goodstein, "Military Clerics Balance Arms and Allah," *New York*

Times, October 7, 2001; Tara Bahrampour, "Where Islam Meets 'Brave New World,'" *New York Times*, November 4, 2001; Blaine Harden, "A Network for Arabs Presents Programming with Attitude," *New York Times*, October 15, 2001.

47. Daniel J. Wakin, "Moderates Start Speaking Out against Islamic Intolerance," *New York Times*, October 28, 2001; Laurie Goodstein, "Stereotyping Rankles Silent, Secular Majority of American Muslims," *New York Times*, December 23, 2001.

48. Matthew Purdy, "For Arab-Americans, Flag-Flying and Fear," *New York Times*, September 14, 2001; John Rather, "Uneasy Times for Muslims on Island," *New York Times*, September 23, 2001; Sengupta, "Arabs and Muslims Steer through an Unsettling Scrutiny"; Daniel J. Wakin and Charles LeDuff, "Among New York Muslims, Support for U.S. Strikes," *New York Times*, October 8, 2001; Yilu Zhao, "Police Officer Visits to Reassure a Queens Mosque," *New York Times*, September 22, 2001.

49. Zhao, "Police Officer Visits to Reassure a Queens Mosque."

50. Zhao.

51. Worth, "For Arab-Americans, a Time of Disquiet."

52. Jodi Wilgoren, "Swept up in a Dragnet, Hundreds Sit in Custody and Ask, 'Why?,'" *New York Times*, November 25, 2001.

53. Deborah Sontag, "'Who Is This Kafka That People Keep Mentioning?,'" *New York Times Magazine*, October 21, 2001.

54. Christopher Drew and Judith Miller, "Though Not Linked to Terrorism, Many Detainees Cannot Go Home," *New York Times*, February 18, 2001.

55. Talal Asad, *On Suicide Bombing* (New York: Columbia University Press, 2007).

56. Goodstein, "Military Clerics Balance Arms and Allah"; Douglas Jehl, "A Navy Man and Muslim Reconciles Two Worlds," *New York Times*, October 10, 2001; Corey Kilgannon, "Muslims in Gray," *New York Times*, November 25, 2001; Susan Sachs and Blaine Harden, "A Family, Both Arab and Arab-American, Divided by a War," *New York Times*, October 29, 2001; Daniel J. Wakin, "Thanksgiving in a Time of Fasting: In Brooklyn, Healing Rhythms of Ramadan," *New York Times*, November 21, 2001.

57. McAlister, *Epic Encounters*.

58. Kilgannon, "Muslims in Gray."

59. Kilgannon.

60. Two were Sikh Indians, one was Hindu Indian, one was a (Muslim) Pakistani, and one was a Christian Arab. Muneer Ahmad, "Homeland Insecurities: Racial Violence the Day after September 11," *Social Text* 20, no. 3 (2002): 101–15.

61. Worth, "For Arab-Americans, a Time of Disquiet"; Wakin and LeDuff,

"Among New York Muslims, Support for U.S. Strikes"; Purdy, "For Arab-Americans, Flag-Flying and Fear"; Sengupta, "Arabs and Muslims Steer through an Unsettling Scrutiny."

62. Steven George Salaita, *Anti-Arab Racism in the USA: Where It Comes from and What It Means for Politics Today* (London: Pluto Press, 2006).

63. Felicia Lee, "Trying to Soothe the Fears Hiding behind the Veil," *New York Times*, September 23, 2001.

64. Worth, "For Arab-Americans, a Time of Disquiet"; Fountain, "Sadness and Fear as a Group Feels Doubly at Risk"; Lee, "Trying to Soothe the Fears Hiding behind the Veil."

65. Laurie Goodstein, "Muslims Nurture Sense of Self on Campus," *New York Times*, November 3, 2001.

66. Evelyn Nieves, "Slain Arab-American May Have Been Hate-Crime Victim," *New York Times*, October 6, 2001.

67. Worth, "For Arab-Americans, a Time of Disquiet."

68. Greg Winter, "F.B.I. Visits Provoke Waves of Worry in Middle Eastern Men," *New York Times*, November 16, 2001.

69. Sachs and Harden, "A Family, Both Arab and Arab-American, Divided by a War."

70. John W. Fountain, "Carrying 27 Years of Civic Passion to the Mayor's Office," *New York Times*, November 17, 2001.

71. Laurie Goodstein, "Terrorist from Central Casting Has Hard Lessons to Teach," *New York Times*, December 12, 2001.

72. Goodstein.

73. Paul Krugman, "Lifting the Shroud," *New York Times*, March 23, 2004, http://www.nytimes.com/2004/03/23/opinion/23KRUG.html.

74. Rather, "Uneasy Times for Muslims on Island."

75. Linda Silverstein, "A Disquieting Remark by a Muslim Woman," *New York Times*, October 7, 2001.

76. Susan Sachs, "The 2 Worlds of Muslim American Teenagers," *New York Times*, October 7, 2001.

77. Laurie Goodstein, "Stereotyping Rankles Silent, Secular Majority of American Muslims," *New York Times*, December 23, 2001, A20.

78. Daniel J. Wakin, "Moderates Start Speaking Out against Islamic Intolerance," *New York Times*, October 28, 2001, B5.

79. Hilarie M. Sheets, "Stitch by Stitch, a Daughter of Islam Takes On Taboos," *New York Times*, November 25, 2001.

80. Robin Finn, "A Daughter of Islam, and an Enemy of Terror," *New York Times*, October 25, 2001.

81. Lynda Richardson, "Strains on a Man and the City, Distilled in 10 Minutes," *New York Times,* October 16, 2001.

82. Pew Research Center, *Muslim Americans: Middle Class and Mostly Mainstream* (Washington, D.C.: Pew Research Center, 2007).

83. Some examples of this kind of analysis: Herbert Mack, "Countering Violent Extremism in the United States: Law Enforcement's Approach to Preventing Terrorism through Community Partnerships," *Journal of Physical Security* 7, no. 1 (2014): 51–56; Jerrold M. Post and Gabriel Sheffer, "The Risk of Radicalization and Terrorism in U.S. Muslim Communities," *Brown Journal of World Affairs* 13, no. 2 (2007): 101–12; Clark McCauley, "Testing Theories of Radicalization in Polls of U.S. Muslims," *Analyses of Social Issues and Public Policy* 12, no. 1 (2012): 296–311; John Tirman, "Security and Antiterror Policies in America and Europe," in *Managing Ethnic Diversity after 9/11: Integration, Security, and Civil Liberties in Transatlantic Perspective,* ed. Ariane Chebel d'Appollonia and Simon Reich (New Brunswick, N.J.: Rutgers University Press, 2014).

84. Pew Research Center, *Muslim Americans: No Sign of Growth in Alienation or Support for Extremism* (Washington, D.C.: Pew Research Center, 2011).

85. Kate Parry, "Poll of Muslims Presents a Conundrum; Two Fascinating Findings Had Newspapers Struggling to Decide Which Was Most Important," *Star Tribune* (Minneapolis), May 27, 2007; Brian Knowlton, "U.S. Muslims Largely Content, Poll Finds," *New York Times,* May 24, 2007.

86. Alan Cooperman, "Survey: U.S. Muslims Assimilated, Opposed to Extremism," *Washington Post,* May 23, 2007; Ewen MacAskill, "US Muslims More Assimilated than British," *Guardian,* May 23, 2007.

87. Douglas Montero and Andy Soltis, "Time Bombs in Our Midst—26% of Young U.S. Muslims Back Killings," *New York Post,* May 23, 2007.

88. Pew Research Center, *Muslim Americans: Middle Class and Mostly Mainstream,* 54.

89. Rachel Monahan, "1 in 4 Muslims Say Bombers OK," *Daily News,* May 23, 2007.

90. *Investor's Business Daily,* "What Muslims Really Think," May 23, 2007.

91. Kathleen M. Woodward, *Statistical Panic: Cultural Politics and Poetics of the Emotions* (Durham, N.C.: Duke University Press, 2009), 26.

92. Sara Ahmed, *The Cultural Politics of Emotion* (New York: Routledge, 2004); Woodward, *Statistical Panic.*

93. Woodward, *Statistical Panic,* 209–10.

94. *Investor's Business Daily,* "What Muslims Really Think."

95. Kim Vo, "Some American Muslims Back Suicide Attacks," *Inside Bay Area,*

May 23, 2007; "Most Muslim Americans Oppose Suicide Bombings," *Capital* (Annapolis, MD), May 22, 2007.

96. Michelle Malkin, "Tiny Minority, Big Problem," *Lowell Sun,* May 26, 2007.

97. Leerom Medovoi, "Dogma-Line Racism: Islamophobia and the Second Axis of Race," *Social Text* 30, no. 2 (2012): 43–74.

98. Arjun Appadurai, *Fear of Small Numbers: An Essay on the Geography of Anger,* Public Planet Books (Durham, N.C.: Duke University Press, 2006), 62.

99. Steven Kull, *Public Opinion in Iran and America on Key International Issues* (Washington, D.C.: WorldPublicOpinion.org, Program on International Policy Attitudes, 2007). It is telling that the analysis plays down this large difference, suggesting that Iranians and Americans are more or less similar in their views.

100. *CBS News,* "Poll: WWII Atom Bombs 'Right Thing to Do,'" 2009, https://www.cbsnews.com/news/poll-wwii-atom-bombs-right-thing-to-do/; "Bombing Hiroshima Was Right, Amercian Voters Say 3–1, Quinnipiac University National Poll Finds," Quinnipiac University Poll, August 4, 2009, https://poll.qu.edu/national/release-detail?releaseid=1356.

101. Pew Research Center, *U.S. Muslims Concerned about Their Place in Society, but Continue to Believe in the American Dream* (Washington, D.C.: Pew Research Center, 2017).

102. Hakimeh Saphaye-Biria, "American Muslims as Radicals? A Critical Discourse Analysis of the US Congressional Hearing on 'the Extent of Radicalization in the American Muslim Community and That Community's Response,'" *Discourse and Society* 23, no. 5 (2012): 508–24.

103. Saphaye-Biria, 514.

104. Saphaye-Biria, 519.

105. Mahmood Mamdani, *Good Muslim, Bad Muslim: America, the Cold War, and the Roots of Terror* (New York: Pantheon Books, 2004).

2. FROM READING LOLITA TO READING MALALA

1. Malala Yousafzai and Christina Lamb, *I Am Malala: The Girl Who Stood Up for Education and Was Shot by the Taliban* (New York: Back Bay Books, 2015); Davis Guggenheim, dir., *He Named Me Malala* (Twentieth Century Fox, 2015). *I Am Malala* by Yousafzai and Lamb spent twenty-four weeks among the top fifteen on the *New York Times* hardcover best-seller list, debuting at number 4 on October 27, 2013. "Books: Best Sellers: Combined Print and E-Book Nonfiction," *New York Times,* October 27, 2013, https://www.nytimes.com/books/best-sellers/combined-print-and-e-book-nonfiction/2013/10/27.

2. These books include *Malala's Magic Pencil* by Malala Yousafzai, *For the Right to Learn* by R. Langston-George, *Who Is Malala Yousafzai?* by Dinah Brown, *Malala: Activist for Girls' Education* by Raphaele Frier, *Malala: A Hero for All* by Shana Corey, *Malala Yousafzai: Warrior with Words* by Karen Leggett Abouraya, *Malala, a Brave Girl from Pakistan* by Jeanette Winter, *Dear Malala, We Stand with You* by Rosemary McCarney, and *Free as a Bird: The Story of Malala* by Lina Maso.

3. Shenila Khoja-Moolji, *Forging the Ideal Educated Girl: The Production of Desirable Subjects in Muslim South Asia* (Oakland: University of California Press, 2018), 3.

4. "The War in Iraq: 10 Years and Counting: Analysis of Deaths in a Decade of Violence," *Iraq Body Count* (blog), March 19, 2013, https://www.iraqbody count.org/analysis/numbers/ten-years/.

5. Hay and Rowe report that the book was the freshman reading selection at Connecticut College, Mount Holyoke College, Oglethorpe University, Ramapo College of New Jersey, Wake Forest University, Case Western Reserve University, McKendree College, and the University of Montana–Missoula. Donadey and Ahmed-Ghosh report that the book is assigned in many women's studies courses. Simon Hay, "Why Read *Reading Lolita*? Teaching Critical Thinking in a Culture of Choice," *Pedagogy* 8, no. 1 (2008): 5–24; John Carlos Rowe, "Reading *Reading Lolita in Tehran* in Idaho," *American Quarterly* 59, no. 2 (2007): 253–75; *New York Times*, "Paperback Best Sellers: September 3, 2006," September 3, 2006; Anne Donadey and Huma Ahmed-Ghosh, "Why Americans Love Azar Nafisi's *Reading Lolita in Tehran*," *Signs: Journal of Women in Culture and Society* 33, no. 3 (2008): 623–46.

6. R. Shareah Taleghani, "'Axising' Iran: The Politics of Domestication and Cultural Translation," in *Between the Middle East and the Americas: The Cultural Politics of Diaspora,* ed. Evelyn Alsultany and Ella Shohat (Ann Arbor: University of Michigan Press, 2013).

7. Evelyn Alsultany, *Arabs and Muslims in the Media: Race and Representation after 9/11,* Critical Cultural Communication (New York: New York University Press, 2012), 71.

8. Alsultany; Jasbir K. Puar and Amit Rai, "Monster, Terrorist, Fag: The War on Terrorism and the Production of Docile Patriots," *Social Text* 20, no. 3 (2002): 117–48.

9. See, e.g., Laura Sjoberg and Sandra Via, *Gender, War, and Militarism: Feminist Perspectives,* Praeger Security International (Santa Barbara, Calif.: Praeger, 2010).

10. Hamid Dabashi, *Brown Skin, White Masks* (London: Pluto, 2011), 15.

11. Azar Nafisi, "Women, Culture, Human Rights: The Case of Iran," paper

presented at the New York Democracy Forum: Foreign Policy Association, New York, April, 20, 2005.

12. Samuel P. Huntington, "The Clash of Civilizations?," *Foreign Affairs* 72, no. 3 (1993): 25.

13. Huntington, 40.

14. Huntington, 35.

15. Mamdani, *Good Muslim, Bad Muslim.*

16. Frederick Kempe, "Lewis's 'Liberation' Doctrine for Mideast Faces New Tests," *Wall Street Journal,* December 13, 2005.

17. Said, *Orientalism.*

18. Melani McAlister, *Epic Encounters: Culture, Media, and U.S. Interests in the Middle East, 1945–2000,* American Crossroads (Berkeley: University of California Press, 2005), 304.

19. For *Reading Lolita in Tehran,* I analyzed approximately sixty reviews, interviews, and articles published in the year and a half following the publication of the book. While the vast majority of reviews (forty-three) I analyzed were in U.S.-based publications, a number were published in other countries: the United Kingdom (six), Canada (four), Australia (two), and New Zealand (one). In relation to Malala Yousafzai, I analyzed a variety of print, television, filmic, and internet-based representations, including twenty-nine reviews and articles published in newspapers on the book *I Am Malala* between October and December 2013. Searches through the end of 2014 did not elicit more sources on the book.

20. Mary Louise Pratt, *Imperial Eyes: Travel Writing and Transculturation* (London: Taylor and Francis, 2007), 9.

21. David Butz and Kenneth I. MacDonald, "Serving Sahibs with Pony and Pen: The Discursive Uses of 'Native Authenticity,'" *Society and Space* 19 (2001): 184.

22. Mary Feely, "*Reading Lolita in Tehran*: A Memoir in Books, Azar Nafisi, Fourth Estate," *Irish Times,* February 21, 2004; Paul Allen, "International Politics: Through the Veil: Paul Allen Is Intrigued by a Book Club with a Difference: *Reading Lolita in Tehran*: A Story of Love, Books and Revolution by Azar Nafisi," *Guardian,* September 13, 2003; Nan Levinson, "Literature, as Survival," *Women's Review of Books,* July 2003; Helen Rumbelow, "Pride, Prejudice and Defiance," *London Times,* February 21, 2004.

23. Azar Nafisi, *Reading Lolita in Tehran: A Memoir in Books* (New York: Random House, 2003), 57.

24. Feely, "*Reading Lolita in Tehran.*"

25. Judy Stoffman, "For a Love of Books," *Toronto Star,* October 19, 2003.

26. Shusha Guppy, "Revolutionary Reading: A Group of Iranian Women

Reminds Shusha Guppy of the Universality and Timelessness of Literature," *Financial Times*, August 2, 2003.

27. Susan Larson, "Books about Books; War of Words and Eyre Apparent," *Times-Picayune*, March 30, 2003; Mona Simpson, "Book Group in Chadors: An Outstanding and Unusual Memoir of Post-revolutionary Iran," *Atlantic Monthly*, June 2003; Heather Hewett, "A Woman Passionately Defends Books in a Repressed Land," *Seattle Times*, April 18, 2003.

28. Nafisi, *Reading Lolita*, 111.

29. Azar Nafisi, "A Reader's Guide," in *Reading Lolita in Tehran*, 360.

30. Jodi Melamed, *Represent and Destroy: Rationalizing Violence in the New Racial Capitalism*, Difference Incorporated (Minneapolis: University of Minnesota Press, 2011), 141.

31. Taleghani, "'Axising' Iran," 289.

32. At the time of compiling these reviews (September 2011), a total of 410 reviews were posted on Amazon's *Reading Lolita in Tehran* web pages for the 2003 and 2008 editions of the book. Of the thirty top-rated reviews, twenty-four were written in 2003 or 2004.

33. T. Kelly, review of *Reading Lolita in Tehran* by Azar Naifisi, Amazon, July 11, 2008, https://www.amazon.com/Reading-Lolita-Tehran-Memoir-Books -ebook/product-reviews/B000FC0XY6; Stacy Allen, review of *Reading Lolita in Tehran* by Azar Naifisi, Amazon, September 21, 2004, https://www.amazon.com/ Reading-Lolita-Tehran-Memoir-Books-ebook/product-reviews/B000FC0XY6.

34. "Malala Yousafzai," *The Daily Show with Jon Stewart*, October 8, 2013, available at http://www.cc.com/video-clips/a335nz/the-daily-show-with-jon-stewart -malala-yousafzai.

35. Yousafzai and Lamb, *I Am Malala*, 194.

36. Guggenheim, "He Named Me Malala."

37. CBC, "Malala Yousafzai's Shooting by Taliban Made 'Millions of Malalas' Speak Up," October 9, 2013, https://www.cbc.ca/news/world/malala-yousafzai-s -shooting-by-taliban-made-millions-of-malalas-speak-up-1.1929982.

38. "Malala Yousafzai—Nobel Lecture," Nobel Foundation, December 10, 2014, https://www.nobelprize.org/prizes/peace/2014/yousafzai/26074-malala -yousafzai-nobel-lecture-2014/.

39. Elizabeth Renzetti, "About a Girl, and a Hero," *Globe and Mail*, October 12, 2013.

40. "The Bravest Girl in the World: In This Exclusive Excerpt from Her Autobiography, I Am Malala, Young Activist Malala Yousafzai Recounts the Day She Was Shot by the Taliban," *Dayton Daily News*, October 6, 2013; Jill Lawless, "Taliban Shooting Survivor Describes Journey from Schoolgirl to Activist," *Pittsburgh*

Post, October 8, 2013; "Education Crusader Recalls Surviving Taliban Shooting," *Courier-Mail,* October 10, 2013; Catherine Bennett, "Comment: Remember the Young Girl behind the Public Malala: With Her Huge Intelligence and Courage It's Easy to Forget That She Is Still a Teenager. Let's Give Her Space to Grow," *Observer,* October 13, 2013; "Malala Yousafzai—the National (CBC News)— Oct 9, 2013," YouTube video, 22:05, October 15, 2013, https://www.youtube .com/watch?v=q5M9L4k-HTI#t=167.467686.

41. "Malala Yousafzai—the National (CBC News)—Oct 9, 2013."

42. Gordon Brown, "Malala Yousafzai's Courage Can Start New Movement for Global Education," *Guardian,* October 25, 2012, https://www.theguardian.com /global-development/poverty-matters/2012/oct/25/malala-yousafzai-courage -global-education.

43. Sayres S. Rudy, "Pros and Cons: Americanism against Islamism in the 'War on Terror,'" *Muslim World* 97 (2007): 39.

44. Rudy.

45. John L. Esposito, *Islam and Politics* (Syracuse, N.Y.: Syracuse University Press, 1984).

46. McAlister, *Epic Encounters,* 203–4.

47. Nafisi, *Reading Lolita,* 262, 67.

48. Samira Haj, *Reconfiguring Islamic Tradition: Reform, Rationality, and Modernity* (Stanford, Calif.: Stanford University Press, 2009), 197.

49. Minoo Moallem, *Between Warrior Brother and Veiled Sister: Islamic Fundamentalism and the Politics of Patriarchy in Iran* (Berkeley: University of California Press, 2005).

50. Samela Harris, "Reading Lolita in Tehran," *Advertiser,* April 3, 2004.

51. Janet Saidi, "Years of Reading Dangerously: Western Literature Takes on the Luster of Forbidden Fruit in an Islamic Republic," *San Diego Union-Tribune,* April 27, 2003.

52. Saadia Toor, *The State of Islam: Culture and Cold War Politics in Pakistan* (London: Pluto Press, 2011).

53. Yousafzai and Lamb, *I Am Malala,* 31.

54. Yousafzai and Lamb, 33.

55. Yousafzai and Lamb, 35.

56. Yousafzai and Lamb, 111.

57. Sawyer says it is "a battle between dark and light," that "the Taliban came out of the shadows," and that "we traveled one dark evening to meet with a group of extreme, hard line fundamentalists there." "Diane Sawyer Reports—Unbreakable: One Girl Changing the World," Vimeo video, 39:35, October 12, 2013, https:// vimeo.com/238429892.

58. Yousafzai and Lamb, *I Am Malala*, 299.

59. International Human Rights and Conflict Resolution Clinic at Stanford Law School and Global Justice Clinic at NYU Law School, *Living under Drones: Death, Injury, and Trauma to Civilians from Drone Practices in Pakistan* (Stanford, Calif.: Standford Law School and NYU Law School, 2012).

60. Chris Woods, "The Day 69 Children Died," *Express Tribune*, August 12, 2011, https://tribune.com.pk/story/229844/the-day-69-children-died/.

61. Yousafzai and Lamb, *I Am Malala*, 209.

62. International Human Rights and Conflict Resolution Clinic at Stanford Law School and Global Justice Clinic at NYU Law School, *Living under Drones*.

63. Yousafzai and Lamb, *I Am Malala*, 312.

64. Peter Hart, "Missing Malala's Message of Peace: Drones Fuel Terrorism," Fairness and Accuracy in Reporting, October 14, 2014, https://fair.org/home/missing-malalas-message-of-peace-drones-fuel-terrorism/.

65. CBS This Morning, "Malala: Fearless Teen Leads Fight for Global Education," YouTube video, 5:53, November 12, 2013, https://www.youtube.com/watch?v=lIeGlEyaPQw.

66. Arzoo Osanloo, *The Politics of Women's Rights in Iran* (Princeton, N.J.: Princeton University Press, 2009); Lila Abu-Lughod, "Do Muslim Women Really Need Saving? Anthropological Reflections on Cultural Relativism and Its Others," *American Anthropologist* 104, no. 3 (2002): 783–90.

67. Mamdani, *Good Muslim, Bad Muslim*.

68. Joseph Andoni Massad, *Islam in Liberalism* (Chicago: University of Chicago Press, 2015), 113–15.

69. Chandra Talpade Mohanty, "Under Western Eyes: Feminist Scholarship and Colonial Discourses," in *Third World Women and the Politics of Feminism*, ed. Chandra Talpade Mohanty, Ann Russo, and Lourdes Torres (Bloomington: Indiana University Press, 1991); Abu-Lughod, "Do Muslim Women Really Need Saving?"

70. Nafisi, "A Reader's Guide," 366.

71. Nafisi, *Reading Lolita*, 26.

72. Guppy, "Revolutionary Reading"; Rumbelow, "Pride, Prejudice and Defiance"; Harris, "Reading Lolita in Tehran"; Rory Stewart, "Secret Texts: Reading Lolita in Tehran; a Story of Love, Books and Revolution," *New Statesman*, July 2003.

73. Nafisi, *Reading Lolita*, 329.

74. Stephen J. Lyons, "'Lolita in Tehran' Lifts a Veil on Oppression," *USA Today*, May 8, 2003.

75. Valentine M. Moghadam, *Modernizing Women: Gender and Social Change in the Middle East* (Boulder, Colo.: Lynne Rienner, 2003), 138.

76. Rumbelow, "Pride, Prejudice and Defiance"; Colleen Kelly Warren, "In Iran, Women 'Shed Their Veils' to Worship Novel," *St. Louis Post-Dispatch,* June 1, 2003; Valerie Ryan, "Nonfiction Review behind the Veil, an English Lit Class," *Sunday Oregonian,* March 30, 2003.

77. Haleh Esfandiari, *Reconstructed Lives: Women and Iran's Islamic Revolution* (Washington, D.C.: Woodrow Wilson Center Press, 1997); Osanloo, *Politics of Women's Rights in Iran.*

78. "At a Glance: Iran (Islamic Republic of): The Big Picture," UNICEF, 2005, http://www.unicef.org/infobycountry/iran.html; "Students at Universities and Higher Education Institutes by Broad Field of Study, Sex and Academic Level," Statistical Centre of Iran, 2005, http://www.sci.org.ir/index.htm.

79. "At a Glance"; United Nations Development Programme, "Iran, Islamic Rep. Of: The Human Development Index: Going beyond Income," Human Development Report: Country Fact Sheets, 2005, http://hdr.undp.org/statistics/data/country_fact_sheets/cty_fs_IRN.html.

80. Moghadam, *Modernizing Women.*

81. Nafisi, *Reading Lolita,* 268.

82. Nafisi, 194, 240, 103.

83. Yousafzai and Lamb, *I Am Malala,* 133.

84. Yousafzai and Lamb, 128.

85. Yousafzai and Lamb, 116.

86. Yousafzai and Lamb, 127.

87. Sayeeda Warsi, "Baroness Warsi: 'Malala Has Turned a Tragedy into Something Positive,'" *Telegraph,* October 8, 2013.

88. Yvonne Roberts, "The New Review: Books: Biography: One Girl among Many, but a Truly Extraordinary One: I Am Malala Malala Yousafzai," *Observer,* October 13, 2013.

89. Warsi, "Baroness Warsi."

90. Ziauddin Sardar, "For Malala, the World Can Wait: The Schoolgirl Campaigner Who Defied the Taleban Is Admirable, Ziauddin Sardar Writes, but Forget the Nobel Peace Prize—She Needs an Excellent Education First," *Times,* October 14, 2013.

91. "Diane Sawyer Reports."

92. "Diane Sawyer Reports."

93. Khoja-Moolji, *Forging the Ideal Educated Girl,* 98.

94. Kathryn Moeller, *The Gender Effect: Capitalism, Feminism, and the Corporate Politics of Development* (Oakland: University of California Press, 2018), 38.

95. Cynthia M. Caron and Shelby A. Margolin, "Rescuing Girls, Investing in Girls: A Critique of Development Fantasies," *Journal of International Development* 27 (2015): 891.

96. Caron and Margolin, 893.

97. Moeller, *Gender Effect*, xvi.

98. Guppy, "Revolutionary Reading"; Noreen Shanahan, "Reading Lolita in Tehran," *Herizons*, Fall 2004; Warren, "In Iran"; Hewett, "A Woman Passionately"; "Azar Nafisi: Reading Lolita in Tehran," January 15, 2004; Fiona Hook, "Words of Freedom," *Times*, August 16, 2003; Moni Basu, "Books: Literature Provides a Sliver of Freedom," *Atlanta Journal-Constitution*, May 4, 2003; Christine Sismondo, "Lolita, under the Veil," *Toronto Star*, May 4, 2003; Ryan, "Nonfiction Review behind the Veil"; Larson, "Books about Books."

99. Moallem, *Between Warrior Brother and Veiled Sister.*

100. Stoffman, "For a Love of Books"; Hewett, "A Woman Passionately"; Ellen Goodman, "Will U.S. Remember the Ladies?," *Boston Globe*, September 7, 2003.

101. Nafisi, *Reading Lolita,* 187; see also Asghar Massombagi, "Being Lolita in Tehran: Azar Nafisi's Observations of Post-revolution Iran from Olympian Heights," Iranian.com, June 30, 2005, http://www.iranian.com/AsgharMassom bagi/2005/June/Lolita/index.html.

102. Stoffman, "For a Love of Books."

103. Nafisi, *Reading Lolita,* 25.

104. Nafisi, 262; Ziba Mir-Hosseini, "Stretching the Limits: A Feminist Reading of the *Shari'a* in Post-Khomeini Iran," in *Feminism and Islam: Legal and Literary Perspectives,* ed. Mai Yamani (New York: New York University Press, 1996), 285–319. Moghadam has written cogently on differing views on the implications and tenability of "Islamic feminism." Valentine M. Moghadam, "Islamic Feminism and Its Discontents: Toward a Resolution of the Debate," *Signs* 27, no. 4 (2002): 1135–71.

105. Azar Nafisi, Samantha Ravich, and Tahir-Kheli Shirin, "Roundtable: Three Women, Two Worlds, One Issue," *SAIS Review* 20, no. 2 (2000): 31–50.

106. Marie Arana, "She Didn't Win the Nobel, but She's Winning Her Fight," *Washington Post*, October 13, 2013.

107. Yousafzai and Lamb, *I Am Malala,* 195.

108. Christina Lamb, "My Year with Malala: In January, Malala Yousafzai, the Pakistani Schoolgirl Shot by the Taliban, Asked Christina Lamb to Write Her Book. From Theatre Trips to a Visit from Angelina Jolie, This Is the Story of Their Remarkable Time Together," *Sunday Times* (London), October 13, 2013.

109. CNN, "Full Amanpour Malala Interview," YouTube video, 54:20, October 22, 2013, https://www.youtube.com/watch?v=aKIQ_AyLi30.@39:20.

110. Warsi, "Baroness Warsi."

111. Yousafzai and Lamb, *I Am Malala,* 72, 180.

112. "Malala Yousafzai: Malala: Using Islam to Promote Education," Times-

Video, August 19, 2014, https://www.nytimes.com/video/multimedia/1000000 03153147/malala-using-islam-to-promote-education.html.

113. Yousafzai and Lamb, *I Am Malala,* 28.

114. Shenila Khoja-Moolji, "The Making of Humans and Their Others in and through Transnational Human Rights Advocacy: Exploring the Cases of Mukhtar Mai and Malala Yousafzai," *Signs: Journal of Women in Culture and Society* 42, no. 2 (2017): 378.

115. Khoja-Moolji, 379–80.

116. Said, *Orientalism.*

117. Azar Nafisi, "Introductory Essay," 2004, http://dialogueproject.sais-jhu .edu/ (no longer online).

3. "IRAN, STOP KILLING GAYS"

1. Although the vast majority of key participants were gay men, this term reflects the identities of organizations and the fact that the identities of individuals who participated in circulating the information via the internet are not necessarily obvious but express an affinity with LGBTQ politics.

2. I use the term *Western* to refer to activists who appear to be primarily based in the United States and the United Kingdom. However, some activists were clearly from other parts of the world, and discourses on the internet are not always easily sourced. However, the "Western" identity here also refers to a particular construction of the "West" as distinct from Islamic cultures that is evident in these discourses. I also used *Western* as distinct from *Iranian,* despite the existence of Iranian American and British communities, as I largely exclude diasporic Iranian discourses from my analysis.

3. Office of the United Nations High Commissioner for Human Rights, "Convention on the Rights of the Child," September 2, 1990, https://www.ohchr .org/EN/ProfessionalInterest/Pages/CRC.aspx; Office of the United Nations High Commissioner for Human Rights, "Status of Ratification: Interactive Dashboard," September 2, 2014, http://indicators.ohchr.org/.

4. Saba Mahmood, "Is Critique Secular? A Symposium at UC Berkeley," *Public Culture* 20, no. 3 (2008): 451.

5. Ann Pellegrini, "Feeling Secular," *Women and Performance: A Journal of Feminist Theory* 19, no. 2 (2009): 212.

6. Tariq Ali, *The Clash of Fundamentalisms: Crusades, Jihads and Modernity* (London: Verso, 2002).

7. Bernard Lewis, *What Went Wrong? Western Impact and Middle Eastern Response* (New York: Oxford University Press, 2002); Robert Neelly Bellah, *Beyond*

Belief: Essays on Religion in a Post-traditional World (Berkeley: University of California Press, 1991).

8. Talal Asad, *Formations of the Secular: Christianity, Islam, Modernity* (Stanford, Calif.: Stanford University Press, 2003).

9. Afsaneh Najmabadi, *Women with Mustaches and Men without Beards: Gender and Sexual Anxieties of Iranian Modernity* (Berkeley: University of California Press, 2005); Joseph A. Massad, *Desiring Arabs* (Chicago: University of Chicago Press, 2007).

10. Lewis, *What Went Wrong?*; Daniel Pipes, "Strange Sex Stories from the Muslim World," November 3, 2008, http://www.danielpipes.org/blog/2008/04/strange-sex-stories-from-the-muslim-world.html; Ronald Inglehart and Pippa Norris, *Rising Tide: Gender Equality and Cultural Change around the World* (Cambridge: Cambridge University Press, 2003).

11. Jasbir K. Puar, *Terrorist Assemblages: Homonationalism in Queer Times* (Durham, N.C.: Duke University Press, 2007).

12. Jin Haritaworn, Adi Kuntsman, and Silvia Posocco, Introduction to *Queer Necropolitics,* ed. Jin Haritaworn, Adi Kuntsman, and Silvia Posocco (New York: Routledge, 2014).

13. Sima Shakhsari, "Killing Me Softly with Your Rights: Queer Death and the Politics of Rightful Killing," in *Queer Necropolitics,* ed. Jin Haritaworn, Adi Kuntsman, and Silvia Posocco (New York: Routledge, 2014).

14. Jasbir Puar, "Israel's Gay Propaganda War," *Guardian,* July 1, 2010, http://www.guardian.co.uk/commentisfree/2010/jul/01/israels-gay-propaganda-war.

15. Marcel Mausse, "Anti-Muslim Sentiments and Mobilization in the Netherlands. Discourse, Policies and Violence," in *Securitization and Religious Divides in Europe: Muslims in Western Europe after 9/11: Why the Term Islamophobia Is More a Predicament than an Explanation,* ed. Jocelyne Cesar, submission to "Changing Landscape of Citizenship and Security," 6th PCRD of European Commission, 2006, 122.

16. Lucas Grindley, "Donald Trump Wants to Test Muslim Immigrants on Gay Equality," *Advocate,* March 12, 2019, https://www.advocate.com/election/2016/8/15/donald-trump-wants-test-muslim-immigrants-gay-equality.

17. Hadi Ghaemi and Michael Bochenek, "Human Rights Watch Letter to Iran's Head of Judiciary," Human Rights Watch, July 27, 2005, http://www.hrw.org/en/news/2005/07/26/human-rights-watch-letter-irans-head-judiciary; *Chicago Tribune,* "Nobel Laureate Condemns Hanging of 2 Teenage Boys," July 24, 2005, https://www.chicagotribune.com/news/ct-xpm-2005-07-24-0507240331-story.html.

18. Erica Templeton, "Note: Killing Kids: The Impact of Domingues v. Nevada on the Juvenile Death Penalty as a Violation of International Law," *Boston College Law Review* 41 (2000): 1190.

19. Richard Kim, "Witnesses to an Execution," *Nation*, August 15, 2005, http://www.thenation.com/article/witnesses-execution.

20. OutRage!, "Execution of Gay Teens in Iran," July 27, 2005, http://www.petertatchell.net/international/iranexecution.htm (last accessed 2012 but no longer online).

21. Kim, "Witnesses to an Execution."

22. Scott Long, "Human Rights Watch Memo on Iran 'Gay Killing,'" August 15, 2006, http://karmalised.com/?p=1569.

23. See the July 27, 2006, issue of *Gay City News* covering various perspectives in the debate.

24. Duncan Osborne, "Mashad Hangings Anniversary Marked in Midtown Vigil," *Gay City News*, July 20, 2006, https://www.gaycitynews.com/mashad hangings-anniversary-marked-in-midtown-vigil/; Michael Petrelis, "Reports, Pix from July 19 Cities," *Petrelis Files*, July 19, 2006, http://mpetrelis.blogspot.com/2006/07/reports-pix-from-july-19-cities-this.html; Doug Ireland, "Global Protests July 19 to Commemorate Hanging of 2 Iranian Teens (Updated)," *DIRELAND*, July 28, 2006, http://direland.typepad.com/direland/2006/06/global_protests.html.

25. Ireland, "Global Protests."

26. "Under the Pale Blue Sky," YouTube video, 4:29, November 7, 2006, https://www.youtube.com/watch?v=2dgsZYA1mPY; "To Mahmoud Asgari and Ayaz Marhoni with Sorrow (Engl. Ver.)," YouTube video, January 24, 2008, http://www.youtube.com/watch?v=BPsT9QnshJM (last accessed 2008 but no longer online); "The Vista Festival," Opera Vista, 2009, http://www.operavista.org/festival.php?show=operas (last accessed 2009 but no longer online); "Haram Iran," 2009, http://www.haramiran.com/ (last accessed 2009 no longer online).

27. Amber Dowling, "'The Handmaid's Tale': Rape, Mutilation and That Shocking Death Explained," *Hollywood Reporter*, April 26, 2017, https://www.hollywoodreporter.com/live-feed/handmaids-tale-shocking-death-rape-mutilation-explained-995751; Emily Gaudette, "The 'Gender Crime' in 'Handmaid's Tale' Isn't Fictional," *Inverse*, May 2, 2017, https://www.inverse.com/article/31005-handmaid-s-tale-alexis-bledel-which-countries-kill-gay-people-queer-panic-trans-panic-defense; Sarah Jones, "The Handmaid's Tale Is a Warning to Conservative Women," *New Republic*, April 20, 2017, https://newrepublic.com/article/141674/handmaids-tale-hulu-warning-conservative-women.

28. Philip Kennicott, "Pictures from an Execution Come into Focus,"

Washington Post, July 20, 2006, http://www.washingtonpost.com/wp-dyn/content/article/2006/07/19/AR2006071902061.html.

29. Anne Penketh, "Brutal Land Where Homosexuality Is Punishable by Death," *Independent,* March 6, 2008, http://www.independent.co.uk/news/world/middle-east/brutal-land-where-homosexuality-is-punishable-by-death-792057.html; Democracy Now!, "Iranian President Mahmoud Ahmadinejad on Iran-Iraq Relations, Iran's Persecution of Gays and the Future of Israel-Palestine," September 26, 2008, http://www.democracynow.org/2008/9/26/iranian_president_mahmoud_ahmedinejad_on_iran.

30. Nazila Fathi, "Rights Advocates Condemn Iran for Executing 2 Young Men," *New York Times,* July 29, 2005, http://www.nytimes.com/2005/07/29/international/middleeast/29hangings.html; Nazila Fathi, "Despite Denials, Gays Insist They Exist, If Quietly, in Iran," *New York Times,* September 30, 2007, http://www.nytimes.com/2007/09/30/world/middleeast/30gays.html.

31. Michael Petrelis, "Iran's Ex President Defends Killing Gays in Harvard Talk," *Petrelis Files,* September 12, 2006, http://mpetrelis.blogspot.com/2006/09/irans-ex-president-defends-killing.html; Janet Afary, *Sexual Politics in Modern Iran* (Cambridge: Cambridge University Press, 2009), 287.

32. "President Khatami and Homosexuals in Iran," YouTube video, 6:22, April 3, 2008, https://www.youtube.com/watch?v=H99du1-u2-o; International Gay and Lesbian Human Rights Commission, "Iran: Stop Executions for Sodomy Charges," November 25, 2009, http://www.iglhrc.org/cgi-bin/iowa/article/takeaction/globalactionalerts/1028.html.

33. Afary, *Sexual Politics in Modern Iran.*

34. Pardis Mahdavi, *Passionate Uprisings: Iran's Sexual Revolution* (Stanford, Calif.: Stanford University Press, 2009), 135.

35. Afsaneh Najmabadi, "Transing and Transpassing across Sex-Gender Walls in Iran," *Women's Studies Quarterly* 36, no. 3/4 (2008): 23–42; Afsaneh Najmabadi, *Professing Selves: Transsexuality and Same-Sex Desire in Contemporary Iran* (Durham, N.C.: Duke University Press, 2013).

36. Nikolai Alekseev, "An Interview with Gay Activists in Iran," International Lesbian and Gay Association, July 26, 2005, http://www.ilga.org/news_results.asp?FileCategory=9&ZoneID=3&FileID=681 (last accessed 2009 but no longer online).

37. Western activists mobilized in 2007 in response to the death sentence of Makwan Moloudzadeh, who was accused of raping three boys when he was thirteen years old. Moloudzadeh was executed despite the fact that the plaintiffs recanted their statements and a judge issued a stay of execution. A number of instances of executions for sodomy have since been reported by human rights

organizations. International Gay and Lesbian Human Rights Commission, "Iran: Stop Executions for Sodomy Charges." In addition, high-profile asylum cases, such as that of Pegah Emambakhsh and Mehdi Kazemi in the United Kingdom, have focused on the threat of execution in Iran.

38. Sianne Ngai, *Ugly Feelings* (Cambridge, Mass.: Harvard University Press, 2005).

39. Ahmed, *Cultural Politics of Emotion,* 56.

40. Marjorie Garber, "Compassion," in *Compassion: The Culture and Politics of an Emotion,* ed. Lauren Gail Berlant (New York: Routledge, 2004), 23.

41. Amit Rai, *Rule of Sympathy: Sentiment, Race, and Power, 1750–1850* (New York: Palgrave, 2002).

42. Ahmed, *Cultural Politics of Emotion,* 11.

43. Jasbir K. Puar, "Abu Ghraib: Arguing against Exceptionalism," *Feminist Studies* 30, no. 2 (2004): 532.

44. Andrew Sullivan, "Quote for the Day II," *Daily Dish,* July 26, 2006, http://andrewsullivan.theatlantic.com/the_daily_dish/2006/07/quote_for_the_d_24.html (no longer online).

45. Peter Schworm, "Study Faults Treatment of Juvenile Offenders: Detention as Adults Harmful, Report Says," *Boston Globe,* March 14, 2005; Adam Liptak, "Serving Life, with No Chance of Redemption," *New York Times,* October 5, 2005.

46. Simon Forbes, "Mashhad: Place of Martyrdom," OutRage!, 2006, http://www.irqr.net/English/files/MASHHAD%20PLACE_OF_MARTYRDOM.pdf (no longer online).

47. Osborne, "Mashad Hangings."

48. "To Mahmoud Asgari."

49. Ahmed, *Cultural Politics of Emotion.*

50. Scott Long, "Unbearable Witness: How Western Activists (Mis)Recognize Sexuality in Iran," *Contemporary Politics* 15, no. 1 (2009): 130.

51. Forbes, "Mashhad."

52. "Emory Student's Opera Examines Gay Hangings in Iran," *Southern Voice,* April 6, 2007, http://www.sovo.com/2007/4-6/locallife/feature/6764.cfm (last accessed 2009 but no longer online).

53. Elizabeth A. Povinelli, *The Empire of Love: Toward a Theory of Intimacy, Genealogy, and Carnality,* Public Planet Books (Durham, N.C.: Duke University Press, 2006), 177–78.

54. Lila Abu-Lughod, "Seductions of the 'Honor Crime,'" *differences: A Journal of Feminist Cultural Studies* 22, no. 1 (2011): 17–63; Lila Abu-Lughod, *Do Muslim Women Need Saving?* (Cambridge, Mass.: Harvard University Press, 2013).

55. Abu-Lughod, "Seductions of the 'Honor Crime,'" 33.

56. Abu-Lughod, 32.

57. Anna Gibbs, "Disaffected," *Continuum: Journal of Media and Cultural Studies* 16, no. 3 (2002): 338.

58. Ahmed, *Cultural Politics of Emotion*, 65.

59. Ahmed, 63.

60. The images were of a young man crying and a close-up image of a man awaiting execution. The images were originally published by Iranian.com. "Photo of the Day (Unidentified Boy Cries)," 2002, http://www.iranian.com/Photo Day/2002/September/hang55.html; "Photo of the Day (Payam Amini)," 2002, http://www.iranian.com/PhotoDay/2002/September/hang2.html.

61. Forbes, "Mashhad."

62. "Under the Pale; Real Execution :((Stop the Gay Crime, Iran!! :(((," YouTube video, 4:59, February 28, 2009.

63. "To Mahmoud Asgari"; Gibbs, "Disaffected," 338.

64. OutRage!, "Execution."

65. Doug Ireland, "Two More Executions Planned in Iran," *Gay City News*, August 18, 2005, https://www.gaycitynews.com/two-more-executions-planned -in-iran/.

66. Ireland.

67. Kennicott, "Pictures from an Execution."

68. Gibbs, "Disaffected," 339.

69. Beth Loffreda, *Losing Matt Shepard: Life and Politics in the Aftermath of Anti-gay Murder* (New York: Columbia University Press, 2000), 127. Loffreda's analysis highlights another parallel, describing the media as "a closed loop feeding off their own energies" (13), where the dominant narrative was produced through the repetition of particular ideas and images.

70. Pellegrini, "Feeling Secular," 213.

71. Ahmed, *Cultural Politics of Emotion*, 69.

72. Lawrence D. Mass, "I Was Afraid to Speak Out about Iran," *Gay City News*, August 23, 2006, https://www.gaycitynews.com/i-was-afraid-to-speak-out -about-iran-2/.

73. Osborne, "Mashad Hangings."

74. Doug Ireland, "Hangings Awaken Long-Overdue Outrage," *Gay City News*, July 28, 2005, https://www.gaycitynews.com/hangings-awaken-long-over due-outrage/; OutRage!, "Execution."

75. Kennicott, "Pictures from an Execution."

76. Duncan Osborne, "Iran Executes Two Teens," *Gay City News*, July 28, 2005, https://www.gaycitynews.com/iran-executes-two-teens/.

77. Doug Ireland, "Iran: Setting the Record Straight," *Gay City News,* August 3, 2006, https://www.gaycitynews.com/iran-setting-the-record-straight-2/.

78. Peter Tatchell, "Far Left Collusion with Islamo-Fascism," November 18, 2005, http://www.petertatchell.net/international/islamo-fascism.htm.

79. Michel Foucault, *Discipline and Punish: The Birth of the Prison,* 2nd Vintage Books ed. (New York: Vintage Books, 1995).

80. Asad, *Formations of the Secular.*

81. Darius M. Rejali, *Torture and Modernity: Self, Society, and State in Modern Iran* (Boulder, Colo.: Westview Press, 1994).

82. Rejali.

83. *BBC News,* "Mid-East Executions Are Condemned," April 20, 2006, http://news.bbc.co.uk/2/hi/middle_east/4925922.stm; Nina Totenberg, "Supreme Court Ends Death Penalty for Juveniles," *NPR,* March 2, 2005, http://www.npr.org/templates/story/story.php?storyId=4518051.

84. Doug Ireland, "Iran: Man Hanged for 'Sodomy'," *Gay City News,* November 21, 2006, https://www.gaycitynews.com/iran-man-hanged-for-sodomy/.

85. Kennicott, "Pictures from an Execution."

86. Mass, "I Was Afraid"; Ireland, "Hangings Awaken"; Ireland, "Two More Executions Planned in Iran."

87. Mick Meenan, "Torture in Iraq from Homophobia at Home," *Gay City News,* May 6, 2004, http://gaycitynews.com/site/index.cfm?newsid=17005479&BRD=2729&PAG=461&dept_id=568864&rfi=8 (last accessed 2009 but no longer online); *Gay City News,* "Pentagon Uses Gay Sex as Tool of Humiliation: Military Culture of Homophobia at Heart of Scandal," May 13, 2004, https://www.gaycitynews.com/pentagon-uses-gay-sex-as-tool-of-humiliation/; Paul Schindler, "Rumsfeld Must Go: Homophobia at the Heart of the Matter," *Gay City News,* May 13, 2004, https://www.gaycitynews.com/head/.

88. Matthew Rothschild, "America's Amnesia," *Progressive,* July 2004; Naomi Klein, "'Never Before!': Our Amnesiac Torture Debate," *Nation,* December 26, 2005; Anne-Marie Cusac, "Abu Ghraib, USA," *Progressive,* July 2004.

89. Faisal Alam, "Shock and Awe Has Become Terrorize and Disgust," *Gay City News,* May 13, 2004, https://www.gaycitynews.com/shock-and-awe-has-become-terrorize-and-disgust/.

90. Meenan, "Torture in Iraq"; Schindler, "Rumsfeld Must Go"; Andrew Sullivan, "Atrocities in Plain Sight," *New York Times,* January 13, 2005, http://www.nytimes.com/2005/01/13/books/review/books-sullivan.html.

91. Katha Pollitt, "Sweatin' to the Koran?," *Nation,* April 28, 2008.

92. Scott Long, "Debating Iran," *Gay City News,* August 2, 2006, https://www.gaycitynews.com/debating-iran-2/.

93. "Mid-East Executions"; *BBC News*, "Tehran Killers Hanged in Public," August 2, 2007, http://news.bbc.co.uk/2/hi/middle_east/6927434.stm; *BBC News*, "Iran to Limit Execution in Public," January 30, 2008, http://news.bbc.co.uk/2/hi/middle_east/7217509.stm; *Washington Post*, "President Ahmadinejad Delivers Remarks at Columbia University," September 24, 2007, http://www.washingtonpost.com/wp-dyn/content/article/2007/09/24/AR2007092401042.html.

94. See, e.g., Gil Z. Hochberg, Haneen Maikey, Rima, and Samira Saraya, "No Pride in Occupation: A Roundtable Discussion," *GLQ: A Journal of Lesbian and Gay Studies* 16, no. 4 (2010): 605.

95. Haj, *Reconfiguring Islamic Tradition*.

96. Osanloo, *Politics of Women's Rights in Iran*.

4. DEFAMED AND DEFENDED

1. Rey Chow, *The Protestant Ethnic and the Spirit of Capitalism* (New York: Columbia University Press, 2002).

2. Sarah Palin (@SarahPalinUSA), "Peace-seeking Muslims, pls understand," Twitter, July 18, 2010, 2:57 P.M., http://twitter.com/sarahpalinusa/status/18858128918.

3. Michael Barbaro, "Debate Heats Up about Mosque near Ground Zero," *New York Times*, July 30, 2010, http://www.nytimes.com/2010/07/31/nyregion/31mosque.html.

4. Jen Chung, "Fareed Zakaria: ADL's Mosque Opposition Is 'Bizarre,'" *Gothamist*, August 7, 2010, https://gothamist.com/news/fareed-zakaria-adls-mosque-opposition-is-bizarre; Paul Krugman, "Bad for the Jews," *New York Times*, July 30, 2010, http://krugman.blogs.nytimes.com/2010/07/30/bad-for-the-jews/.

5. "Interfaith Coalition on Mosques (ICOM): Statement of Purpose," Anti-Defamation League, September 10, 2010, http://www.adl.org/main_interfaith/ICOM_Statement_of_Purpose.htm (no longer online).

6. Greg Gutfeld, "Monday's Gregalogue: My New Gay Bar," *Daily Gut*, October 27, 2010, http://www.dailygut.com/?i=4696 (no longer online).

7. "Red Eye: Greg Gutfeld's Gay Bar—Part 2," private YouTube video, August 13, 2010.

8. Elizabeth Weiss Green, "Klein Relieves Some Critics' Concerns about Arab School," *New York Sun*, May 16, 2007, http://www.nysun.com/new-york/klein-relieves-some-critics-concerns-about-arab/54557/.

9. Donna Nevel, "The Slow Death of Khalil Gibran International Academy," *Chalkbeat*, April 20, 2011, http://gothamschools.org/2011/04/20/the-slow-death-of-khalil-gibran-international-academy/.

10. Randi Weingarten, "Letter to Editor," *New York Post,* August 9, 2007, http://www.nypost.com/p/news/opinion/letters/item_SRVPeVmbjx1ivewP eVlw3M.

11. Tiziana Terranova, *Network Culture: Politics for the Information Age* (Ann Arbor, Mich.: Pluto Press, 2004).

12. Terranova, 140.

13. Janice M. Irvine, "Transient Feelings: Sex Panics and the Politics of Emotions," *GLQ: A Journal of Lesbian and Gay Studies* 14, no. 1 (2008): 2.

14. Terranova, *Network Culture.*

15. I surveyed media coverage about the school and Debbie Almontaser in a wide range of "mainstream" media reaching broad audiences available on the World Wide Web and via Lexis Nexis, including the major New York City papers (*New York Post, New York Sun, Daily News,* and *New York Times*), other major U.S. and world newspapers, and transcripts and clips of radio and television sources (e.g., WNYC, NPR, CNN, *Fox News*). I also surveyed many more specialized sources, including right-wing blogs that purport to monitor Islamic extremism (e.g., DanielPipes.org, MilitantIslamMonitor.org, PipelineNews.org, Atlas Shrugs, JihadWatch.org), neighborhood newspapers (*Brooklyn Daily Eagle* and *Brooklyn Paper*), newspapers serving Arab or Jewish communities in New York (e.g., *Aramica, Jewish Week*), the websites of opposing and supportive grassroots organizations (e.g., Stop the Madrassa, Communities in Support of Khalil Gibran International Academy, Arab Women Active in the Arts and Media), education-focused websites (e.g., Edwize, InsideSchools.org), and progressive media (e.g., *Democracy Now!, Colorlines*).

16. See Paley's ethnographic study of activism surrounding the controversy, which she sees as a reenactment of the Israeli–Palestinian conflict through diasporic Arabs, Muslims, and Jews. Naamah Paley, "The Khalil Gibran International Academy: Diasporic Confrontations with an Emerging Islamophobia," in *Islamophobia/Islamophilia: Beyond the Politics of Enemy and Friend,* ed. Andrew Shryock, 53–78 (Bloomington: Indiana University Press, 2010).

17. Larry Cohler-Esses, "Jewish Shootout over Arab School," *New York Jewish Week,* August 17, 2007.

18. Samuel G. Freedman, "Critics Ignored Record of a Muslim Principal," *New York Times,* August 29, 2007.

19. Mamdani, *Good Muslim, Bad Muslim.*

20. Julie Bosman and Jennifer Medina, "How a New Arabic School Roused the City's Old Rivalries," *New York Times,* August 15, 2007.

21. Andrea Elliott, "Her Dream, Branded as a Threat," *New York Times,* April 28, 2008.

22. Julie Bosman, "Plan to Open an Arabic School in Brooklyn Arouses Protests," *New York Times,* May 4, 2007.

23. Mary Frost, "Park Slope School's Parents Protest Incoming Arab-Themed Upper School," *Brooklyn Daily Eagle,* March 20, 2007, http://www.brooklyneagle .com/categories/category.php?category_id=27&id=11854 (accessed 2011 but no longer online).

24. Joel J. Levy, "Letter to the Editor," *New York Sun,* May 9, 2007, http:// www.adl.org/media_watch/newspapers/20070507-NYSun.htm (accessed 2011 but no longer online).

25. David Andreatta, "Iraq GI Salutes City Arab School," *New York Post,* May 28, 2007.

26. Jonathan Zimmerman, "Arabic School's Critics Are the True Zealots," *Daily News* (New York), May 9, 2007, https://www.nydailynews.com/opinion/ arabic-school-critics-true-zealots-article-1.251464.

27. Richard D. Kahlenberg, "Americanization 101," *New York Times,* August 19, 2007; Alicia Colon, "Madrassa Plan Is Monstrosity," *New York Sun,* May 1, 2007.

28. Adam Dickter, "Hebrew, Arabic Schools Seen Stretching Boundaries," *New York Jewish Week,* August 3, 2007.

29. Noah Feldman, "Universal Faith," *New York Times Magazine,* August 26, 2007.

30. Daniel Pipes, "A Madrassa Grows in Brooklyn," *New York Sun,* April 24, 2007.

31. Anthony DiMaggio, "The Right-Wing's War on the Gibran Academy: Arabic as a Terrorist Language," *CounterPunch,* August 30, 2007, http://www .counterpunch.org/2007/08/30/arabic-as-a-terrorist-language/.

32. Dickter, "Hebrew, Arabic Schools Seen Stretching Boundaries"; Levy, "Letter to the Editor"; Frost, "Park Slope School's Parents Protest Incoming Arab-Themed Upper School."

33. See, e.g., Daniel Pipes, "The Real Arab School Fear," *New York Sun,* May 22, 2007.

34. Sarah Garland, "Arab School to Face Scrutiny at Emergency Parent Meeting," *New York Sun,* May 14, 2007, http://www.nysun.com/new-york/arab -school-to-face-scrutiny-at-emergency-parent/54400/.

35. Bosman, "Plan to Open an Arabic School in Brooklyn Arouses Protests."

36. Richard Bernstein, "'Madrasa' in New York? Hysteria Trumps Reason; Letter from America," *International Herald Tribune,* May 7, 2007.

37. "Khalil Gibran Principal Almontaser Undergoes PR Makover Switches Clothes and Headcovering in Attempt to Disquise Islamist Agenda," *Militant Islam Monitor,* April 16, 2007, http://www.militantislammonitor.org/article/id/2823.

38. See, e.g., Sarah Garland, "'Screaming and Crying' Greet Arab School Plan," *New York Sun,* March 14, 2007.

39. Anne Barnard and Alan Feuer, "Outraged, and Outrageous," *New York Times,* October 10, 2010, http://www.nytimes.com/2010/10/10/nyregion/10geller.html?scp=1&sq=Outraged,%20And%20Outrageous&st=cse; Steve Rendall, Isabel Macdonald, Veronica Cassidy, and Dina Marguerite Jacir, *Smearcasting: How Islamophobes Spread Fear, Bigotry, and Misinformation* (New York: Fairness and Accuracy in Reporting, 2008).

40. Dana Rubinstein, "Holy War! Slope Parents Protest Arabic School Plan," *Brooklyn Paper,* March 17, 2007, http://www.brooklynpaper.com/stories/30/11/30_11holywar.html.

41. See, e.g., Dana Rubinstein, "Media Descends on Gibran as Arabic School Opens," *Brooklyn Paper,* September 8, 2007, http://www.brooklynpaper.com/stories/30/35/30_35gibranopening.html.

42. Frost, "Park Slope School's Parents Protest Incoming Arab-Themed Upper School."

43. Sarah Wolff, "'Joining the East and West': Brooklyn Activist Building Bridges in Iraq Shares Vision for International School Here," *Brooklyn Daily Eagle,* March 20, 2007, http://www.brooklyneagle.com/categories/category.php?category_id=18&id=11861 (accessed 2011 but no longer online).

44. Scott Sherman, "*Sun*-Rise in New York," *Nation,* April 18, 2007, http://www.thenation.com/article/sun-rise-new-york.

45. In 2007, the *New York Post* had a circulation of 725,000 papers per day. Burrelles*Luce,* "Top 100 US Daily Newspapers," 2007, http://www.burrellesluce.com/top100/2007_Top_100List.pdf.

46. Garland, "Screaming and Crying"; David Andreatta, "Brooklyn School in Space War," *New York Post,* April 10, 2007; Sarah Garland, "New Brooklyn School to Offer Middle East Studies," *New York Sun,* March 7, 2007.

47. Andrew Wolf, "Out of Many, One," *New York Sun,* March 16, 2007; Wolf, "Where Radical Politics and Education Intersect," *New York Sun,* April 17, 2007.

48. Pipes, "A Madrassa Grows in Brooklyn"; Colon, "Madrassa Plan Is Monstrosity."

49. *New York Sun,* "Brooklyn Arabic School," May 8, 2007.

50. Levy, "Letter to the Editor."

51. Zimmerman, "Arabic School's Critics Are the True Zealots"; Diane Ravitch, "Arabic School Fails the Test: A United City Demands We Educate Kids Together," *Daily News* (New York), May 14, 2007; *Daily News,* "Culture in the Classroom," May 13, 2007.

52. Raanan Geberer, "Critics of Khalil Gibran School Unfairly Target Islam, Arabic Culture," *Brooklyn Daily Eagle,* May 14, 2007, http://www.brooklyneagle

.com/categories/category.php?category_id=10&id=12879 (accessed 2011 but no longer online).

53. CNN, September 4, 2007.

54. See, e.g., Pipes, "A Madrassa Grows in Brooklyn." Pipes used a truncated quotation to falsely imply that she did not believe that Muslims or Arabs were responsible for the 9/11 attacks.

55. Pipes.

56. *New York Sun*, "Brooklyn Arabic School."

57. Terranova, *Network Culture*, 142.

58. Terranova, 141.

59. Doug Chandler and Larry Cohler-Esses, "Tables Turn on Arab School Critics," *New York Jewish Week*, August 24, 2007.

60. Justin Elliott, "Arabic for Right-Wingers," *Salon*, January 16, 2011, https://www.salon.com/2011/06/17/right_wing_arabic_glossary/.

61. Ahmad Atif Ahmad, *Islam, Modernity, Violence, and Everyday Life* (New York: Palgrave Macmillan, 2009).

62. Andy Soltis, Leonard Greene, and Dareh Gregorian, "Muslim Major Screamed 'Allahu Akbar' before Slaughtering 13 at Ft. Hood," *New York Post*, November 6, 2009, http://www.nypost.com/p/news/national/muslim_major _screamed_allahu_akbar_XGrZPwVI9UdcsxpV42AdnK.

63. See, e.g., Beila Rabinowitz, "New York Set to Open Khalil Gibran 'Jihad' School—Connected to Saudi Funded ADC—Principal Won CAIR Award," *Militant Islam Monitor*, March 10, 2007, http://www.militantislammonitor.org/article/id/2755.

64. Mary Frost, "Learning Curves: Proposed Brooklyn Arabic School Becomes Target of Media Campaign," *Brooklyn Daily Eagle*, May 9, 2007, http://www.brooklyneagle.com/categories/category.php?category_id=27&id=11854 (accessed 2011 but no longer online).

65. A wide range of scholarly and popular books published on "jihad" and "jihadism" demonstrate the broad legitimacy and usage of these terms: Gilles Kepel's *Jihad: The Trail of Political Islam* (2002), Fawaz Gerge's *Journey of the Jihadist: Inside Muslim Militancy* (2006), Walid Phares's *The War of Ideas: Jihad against Democracy* (2008), Jarret Brachman's *Global Jihadism: Theory and Practice* (2008), Marc Sageman's *Leaderless Jihad: Terror Networks in the Twenty-First Century* (2008), Farhad Khosrokhavar's *Inside Jihadism: Understanding Jihadi Movements Worldwide* (2009), and Reza Aslan's *Global Jihadism: A Transnational Social Movement* (2010).

66. Frontline, "Analysis: Madrassas," *Saudi Time Bomb?*, PBS, 2011, http://www.pbs.org/wgbh/pages/frontline/shows/saudi/analyses/madrassas.html.

67. "CNN Debunks False Report about Obama," January 22, 2007, https:// www.cnn.com/2007/POLITICS/01/22/obama.madrassa/.

68. See, e.g., Frost, "Learning Curves."

69. Colon, "Madrassa Plan Is Monstrosity."

70. Chuck Bennett and Jana Winter, "City Principal Is 'Revolting'—Tied to 'Intifada NYC' Shirts," *New York Post,* August 6, 2007.

71. In contrast to the *Post*'s presentation of this as a defense of the T-shirt, Almontaser says that she never spoke directly about the T-shirts but was responding first to a question about the "origins of the word intifada" and later to the reporter's depiction of the girls as advocating terrorism. Andrea Elliott, "Critics Cost Muslim Educator Her Dream School," *New York Times,* April 28, 2008, http://www .nytimes.com/2008/04/28/nyregion/28school.html; Jennifer Medina, "Principal of Arabic School Says She Was Forced Out," *New York Times,* October 16, 2007, http://cityroom.blogs.nytimes.com/2007/10/16/principal-of-citys-arabic -school-says-she-was-forced-out/. Although Almontaser did not speak to the press in the month following her resignation, Larry Cohler-Esses on August 17 recounted this version of events based on other sources who had spoken with Almontaser. Cohler-Esses, "Jewish Shootout over Arab School."

72. Andrea Peyser, "Shirting the Issue—'Sorry' Principal First Defends 'Intifada'-Wear," *New York Post,* August 7, 2007.

73. *New York Post,* "Joel Klein's Choice," August 7, 2007.

74. Elizabeth Green, "Arab School Principal Says She Regrets Intifada Remarks," *New York Sun,* August 7, 2007.

75. Bradley Burston, "Let Arabs Tell the Truth," *Haaretz,* August 21, 2007, http://www.haaretz.com/news/let-arabs-tell-the-truth-1.227895.

76. Weingarten, "Letter to Editor."

77. Green, "Arab School Principal Says She Regrets Intifada Remarks."

78. Green.

79. Julie Bosman, "Under Fire, Arabic-Themed School's Principal Resigns," *New York Times,* August 13, 2007, http://cityroom.blogs.nytimes.com/ 2007/08/10/under-fire-arabic-themed-school-principal-resigns/.

80. CNN, September 4, 2007.

81. Corky Siemaszko and Thomas Zambito, "NY Minute," *Daily News* (New York), December 5, 2007.

82. CNN, August 15, 2007.

83. Rubinstein, "Media Descends on Gibran as Arabic School Opens."

84. Robin Shulman, "In New York, a Word Starts a Fire; Arabic Educator's Brief Defense of 'Intifada' T-Shirts Makes Her a Target," *Washington Post,* August 24, 2007.

85. Fox News Network, September 26, 2007.

86. Zimmerman, "Arabic School's Critics Are the True Zealots."

87. Bernstein, "'Madrasa' in New York?"

88. DiMaggio, "The Right-Wing's War on the Gibran Academy."

89. Deborah Howard, "KGIA Design Team Member Speaks Out," AWAAM: Arab Women Active in the Arts and Media, 2007, http://www.awaam.org/index .php?name=pagetool_news&news_id=7 (accessed 2011 but no longer online); Communities in Support of the Khalil Gibran International Academy, "cisKGIA Statement," AWAAM: Arab Women Active in the Arts and Media, August 15, 2007, http://awaam.org/index.php?name=ciskgiastatement1 (accessed 2011 but no longer online); "Open Letter from Educators in Support of the Khalil Gibran International Academy and Principal Debbie Almontaser to Michael Bloomberg and Joel Klein," Communities in Support of KGIA, 2008, http://kgia.wordpress .com/2008/04/05/open-letter-from-educators-in-support-of-the-khalil-gibran -international-academy-and-principal-debbie-almontaser-to-michael-bloomberg -and-joel-klein/.

90. Mary Frost, "Principal of Controversial Arabic-Themed Brooklyn School Resigns," *Brooklyn Daily Eagle*, August 10, 2007, http://www.brooklyneagle.com/ categories/category.php?category_id=27&id=14771 (accessed 2011 but no longer online), emphasis added.

91. Bosman and Medina, "How a New Arabic School Roused the City's Old Rivalries."

92. Bosman and Medina; see also Bosman, "Under Fire, Arabic-Themed School's Principal Resigns"; Julie Bosman, "Head of City's Arabic School Steps Down under Pressure," *New York Times*, August 11, 2007; Jennifer Medina, "Protesters Seek Leader's Return to Arabic School," *New York Times*, August 21, 2007; Medina, "Arabic School Ex-Prinipal Fights to Get Her Job Back," *New York Times*, October 17, 2007; Medina, "Manhattan: Principal of Arabic School Sues City," *New York Times*, November 20, 2007.

93. In the statement, Almontaser says, "During the interview, the reporter asked about the Arabic origin of the word 'intifada.' I told him that the root word from which the word intifada originates means 'shake off' and that the word intifada has different meanings for different people, but certainly for many, given its association with the Palestinian/Israeli conflict, it implied violence. I reiterated that I would never affiliate myself with an individual or organization that would condone violence in any shape, way, or form. In response to a further question, I expressed the belief that the teenage girls of AWAAM did not mean to promote a 'Gaza-style uprising' in New York City." Medina, "Principal of Arabic School Says She Was Forced Out."

94. Freedman, "Critics Ignored Record of a Muslim Principal."

95. Cohler-Esses, "Jewish Shootout over Arab School."

96. Raanan Geberer, "Brooklyn Arabic School: Not 'Jew vs. Arab,'" *Brooklyn Daily Eagle*, August 31, 2007, http://www.brooklyneagle.com/categories/category.php?category_id=10&id=12879 (accessed 2011 but no longer online).

97. Shulman, "In New York, a Word Starts a Fire."

98. Steve Light, "New York City: Right-Wing Zionist Witch-Hunt Ousts Principal of New Arabic School," World Socialist Web Site, September 1, 2007, http://www.wsws.org/articles/2007/sep2007/kgia-s01.shtml.

99. Elliott, "Her Dream, Branded as a Threat."

100. Elliott, "Critics Cost Muslim Educator Her Dream School."

101. Antoine Faisal, "Zionist Organization Supports Gibran School Principal: ADL Support Could Affect School's Success!," *Aramica*, June 29–July 11, 2007, http://www.viewda.com/webpaper/aramica/ (accessed 2011 but no longer online).

102. Aref Assaf, "Questioning Motives?," *American Arab Forum*, September 4, 2007, http://www.aafusa.org/questioning_motives.htm (accessed 2011 but no longer online).

103. See, e.g., "Ruining People Is Considered Sport," *No More Mister Nice Blog*, April 28, 2008, http://nomoremister.blogspot.com/2008/04/ruining-people-is-considered-sport-in.html; "Pipes," *Rubber Hose* (blog), April 28, 2008, http://upyernoz.blogspot.com/2008/04/pipes.html; "Discouraged," *Mahablog*, April 28, 2008, http://www.mahablog.com/2008/04/28/discouraged/; "Monday, April 28, 2008," *Through the Looking Glass: A Chronicle of the Absurd, in Politics and Life* (blog), April 28, 2008, http://thelookingglass.blogspot.com/2008/04/today-in-new-york-times-story-of-debbie.html.

104. Seth Freed Wessler, "Silenced in the Classroom," *Colorlines*, December 3, 2008, https://www.colorlines.com/articles/silenced-classroom.

105. Josh Nathan-Kazis, "The Leading Jew in Labor Wears Pearls: As Teacher Layoffs Loom, Weingarten Takes Center Stage," *Forward*, May 12, 2010, http://www.forward.com/articles/127978/.

5. MAKING MUSLIMS WORTH SAVING

1. "Aylan Kurdi" was the name initially given by the Turkish press and the name used most frequently in the media. His actual name has been reported to be Alan Shenu.

2. F. Vis and O. Goriunova, eds., *The Iconic Image on Social Media: A Rapid Research Response to the Death of Aylan Kurdi* (Visual Social Media Lab, 2015).

3. For examples of reporting on migrant deaths, see Jamie Grierson, Alessandra Bonomolo, and Alan Travis, "Migrant Deaths: Funerals Held as EU Leaders Meet for Crisis Summit," *Guardian*, April 23, 2015, https://www.theguardian.com/world/2015/apr/23/migrant-deaths-funerals-held-after-mediterranean-disaster; Alessandra Bonomolo and Stephanie Kirchgaessner, "UN Says 800 Migrants Dead in Boat Disaster as Italy Launches Rescue of Two More Vessels," *Guardian*, April 20, 2015, https://www.theguardian.com/world/2015/apr/20/italy-pm-matteo-renzi-migrant-shipwreck-crisis-srebrenica-massacre; Luke Harding, "Hungarian Police Arrest Driver of Lorry That Had 71 Dead Migrants Inside," *Guardian*, August 28, 2016, https://www.theguardian.com/world/2015/aug/28/more-than-70-dead-austria-migrant-truck-tragedy.

4. Anne Burns, "Discussion and Action: Political and Personal Responses to the Aylan Kurdi Images," in Vis and Goriunova, *Iconic Image on Social Media*.

5. Lisa Procter and Dylan Yamada-Rice, "Shoes of Childhood: Exploring the Emotional Politics through Which Images Become Narrated on Social Media," in Vis and Goriunova, *Iconic Image on Social Media*.

6. Francesco D'Orazio, "Journey of an Image: From a Beach in Bodrum to Twenty Million Screens across the World," in Vis and Goriunova, *Iconic Image on Social Media*, 18.

7. D'Orazio; Simon Rogers, "What Can Search Data Tell Us about How the Story of Aylan Kurdi Spread around the World?," in Vis and Goriunova, *Iconic Image on Social Media*.

8. Brian Love, "French Opinion Rapidly Swings in Favor of Refugees, Poll Shows," Reuters, September 10, 2015, https://www.reuters.com/article/us-europe-migrants-france/french-opinion-rapidly-swings-in-favor-of-refugees-poll-shows-idUSKCN0RA1MD20150910.

9. Paul Slovic, Daniel Västfjäll, Arvid Erlandsson, and Robin Gregory, "Iconic Photographs and the Ebb and Flow of Empathic Response to Humanitarian Disasters," *PNAS* 114, no. 4 (2017): 640–44.

10. Lin Proitz, "The Strength of Weak Commitment: A Norwegian Response to the Aylan Kurdi Images," in Vis and Goriunova, *Iconic Image on Social Media*.

11. Geordon Omand, "Photo of Alan Kurdi Had Disproportionate Effect on Canada: Observers," *Canadian Press*, September 1, 2016, http://www.ctvnews.ca/canada/photo-of-alan-kurdihad-disproportionate-effect-on-canada-observers-1.3054565.

12. Patrick Kingsley, "The Death of Alan Kurdi: One Year on, Compassion towards Refugees Fades," *Guardian*, September 2, 2016, https://www.theguardian.com/world/2016/sep/01/alan-kurdi-death-one-year-on-compassion-towards-refugees-fades.

13. Luca Mavelli, "Governing Populations through the Humanitarian Government of Refugees: Biopolitical Care and Racism in the European Refugee Crisis," *Review of International Studies* 43, no. 5 (2017): 809–32.

14. Rose Troup Buchanan, "David Cameron Description of Migrant 'Swarm' Condemned as 'Irresponsible' and 'Extremely Inflamatory' by Human Rights Group," *Independent*, July 30, 2015, https://www.independent.co.uk/news/world/europe/calais-crisis-live-david-cameron-says-swarm-of-illegal-migrants-will-not-be-offered-safe-haven-10426083.html.

15. Matt Dathan, "Aylan Kurdi: David Cameron Says He Felt 'Deeply Moved' by Images of Dead Syrian Boy but Gives No Details of Plans to Take In More Refugees," *Independent*, September 3, 2015, https://www.independent.co.uk/news/uk/politics/aylan-kurdi-david-cameron-says-he-felt-deeply-moved-by-images-of-dead-syrian-boy-but-gives-no-10484641.html.

16. Mark Easton and Ben Butcher, "Where Have the UK's 10,000 Syrian Refugees Gone?," *BBC News*, April 24, 2018, https://www.bbc.com/news/uk-43826163.

17. *BBC News*, "Migrant Crisis: One Million Enter Europe in 2015," December 22, 2015, https://www.bbc.com/news/world-europe-35158769; Mavelli, "Governing Populations."

18. *BBC News*, "Paris Attacks: Who Were the Attackers?," April 27, 2016, https://www.bbc.com/news/world-europe-34832512.

19. Nicholas De Genova, *The Borders of "Europe": Autonomy of Migration, Tactics of Bordering* (Durham, N.C.: Duke University Press, 2017), 17.

20. Amanda Meade, "Charlie Hebdo Cartoon Depicting Drowned Child Alan Kurdi Sparks Racism Debate," *Guardian*, January 14, 2016, https://www.theguardian.com/media/2016/jan/14/charlie-hebdo-cartoon-depicting-drowned-child-alan-kurdi-sparks-racism-debate.

21. Mimi Thi Nguyen, *The Gift of Freedom: War, Debt, and Other Refugee Passages*, Next Wave: New Directions in Women's Studies (Durham, N.C.: Duke University Press, 2012).

22. David A. Graham, "Violence Has Forced 60 Million People from Their Homes," *Atlantic*, June 17, 2015, https://www.theatlantic.com/international/archive/2015/06/refugees-global-peace-index/396122/; Adrian Edwards, "Global Forced Displacement Hits Record High," UNHCR, June 20, 2016, https://www.unhcr.org/news/latest/2016/6/5763b65a4/global-forced-displacement-hits-record-high.html.

23. *BBC News*, "Migrant Crisis."

24. "Operational Portal: Refugee Situations: Mediterranean Situation," UNHCR, 2019; Jonathan Clayton and Hereward Holland, "Over One Million

Sea Arrivals Reach Europe in 2015," UNHCR, December 30, 2015, https://www
.unhcr.org/en-us/news/latest/2015/12/5683d0b56/million-sea-arrivals-reach
-europe-2015.html.

25. Jie Zong and Jeanne Batalova, "Syrian Refugees in the United States," *Migration Policy Information Source,* Migration Policy Institute, January 12, 2017, https://www.migrationpolicy.org/article/syrian-refugees-united-states.

26. Phillip Connor, "Most Displaced Syrians Are in the Middle East, and about a Million Are in Europe," Pew Research Center, January 29, 2018, http://pewrsr.ch/2Ekyze4.

27. Jenna Johnson, "Donald Trump: Syrian Refugees Might Be a Terrorist Army in Disguise," *Washington Post,* October 1, 2015; Anthony Zurcher, "Trump Leads Republican 'Bandwagon' against Syrian Refugees," *BBC News,* November 20, 2015, https://www.bbc.com/news/world-us-canada-34884544.

28. David Weigel, "A Renewed Cry in the Gop Primary: Shut the Door on Syrian Refugees," *Washington Post,* November 14, 2015.

29. Daniel C. Vock, "Can Governors Block Syrian Refugees from Their States?," *Tribune,* November 16, 2015; Ashley Fantz and Ben Brumfield, "More than Half the Nation's Governors Say Syrian Refugees Not Welcome," CNN, November 19, 2015, https://www.cnn.com/2015/11/16/world/paris-attacks-syrian-refugees-backlash/index.html.

30. Amy Davidson Sorkin, "Ted Cruz's Religious Test for Syrian Refugees," *New Yorker,* November 16, 2015.

31. James Hohmann, Elise Viebeck, and Michael Smith, "The Daily 202: New Hampshire Democrat's Rejection of Syrian Refugees Underscores the Political Potency of Post-Paris Fear," *Washington Post,* November 17, 2015; Jessica Taylor, "Trump Calls for 'Total and Complete Shutdown of Muslims Entering' U.S.," NPR, December 7, 2015, https://www.npr.org/2015/12/07/458836388/trump-calls-for-total-and-complete-shutdown-of-muslims-entering-u-s.

32. *New York Times,* "Transcript of Donald Trump's Immigration Speech," September 1, 2016, https://www.nytimes.com/2016/09/02/us/politics/transcript-trump-immigration-speech.html.

33. Jenna Johnson, "Conservative Suspicions of Refugees Grow in Wake of Paris Attacks," *Washington Post,* November 15, 2015.

34. Janell Ross, "Suspicious of Syrian Refugees Coming to the U.S.? Here's a Reality Check," *Washington Post,* October 2, 2015.

35. Yen Le Espiritu, *Body Counts: The Vietnam War and Militarized Refugees* (Berkeley: University of California Press, 2014), 12.

36. Nguyen, *Gift of Freedom,* 161.

37. Sheth, *Toward a Political Philosophy of Race,* 119.

38. Lisa Hajjar, "Anatomy of the US Targeted Killing Policy," *Middle East Report,* no. 264 (2012): 10–17.

39. Noah Feldman, "Noah Feldman: We Shouldn't Strip US Terrorists of Citizenship," *West Central Tribune,* November 19, 2019, https://www.wctrib.com/opinion/4776427-Noah-Feldman-We-shouldnt-strip-U.S.-terrorists-of-citizenship; see also Chris C. Bosley and Leanne Erdberg, "Bring Hoda Muthana and Other ISIS Members Home—but for Trial," *Hill,* February 27, 2019, https://thehill.com/opinion/national-security/431479-bring-hoda-muthana-and-other-isis-members-home-but-for-trial.

40. Razack, *Casting Out,* 7.

41. Melamed, *Represent and Destroy,* 2.

42. Nguyen, *Gift of Freedom.*

43. Miriam Iris Ticktin, *Casualties of Care: Immigration and the Politics of Humanitarianism in France* (Berkeley: University of California Press, 2011); see also Ticktin, "The Problem with Humanitarian Borders: Toward a New Framework of Justice," *Public Seminar,* September 18, 2015, http://www.publicseminar.org/2015/09/the-problem-with-humanitarian-borders/; Ticktin, "Humanitarianism's History of the Singular," *Grey Room* 61 (2015): 81–85.

44. Ticktin, "Problem with Humanitarian Borders."

45. Ticktin, *Casualties of Care,* 21.

46. Ticktin, 72.

47. Ticktin, 23.

48. Lilie Chouliaraki, *The Spectatorship of Suffering* (London: Sage, 2006), 88.

49. Chouliaraki, 88.

50. Lilie Chouliaraki and Tijana Stolic, "Rethinking Media Responsibility in the Refugee 'Crisis': A Visual Typology of European News," *Media, Culture, and Society* 39, no. 8 (2017): 1162–77.

51. Daisy Dumas, "Humans of New York Creator Brandon Stanton Pens Open Letter to Donald Trump," *Sydney Morning Herald,* March 15, 2015, https://www.smh.com.au/technology/humans-of-new-york-creator-brandon-stanton-pens-open-letter-to-donald-trump-20160315-gniyah.html.

52. Jonah Engel Bromwich, "Humans of New York Goes Global," *New York Times,* August 18, 2014, https://www.nytimes.com/2014/08/19/arts/design/humans-of-new-york-goes-global.html.

53. Carla Kweifio-Okai, "Humans of New York Blogger Hits the Road for World Tour," *Guardian,* September 5, 2014, https://www.theguardian.com/global-development/2014/sep/05/-sp-humans-new-york-world-brandon-stanton-world-tour; Daisy Dumas, "Humans of New York Creator Brandon Stanton Pens Open Letter to Donald Trump," *Sydney Morning Herald,* March 15, 2015, https://

www.smh.com.au/technology/humans-of-new-york-creator-brandon-stanton
-pens-open-letter-to-donald-trump-20160315-gniyah.html.

54. David Shapiro Jr., "Human by Human, a Following Grows," *Wall Street Journal,* October 14, 2013, https://www.wsj.com/articles/human-by-human-a
-following-grows-1381799311?tesla=y; "Books: Best Sellers: Hardcover Nonfiction," *New York Times,* March 23, 2014, https://www.nytimes.com/books/best-sellers/hardcover-nonfiction/2014/03/23; "Books: Best Sellers: Hardcover Nonfiction," *New York Times,* November 3, 2013, https://www.nytimes.com/books/best-sellers/hardcover-nonfiction/2013/11/03.

55. Neta Alexander, "The Emotional Pornography of Facebook's 'Humans of New York: The Series,'" *Haaretz,* August 31, 2017, https://www.haaretz.com/life/.premium-the-emotional-pornography-of-facebooks-humans-of-new-york
-the-series-1.5447211.

56. Bromwich, "Humans of New York Goes Global."

57. Jennifer Nish, "Representing Precarity, Disavowing Politics: The Exceptional(ist) Appeal of Humans of New York," *Peitho Journal* 20, no. 2 (2018): 364–98.

58. Dominique Mosbergen, "'Humans of New York' Shares Stories of Refugees in Poignant Series," *Huffington Post,* September 29, 2015, http://www.huffingtonpost.com/entry/humans-of-new-york-refugees_us_560a3d15e4b0dd850
3090c35.

59. Brandon Stanton, "Jordan," Humans of New York, https://www.humansofnewyork.com/tagged/jordan.

60. Chouliaraki, *Spectatorship of Suffering,* 89.

61. Chouliaraki, 1168.

62. Bromwich, "Humans of New York Goes Global."

63. Brandon Stanton, "Refugee Stories," Humans of New York, 2015, https://www.humansofnewyork.com/tagged/refugee-stories.

64. Brandon Stanton, "Syrian Americans," Humans of New York, December 2015, https://www.humansofnewyork.com/tagged/syrian-americans.

65. Brandon Stanton, "I Felt So Alone That I Wanted to Kill Myself," Humans of New York, December 2015, https://www.humansofnewyork.com/tagged/syrian-americans#0.

66. Stanton.

67. Stanton, "Syrian Americans."

68. Images and captions as published on Facebook, but without comments, are collected on the Humans of New York website. Brandon Stanton, "I Don't Want the World to Think I'm Over. I'm Still Here," Humans of New York, December 2015, https://www.humansofnewyork.com/tagged/syrian-americans#5.

69. Stanton.

70. Stateside Staff and Jodi Westrick, "What Happened to Dr. Rafaai Hamo, the Syrian Refugee Featured in Humans of New York?," Michigan Radio, 2017, https://www.michiganradio.org/post/what-happened-dr-rafaai-hamo-syrian -refugee-featured-humans-new-york.

71. Stanton, "I Don't Want the World to Think I'm Over."

72. Stanton.

73. Barack Obama, "As a husband and a father," Facebook, December 8, 2015, https://www.facebook.com/humansofnewyork/photos/a.102107073196 735/1144337492307016/?type=1&theater.

74. Espiritu, *Body Counts.*

75. Brandon Stanton, photograph of Dr. Hamo and Barack Obama, Humans of New York, Facebook, January 13, 2016, https://www.facebook.com/humans ofnewyork/photos/a.102107073196735/1167156683358430/?type=3&th eat; Ryan Felton, "Syrian Refugee 'Thrilled' to Be First Lady's Guest at State of the Union Address," *Guardian,* January 11, 2016, https://www.theguardian.com/ world/2016/jan/11/syrian-refugee-thrilled-first-lady-guest-state-of-the-union -address; Stateside Staff and Westrick, "What Happened to Dr. Rafaai Hamo?"

76. Stateside Staff and Westrick, "What Happened to Dr. Rafaai Hamo?"

77. Brandon Stanton, "'They Told Me: 'One Day Aya, You Will Be the Voice of Refugees,'" Humans of New York, December 2015, https://www.humansof newyork.com/tagged/syrian-americans#9.

78. These effects were defended in 1998 by then secretary of state Madeleine Albright, who when asked about the reported deaths of half a million Iraqi children due to sanctions said, "This is a very hard choice, but we think the price is worth it." *Guardian,* "Squeezed to Death," March 4, 2000, https://www.theguardian.com/ theguardian/2000/mar/04/weekend7.weekend9; see also Muhammed Akunjee and Asif Ali, "Healthcare under Sanctions in Iraq: An Elective Experience," *Medicine, Conflict and Survival* 18, no. 3 (2002): 249–57.

79. Stanton, "They Told Me."

80. Stanton.

81. Stanton.

82. Stanton.

83. Stanton.

84. Stanton.

85. Kristina Collins, "I wonder if president Bush," Facebook, December 13, 2015, https://www.facebook.com/humansofnewyork/photos/a.102107073196 735/1147647901975975/?type=3&theater.

86. "How a 'Humans of New York' Blog Post Inspired a Principal and a $1.2 Million Fundraiser," *PBS Newshour,* February 5, 2015, https://www.pbs.org/news hour/education/can-done-everywhere-principal-inspired-1-1-million-fundraiser.

87. Anum Rehman Chagani, "HONY Helps Raise 1.2 Million Dollars to End Bonded Labour in Pakistan," *Dawn,* August 18, 2015, https://www.dawn.com/news/1201220.

88. Nish, "Representing Precarity," 379.

89. Adria Martin Gibbs, "These refugees are really making me," Facebook, December 8, 2015, https://www.facebook.com/humansofnewyork/photos/a.10 2107073196735/1143978592342906/?type=3&theater.

90. George Delgadillo, "Brandon, you are opening the eyes," Facebook, December 15, 2015, https://www.facebook.com/humansofnewyork/photos/a.102 107073196735/1149225948484837/?type=3&theater.

91. Brad Weisman, "A month ago, I was against refugees," Facebook, December 14, 2015, https://www.facebook.com/humansofnewyork/photos/a.1021070 73196735/1148205971920168/?type=3&theater.

92. Chouliaraki and Stolic, "Rethinking Media Responsibility," 1171.

93. "Let's Bring Aya to America," Change.org petition, https://www.change .org/p/president-barackobama-bring-aya-to-america-friendsofaya.

94. Elsa Vulliamy, "Humans of New York Raises $700,000 for Syrian Refugees in Three Days," *Independent,* December 27, 2015, https://www.independent .co.uk/news/humans-of-new-york-raises-700000-for-syrian-refugees-in-three -days-a6787581.html; Brandon Stanton, "Merry Christmas!," photo, Humans of New York, Facebook, December 25, 2015, https://www.facebook.com/humansof newyork/photos/a.102107073196735/1155494721191293/?type=3&theater.

95. "The Scientist," Crowdrise, January 7, 2017, https://cdn.crowdrise.com/ thescientist; Humans of New York, "Yesterday I got an email," Facebook, December 12, 2015, https://www.facebook.com/humansofnewyork/photos/a.1021070 73196735/1147069435367155/?type=3.

96. Waseem Khan, "I'm so sick of reading these stories," Facebook, December 13, 2015, https://www.facebook.com/humansofnewyork/photos/a.1021070 73196735/1147647901975975/?type=3&theater.

97. Fareed Zakaria, "Inside a Refugee's Struggle to Come to America," *On GPS,* CNN, December 12, 2015, https://www.cnn.com/videos/tv/2015/12/12/ exp-gps-brandon-aya-full-interview.cnn.

98. "Humans of New York Gives U.S.-Bound Refugees a Voice," *PBS News-Hour,* YouTube video, 7:28, December 16, 2015, https://www.youtube.com/ watch?v=kxPXKQswY00.

99. Anna L'Abbate, "I have a feeling the father's situation," Facebook, December 15, 2015, https://www.facebook.com/humansofnewyork/photos/a.1021070 73196735/1149225948484837/?type=3&theater.

100. Weiwei Ai, dir., *Human Flow* (Participant Media and Amazon Studios, 2017).

101. Binoy Kampmark, "Art and Exploitation: Ai Weiwei, Dissidence and the Refugee Crisis," *CounterPunch,* March 14, 2018, https://www.counterpunch .org/2018/03/14/art-and-exploitation-ai-weiwei-dissidence-and-the-refugee -crisis/.

102. Hamid Dabashi, "A Portrait of the Artist as a Dead Boy," *Al Jazeera,* February 4, 2016, https://www.aljazeera.com/indepth/opinion/2016/02/portrait -artist-dead-boy-ai-weiwei-aylan-kurdi-refugees-160204095701479.html.

103. Ai, *Human Flow.*

104. Clough, *User Unconscious,* 24.

CONCLUSION

1. The full speech can be viewed at "Khizr Khan's Powerful DNC Speech (Full Speech)," CNN, July 29, 2016, https://www.cnn.com/videos/politics /2016/07/29/dnc-convention-khizr-khan-father-of-us-muslim-soldier-entire -speech-sot.cnn.

2. Kim Ghattas, "The Democratic Party's Silence on Syria," *Foreign Policy,* August 12, 2016, https://foreignpolicy.com/2016/08/12/the-democratic-partys -silence-on-syria/.

3. "Trump to Gold Star Father: 'I've Made a Lot of Sacrifices,'" ABCNews, video, 2:01, July 30, 2016, https://abcnews.go.com/Politics/donald-trump-father -fallen-soldier-ive-made-lot/story?id=41015051.

4. Ghazala Khan, "Ghazala Khan: Donald Trump Knows Nothing about True Sacrifice," *Washington Post,* July 16, 2016.

5. "Trump to Gold Star Father."

6. Nathan Chapman Lean, *The Islamophobia Industry: How the Right Manufactures Fear of Muslims* (New York: Pluto Press, 2012).

7. Said, *Orientalism.*

8. Mamdani, *Good Muslim, Bad Muslim,* 61.

9. Haj, *Reconfiguring Islamic Tradition,* 19.

10. "Freed U.S. Hikers Speak at Occupy Oakland, Express Support for California Prisoners on Hunger Strike," *Democracy Now!,* October 18, 2011, http:// www.democracynow.org/2011/10/18/freed_us_hikers_speak_at_occupy.

11. Allan Smith, "Trump Says Congresswomen of Color Should 'Go Back' and Fix the Places They 'Originally Came From,'" *NBC News,* July 15, 2019, https:// www.nbcnews.com/politics/donald-trump/trump-says-progressive-congress women-should-go-back-where-they-came-n1029676.

12. APAInstitute, "Skirball Talks: Linda Sarsour," YouTube video, 1:22:45, April 23, 2019, https://www.youtube.com/watch?v=sXLsqUmC2yY.

Index

Page numbers in italic refer to illustrations.

MITRA RASTEGAR is clinical associate professor in liberal studies at New York University.